AN ESSAY ON THE
TRIAL BY JURY

A Da Capo Press Reprint Series

CIVIL LIBERTIES IN AMERICAN HISTORY

GENERAL EDITOR: LEONARD W. LEVY
Claremont Graduate School

AN ESSAY ON THE TRIAL BY JURY

By Lysander Spooner

DA CAPO PRESS • NEW YORK • 1971

A Da Capo Press Reprint Edition

This Da Capo Press edition of *An Essay on the Trial by Jury* is an unabridged republication of the first edition published in Boston in 1852. It is reprinted by permission from a copy of the original edition owned by the Library of the University of Michigan.

Library of Congress Catalog Card Number 70-166097

ISBN 0-306-70320-3

Published by Da Capo Press, Inc.
A Subsidiary of Plenum Publishing Corporation
27 West 17th Street, New York, N.Y. 10011
All Rights Reserved

Manufactured in the United States of America

AN ESSAY ON THE
TRIAL BY JURY

AN ESSAY

ON THE

TRIAL BY JURY.

BY LYSANDER SPOONER.

BOSTON:
JOHN P. JEWETT AND COMPANY.
CLEVELAND, OHIO:
JEWETT, PROCTOR & WORTHINGTON.
1852.

NOTICE TO ENGLISH PUBLISHERS.

The author claims the copyright of this book in England, on Common Law principles, without regard to acts of parliament; and if the main principle of the book itself be true, viz., that no legislation, in conflict with the Common Law, is of any validity, his claim is a legal one. He forbids any one to reprint the book without his consent.

Stereotyped by
HOBART & ROBBINS;
New England Type and Stereotype Foundery,
BOSTON.

NOTE.

This volume, it is presumed by the author, gives what will generally be considered satisfactory evidence,— though not all the evidence,— of what the Common Law trial by jury really is. In a future volume, if it should be called for, it is designed to corroborate the grounds taken in this ; give a concise view of the English constitution ; show the unconstitutional character of the existing government in England, and the unconstitutional means by which the trial by jury has been broken down in practice ; prove that, neither in England nor the United States, have legislatures ever been invested by the people with any authority to impair the powers, change the oaths, or (with few exceptions) abridge the jurisdiction, of juries, or select jurors on any other than Common Law principles ; and, consequently, that, in both countries, legislation is still constitutionally subordinate to the discretion and consciences of Common Law juries, in all cases, both civil and criminal, in which juries sit. The same volume will probably also discuss several political and legal questions, which will naturally assume importance if the trial by jury should be reëstablished.

CONTENTS.

TRIAL BY JURY.

CHAPTER I.

THE RIGHT OF JURIES TO JUDGE OF THE JUSTICE OF LAWS.

SECTION I.

FOR more than six hundred years — that is, since **Magna Carta**, in 1215 — there has been no clearer principle of English or American constitutional law, than that, in criminal cases, it is not only the right and duty of juries to judge what are the facts, what is the law, and what was the moral intent of the accused; *but that it is also their right, and their primary and paramount duty, to judge of the justice of the law, and to hold all laws invalid, that are, in their opinion, unjust or oppressive, and all persons guiltless in violating, or resisting the execution of, such laws.*

Unless such be the right and duty of jurors, it is plain that, instead of juries being a "palladium of liberty" — a barrier against the tyranny and oppression of the government — they are really mere tools in its hands, for carrying into execution any injustice and oppression it may desire to have executed.

But for their right to judge of the law, *and the justice of the law,* juries would be no protection to an accused person, *even as to matters of fact;* for, if the government can dictate to a jury any law whatever, in a criminal case, it can certainly dictate to them the laws of evidence. That is, it can dictate what evidence is admissible, and what inadmissible, *and also what force or weight is to be given to the evidence admitted.* And if the government can thus dictate to a jury the laws of evidence, it can not only make it necessary for them to convict on a partial exhibition of the evidence rightfully pertaining to the case, but it can even require them to convict on any evidence whatever that it pleases to offer them.

That the rights and duties of jurors must necessarily be such as are here claimed for them, will be evident when it is considered what the trial by jury is, and what is its object.

" *The trial by jury,*" *then, is a "trial by the country" — that is, by the people — as distinguished from a trial by the government.*

It was anciently called "trial *per pais*" — that is, "trial by the country." And now, in every criminal trial, the jury are told that the accused "has, for trial, put himself upon the *country ;* which *country* you (the jury) are."

The object of this trial "by the country," or by the people, in preference to a trial by the government, is to guard against every species of oppression by the government. In order to effect this end, it is indispensable that the people, or "the country," judge of and determine their own liberties against the government ; instead of the government's judging of and determining its own powers over the people. How is it possible that juries can do anything to protect the liberties of the people against the government, if they are not allowed to determine what those liberties are ?

Any government, that is its own judge of, and determines authoritatively for the people, what are its own powers over the people, is an absolute government of course. It has all the powers that it chooses to exercise. There is no other — or at least no more accurate — definition of a despotism than this.

On the other hand, any people, that judge of, and determine authoritatively for the government, what are their own liberties against the government, of course retain all the liberties they wish to enjoy. *And this is freedom.* At least, it is freedom *to them ;* because, although it may be theoretically imperfect, it, nevertheless, corresponds to *their* highest notions of freedom.

To secure this right of the people to judge of their own liberties against the government, the jurors are taken, (or must be, to make them lawful jurors,) from the body of the people, *by lot,* or by some process that precludes any previous knowledge, choice, or selection of them, on the part of the government.

This is done to prevent the government's constituting a jury
of its own partisans or friends; in other words, to prevent the
government's *packing* a jury, with a view to maintain its own
laws, and accomplish its own purposes.

It is supposed that, if twelve men be taken, *by lot*, from the
mass of the people, without the possibility of any previous
knowledge, choice, or selection of them, on the part of the
government, the jury will be a fair epitome of "the country"
at large, and not merely of the party or faction that sustain
the measures of the government; that substantially all classes
of opinions, prevailing among the people, will be represented
in the jury; and especially that the opponents of the government,(if the government have any opponents,) will be represented there, as well as its friends; that the classes, who are
oppressed by the laws of the government, (if any are thus
oppressed,) will have their representatives in the jury, as well
as those classes, who take sides with the oppressor — that is,
with the government.

It is fairly presumable that such a tribunal will agree to no
conviction except such as *substantially the whole country*
would agree to, if they were present, taking part in the trial.
A trial by such a tribunal is, therefore, in effect, "a trial by
the country." In its results it probably comes as near to a
trial by the whole country, as any trial that it is practicable
to have, without too great inconvenience and expense. And
as unanimity is required for a conviction, it follows that no
one can be convicted, except for the violation of such laws as
substantially the *whole* country wish to have maintained.
The government can enforce none of its laws, (by punishing
offenders, through the verdicts of juries,) except such as substantially the whole people wish to have enforced. The government, therefore, consistently with the trial by jury, can
exercise no powers over the people, (or, what is the same
thing, over the accused person, who represents the rights of
the people,) except such as substantially the whole people
of the country consent that it may exercise. In such a trial,
therefore, "the country," or the people, judge of and determine
their own liberties against the government, instead of the

government's judging of and determining its own powers over the people.

But all this "trial by the country" would be no trial at all "by the country," but only a trial by the government, if the government could either declare who may, and who may not, be jurors, or could dictate to the jury anything whatever, either of law or evidence, that is of the essence of the trial.

If the government may decide who may, and who may not, be jurors, it will of course select only its partisans, and those friendly to its measures. It may not only prescribe who may, and who may not, be eligible to be drawn as jurors; but it may also question each person drawn as a juror, as to his sentiments in regard to the particular law involved in each trial, before suffering him to be sworn on the panel; and exclude him if he be found unfavorable to the maintenance of such a law.*

So, also, if the government may dictate to the jury *what laws they are to enforce*, it is no longer a "trial by the country,"

---

* To show that this supposition is not an extravagant one, it may be mentioned that courts have repeatedly questioned jurors to ascertain whether they were prejudiced *against the government* — that is, whether they were in favor of, or opposed to, such laws of the government as were to be put in issue in the then pending trial. This was done (in 1851) in the United States District Court for the District of Massachusetts, by Peleg Sprague, the United States district judge, in empanelling three several juries for the trials of Scott, Hayden, and Morris, charged with having aided in the rescue of a fugitive slave from the custody of the United States deputy marshal. This judge caused the following question to be propounded to all the jurors separately ; and those who answered unfavorably for the purposes of the government, were excluded from the panel.

"Do you hold any opinions upon the subject of the Fugitive Slave Law, so called, which will induce you to refuse to convict a person indicted under it, if the facts set forth in the indictment, *and constituting the offence*, are proved against him, and the court direct you that the law is constitutional ? "

The reason of this question was, that "the Fugitive Slave Law, so called," was so obnoxious to a large portion of the people, as to render a conviction under it hopeless, if the jurors were taken indiscriminately from among the people.

A similar question was soon afterwards propounded to the persons drawn as jurors in the United States *Circuit* Court for the District of Massachusetts, by Benjamin R. Curtis, one of the Justices of the Supreme Court of the United States, in empanelling a jury for the trial of the aforesaid Morris on the charge before mentioned ; and those who did not answer the question favorably for the government were again excluded from the panel.

It has also been an habitual practice with the Supreme Court of Massachusetts, in empanelling juries for the trial of *capital* offences, to inquire of the persons drawn as jurors whether they had any conscientious scruples against finding verdicts of guilty

but a trial by the government; because the jury then try the accused, not by any standard of their own — not by their own judgments of their rightful liberties — but by a standard dictated to them by the government. And the standard, thus dictated by the government, becomes the measure of the people's liberties. If the government dictate the standard of trial, it of course dictates the results of the trial. And such a trial is no trial by the country, but only a trial by the government; and in it the government determines what are its own powers over the people, instead of the people's determining what are their own liberties against the government. In short, if the jury have no right to judge of the justice of a law of the government, they plainly can do nothing to protect the people against the oppressions of the government; for there are no oppressions which the government may not authorize by law.

The jury are also to judge whether the laws are rightly expounded to them by the court. Unless they judge on this point, they do nothing to protect their liberties against the oppressions that are capable of being practised under cover of a corrupt exposition of the laws. If the judiciary can authoritatively dictate to a jury any exposition of the law, they can dictate to them the law itself, and such laws as they please; because laws are, in practice, one thing or another, according as they are expounded.

---

in such cases ; that is, whether they had any conscientious scruples against sustaining the law prescribing death as the punishment of the crime to be tried ; and to exclude from the panel all who answered in the affirmative.

The only principle upon which these questions are asked, is this — that no man shall be allowed to serve as juror, unless he be ready to enforce any enactment of the government, however cruel or tyrannical it may be.

What is such a jury good for, as a protection against the tyranny of the government ? A jury like that is palpably nothing but a mere tool of oppression in the hands of the government. A trial by such a jury is really a trial by the government itself — and not a trial by the country — because it is a trial only by men specially selected by the government for their readiness to enforce its own tyrannical measures.

If that be the true principle of the trial by jury, the trial is utterly worthless as a security to liberty. The Czar might, with perfect safety to his authority, introduce the trial by jury into Russia, if he could but be permitted to select his jurors from those who were ready to maintain his laws, without regard to their injustice.

This example is sufficient to show that the very pith of the trial by jury, as a safeguard to liberty, consists in the jurors being taken indiscriminately from the whole people, and in their right to hold invalid all laws which they think unjust.

The jury must also judge whether there really be any such law, (be it good or bad,) as the accused is charged with having transgressed. Unless they judge on this point, the people are liable to have their liberties taken from them by brute force, without any law at all.

The jury must also judge of the laws of evidence. If the government can dictate to a jury the laws of evidence, it can not only shut out any evidence it pleases, tending to vindicate the accused, but it can require that any evidence whatever, that it pleases to offer, be held as conclusive proof of any offence whatever which the government chooses to allege.

It is manifest, therefore, that the jury must judge of and try the whole case, and every part and parcel of the case, free of any dictation or authority on the part of the government. They must judge of the existence of the law; of the true exposition of the law; *of the justice of the law ;* and of the admissibility and weight of all the evidence offered; otherwise the government will have everything its own way; the jury will be mere puppets in the hands of the government; and the trial will be, in reality, a trial by the government, and not a "trial by the country." By such trials the government will determine its own powers over the people, instead of the people's determining their own liberties against the government; and it will be an entire delusion to talk, as for centuries we have done, of the trial by jury, as a "palladium of liberty," or as any protection to the people against the oppression and tyranny of the government.

The question, then, between trial by jury, as thus described, and trial by the government, is simply a question between liberty and despotism. The authority to judge what are the powers of the government, and what the liberties of the people, must necessarily be vested in one or the other of the parties themselves — the government, or the people; because there is no third party to whom it can be entrusted. If the authority be vested in the government, the government is absolute, and the people have no liberties except such as the government sees fit to indulge them with. If, on the other hand, that authority be vested in the people, then the people have all liberties, (as against the government,) except such as substantially the whole people (through a jury) choose to disclaim; and the government can exercise no power except such as substantially the whole people (through a jury) consent that it may exercise.

SECTION II.

The force and justice of the preceding argument cannot be evaded by saying that the government is chosen by the people; that, in theory, it represents the people; that it is designed to do the will of the people; that its members are all sworn to observe the fundamental or constitutional law instituted by the people; that its acts are therefore entitled to be considered the acts of the people; and that to allow a jury, representing the people, to invalidate the acts of the government, would therefore be arraying the people against themselves.

There are two answers to such an argument.

One answer is, that, in a representative government, there is no absurdity or contradiction, nor any arraying of the people against themselves, in requiring that the statutes or enactments of the government shall pass the ordeal of any number of separate tribunals, before it shall be determined that they are to have the force of laws. Our American constitutions have provided five of these separate tribunals, to wit, representatives, senate, executive,* jury, and judges; and have made it necessary that each enactment shall pass the ordeal of all these separate tribunals, before its authority can be established by the punishment of those who choose to transgress it. And there is no more absurdity or inconsistency in making a jury one of these several tribunals, than there is in making the representatives, or the senate, or the executive, or the judges, one of them. There is no more absurdity in giving a jury a veto upon the laws, than there is in giving a veto to each of these other tribunals. The people are no more arrayed against themselves, when a jury puts its veto upon a statute, which the other tribunals have sanctioned, than they are when the

---

* The executive has a qualified veto upon the passage of laws, in most of our governments, and an absolute veto, in all of them, upon the execution of any laws which he deems unconstitutional; because his oath to support the constitution (as he understands it) forbids him to execute any law that he deems unconstitutional.

same veto is exercised by the representatives, the senate, the executive, or the judges.

But another answer to the argument that the people are arrayed against themselves, when a jury hold an enactment of the government invalid, is, that the government, and all the departments of the government, *are merely the servants and agents of the people;* not invested with arbitrary or absolute authority to bind the people, but required to submit all their enactments to the judgment of a tribunal more fairly representing the whole people, before they carry them into execution, by punishing any individual for transgressing them. If the government were not thus required to submit their enactments to the judgment of "the country," before executing them upon individuals — if, in other words, the people had reserved to themselves no veto upon the acts of the government, the government, instead of being a mere servant and agent of the people, would be an absolute despot over the people. It would have all power in its own hands; because the power to *punish* carries all other powers with it. A power that can, of itself, and by its own authority, punish disobedience, can compel obedience and submission, and is above all responsibility for the character of its laws. In short, it is a despotism.

And it is of no consequence to inquire how a government came by this power to punish, whether by prescription, by inheritance, by usurpation, or by delegation from the people? *If it have now but got it,* the government is absolute.

It is plain, therefore, that if the people have invested the government with power to make laws that absolutely bind the people, and to punish the people for transgressing those laws, the people have surrendered their liberties unreservedly into the hands of the government.

It is of no avail to say, in answer to this view of the case, that in surrendering their liberties into the hands of the government, the people took an oath from the government, that it would exercise its power within certain constitutional limits; for when did oaths ever restrain a government that was otherwise unrestrained? Or when did a government fail to determine that all its acts were within the constitutional and authorized limits of its power, if it were permitted to determine that question for itself?

Neither is it of any avail to say, that, if the government abuse its power, and enact unjust and oppressive laws, the government may be changed by the influence of discussion, and the exercise of the right of suffrage. Discussion can do nothing to prevent the enactment, or procure the repeal, of unjust laws, unless it be understood that the discussion is to be followed by resistance. Tyrants care nothing for discussions that are to end only in discussion. Discussions, which do not interfere with the enforcement of their laws, are but idle wind to them. Suffrage is equally powerless and unreliable. It can be exercised only periodically; and the tyranny must at least be borne until the time for suffrage comes. Besides, when the suffrage is exercised, it gives no guaranty for the repeal of existing laws that are oppressive, and no security against the enactment of new ones that are equally so. The second body of legislators are liable and likely to be just as tyrannical as the first. If it be said that the second body may be chosen for their integrity, the answer is, that the first were chosen for that very reason, and yet proved tyrants. The second will be exposed to the same temptations as the first, and will be just as likely to prove tyrannical. Who ever heard that succeeding legislatures were, on the whole, more honest than those that preceded them? What is there in the nature of men or things to make them so? If it be said that the first body were chosen from motives of injustice, that fact proves that there is a portion of society who desire to establish injustice; and if they were powerful or artful enough to procure the election of their instruments to compose the first legislature, they will be likely to be powerful or artful enough to procure the election of the same or similar instruments to compose the second. The right of suffrage, therefore, and even a change of legislators, guarantees no change of legislation — certainly no change for the better. Even if a change for the better actually comes, it comes too late, because it comes only after more or less injustice has been irreparably done.

But, at best, the right of suffrage can be exercised only periodically; and between the periods the legislators are wholly irresponsible.　No despot was ever more entirely irresponsible than are republican legislators during the period for which they are chosen.　They can neither be removed from their office, nor called to account while in their office, nor punished after they leave their office, be their tyranny what it may. Moreover, the judicial and executive departments of the government are equally irresponsible *to the people*, and are only responsible, (by impeachment, and dependence for their salaries), to these irresponsible legislators.　This dependence of the judiciary and executive upon the legislature is a guaranty that they will always sanction and execute its laws, whether just or unjust.　Thus the legislators hold the whole power of the government in their hands, and are at the same time utterly irresponsible for the manner in which they use it.

If, now, this government, (the three branches thus really united in one), can determine the validity of, and enforce, its own laws, it is, for the time being, entirely absolute, and wholly irresponsible to the people.

But this is not all.　These legislators, and this government, so irresponsible while in power, can perpetuate their power at pleasure, if they can determine what legislation is authoritative upon the people, and can enforce obedience to it; for they can not only declare their power perpetual, but they can enforce submission to all legislation that is necessary to secure its perpetuity.　They can, for example, prohibit all discussion of the rightfulness of their authority; forbid the use of the suffrage; prevent the election of any successors; disarm, plunder, imprison, and even kill all who refuse submission.　If, therefore, the government (all departments united) be absolute for a day — that is, if it can, for a day, enforce obedience to its own laws — it can, in that day, secure its power for all time — like the queen, who wished to reign but for a day, but in that day caused the king, her husband, to be slain, and usurped his throne.

Nor will it avail to say that such acts would be unconstitutional, and that unconstitutional acts may be lawfully resisted; for everything a government pleases to do will, of course, be determined to be constitutional, if the government itself be permitted to determine the question of the constitutionality of its own acts.　Those who are capable of tyranny, are capable of perjury to sustain it.

The conclusion, therefore, is, that any government, that can, *for a day*, enforce its own laws, without appealing to the people, (or to a tribunal fairly representing the people,) for their consent, is, in theory, an absolute government, irresponsible to the people, and can perpetuate its power at pleasure.

The trial by jury is based upon a recognition of this principle, and therefore forbids the government to execute any of its laws, by punishing violators, in any case whatever, without first getting the consent of "the country," or the people, through a jury. In this way, the people, at all times, hold their liberties in their own hands, and never surrender them, even for a moment, into the hands of the government.

The trial by jury, then, gives to any and every individual the liberty, at any time, to disregard or resist any law whatever of the government, if he be willing to submit to the decision of a jury, the questions, whether the law be intrinsically just and obligatory? and whether his conduct, in disregarding or resisting it, were right in itself? And any law, which does not, in such trial, obtain the unanimous sanction of twelve men, taken at random from the people, and judging according to the standard of justice in their own minds, free from all dictation and authority of the government, may be transgressed and resisted with impunity, by whomsoever pleases to transgress or resist it.*

The trial by jury authorizes all this, or it is a sham and a hoax, utterly worthless for protecting the people against oppression. If it do not authorize an individual to resist the first and least act of injustice or tyranny, on the part of the government, it does not authorize him to resist the last and the greatest. If it do not authorize individuals to nip tyranny in the bud, it does not authorize them to cut it down when its branches are filled with the ripe fruits of plunder and oppression.

Those who deny the right of a jury to protect an individual in resisting an unjust law of the government, deny him all

---

* And if there be so much as a reasonable *doubt* of the justice of the laws, the benefit of that doubt must be given to the defendant, and not to the government. So that the government must keep its laws *clearly* within the limits of justice, if it would ask a jury to enforce them.

legal defence whatsoever against oppression. The right of
revolution, which tyrants, in mockery, accord to mankind, is
no *legal* right *under* a government; it is only a *natural* right
to overturn a government. The government itself never
acknowledges this right. And the right is practically established only when and because the government no longer exists
to call it in question. The right, therefore, can be exercised
with impunity, only when it is exercised victoriously. All
unsuccessful attempts at revolution, however justifiable in
themselves, are punished as treason, if the government be
permitted to judge of the treason. The government itself
never admits the injustice of its laws, as a legal defence for
those who have attempted a revolution, and failed. The right
of revolution, therefore, is a right of no practical value, except
for those who are stronger than the government. So long,
therefore, as the oppressions of a government are kept within
such limits as simply not to exasperate against it a power
greater than its own, the right of revolution cannot be
appealed to, and is therefore inapplicable to the case. This
affords a wide field for tyranny; and if a jury cannot *here*
intervene, the oppressed are utterly defenceless.

It is manifest that the only security against the tyranny of
the government lies in forcible resistance to the execution of
the injustice; because the injustice will certainly be executed,
unless it be forcibly resisted. And if it be but suffered to be
executed, it must then be borne; for the government never
makes compensation for its own wrongs.

Since, then, this forcible resistance to the injustice of the
government is the only possible means of preserving liberty,
it is indispensable to all *legal* liberty that this *resistance*
should be *legalized.* It is perfectly self-evident that where
there is no *legal* right to resist the oppression of the government, there can be no *legal* liberty. And here it is all-impor-
tant to notice, that, *practically speaking,* there can be no *legal*
right to resist the oppressions of the government, unless there
be some *legal* tribunal, other than the government, and wholly
independent of, and *above,* the government, to judge between
the government and those who resist its oppressions; in other
words, to judge what laws of the government are to be

obeyed, and what may be resisted and held for nought. The only tribunal known to our laws, for this purpose, is a jury. If a jury have not the right to judge between the government and those who disobey its laws, and resist its oppressions, the government is absolute, and the people, *legally speaking*, are slaves. Like many other slaves they may have sufficient courage and strength to keep their masters somewhat in check; but they are nevertheless *known to the law* only as slaves.

That this right of resistance was recognized as a common law right, when the ancient and genuine trial by jury was in force, is not only proved by the nature of the trial itself, but is acknowledged by history.*

This right of resistance is recognized by the constitution of the United States, as a strictly legal and constitutional right. It is so recognized, first by the provision that "the trial of all crimes, except in cases of impeachment, shall be by jury" — that is, by the country — and not by the government; secondly, by the provision that "the right of the people to keep and bear arms shall not be infringed." This constitutional security for "the right to keep and bear arms," implies the right to use them — as much as a constitutional security for the right to buy and keep food would have implied the right to eat it. The constitution, therefore, takes it for granted that

---

* *Hallam* says, "The relation established between a lord and his vassal by the feudal tenure, far from containing principles of any servile and implicit obedience, permitted the compact to be dissolved in case of its violation by either party. This extended as much to the sovereign as to inferior lords. * * If a vassal was aggrieved, and if justice was denied him, he sent a defiance, that is, a renunciation of fealty to the king, and was entitled to enforce redress at the point of his sword. It then became a contest of strength as between two independent potentates, and was terminated by treaty, advantageous or otherwise, according to the fortune of war. * * There remained the original principle, that allegiance depended conditionally upon good treatment, and that an appeal might be *lawfully* made to arms against an oppressive government. Nor was this, we may be sure, left for extreme necessity, or thought to require a long-enduring forbearance. In modern times, a king, compelled by his subjects' swords to abandon any pretension, would be supposed to have ceased to reign ; and the express recognition of such a right as that of insurrection has been justly deemed inconsistent with the majesty of law. But ruder ages had ruder sentiments. Force was necessary to repel force ; and men accustomed to see the king's authority defied by a private riot, were not much shocked when it was resisted in defence of public freedom." — 3 *Middle Ages*, 240-2.

the people will judge of the conduct of the government, and that, as they have the right, they will also have the sense, to use arms, whenever the necessity of the case justifies it. And it is a sufficient and *legal* defence for a person accused of using arms against the government, if he can show, to the satisfaction of a jury, *or even any one of a jury*, that the law he resisted was an unjust one.

In the American *State* constitutions also, this right of resistance to the oppressions of the government is recognized, in various ways, as a natural, legal, and constitutional right. In the first place, it is so recognized by provisions establishing the trial by jury; thus requiring that accused persons shall be tried by "the country," instead of the government. In the second place, it is recognized by many of them, as, for example, those of Massachusetts, Maine, Vermont, Connecticut, Pennsylvania, Ohio, Indiana, Michigan, Kentucky, Tennessee, Arkansas, Mississippi, Alabama, and Florida, by provisions expressly declaring that the people shall have the right to bear arms. In many of them also, as, for example, those of Maine, New Hampshire, Vermont, Massachusetts, New Jersey, Pennsylvania, Delaware, Ohio, Indiana, Illinois, Florida, Iowa, and Arkansas, by provisions, in their bills of rights, declaring that men have a natural, inherent, and inalienable right of "*defending*" their lives and liberties." This, of course, means that they have a right to defend them against any injustice *on the part of the government*, and not merely on the part of private individuals; because the object of all bills of rights is to assert the rights of individuals and the people, *as against the government*, and not as against private persons. It would be a matter of ridiculous supererogation to assert, in a constitution of government, the natural right of men to defend their lives and liberties against private trespassers.

Many of these bills of rights also assert the natural right of all men to protect their property — that is, to protect it *against the government*. It would be unnecessary and silly indeed to assert, in a constitution of government, the natural right of individuals to protect their property against thieves and robbers.

The constitutions of New Hampshire and Tennessee also declare that " The doctrine of non-resistance against arbitrary power and oppression is absurd, slavish, and destructive of the good and happiness of mankind."

The legal effect of these constitutional recognitions of the right of individuals to defend their property, liberties, and lives, against the government, is to legalize resistance to all injustice and oppression, of every name and nature whatsoever, on the part of the government.

But for this right of resistance, on the part of the people, all governments would become tyrannical to a degree of which few people are aware. Constitutions are utterly worthless to restrain the tyranny of governments, unless it be understood that the people will, by force, compel the government to keep within the constitutional limits. Practically speaking, no government knows any limits to its power, except the endurance of the people. But that the people are stronger than the government, and will resist in extreme cases, our governments would be little or nothing else than organized systems of plunder and oppression. All, or nearly all, the advantage there is in fixing any constitutional limits to the power of a government, is simply to give notice to the government of the point at which it will meet with resistance. If the people are then as good as their word, they may keep the government within the bounds they have set for it; otherwise it will disregard them — as is proved by the example of all our American governments, in which the constitutions have all become obsolete, at the moment of their adoption, for nearly or quite all purposes except the appointment of officers, who at once become practically absolute, except so far as they are restrained by the fear of popular resistance.

The bounds set to the power of the government, by the trial by jury, as will hereafter be shown, are these — that the government shall never touch the property, person, or natural or civil rights of an individual, against his consent, (except for the purpose of bringing them before a jury for trial,) unless in pursuance and *execution* of a judgment, or decree, rendered by a jury in each individual case, upon such evidence, and such law, as are satisfactory to their own understandings and consciences, irrespective of all legislation of the government.

CHAPTER II.

THAT the trial by jury is all that has been claimed for it in the preceding chapter, is proved both by the history and the language of the Great Charter of English Liberties, to which we are to look for a true definition of the trial by jury, and of which the guaranty for that trial is the vital, and most memorable, part.

SECTION I.

The History of Magna Carta.

In order to judge of the object and meaning of that chapter of Magna Carta which secures the trial by jury, it is to be borne in mind that, at the time of Magna Carta, the king (with exceptions immaterial to this discussion, but which will appear hereafter) was, constitutionally, the entire government; the sole *legislative, judicial,* and executive power of the nation. The executive and judicial officers were merely his servants, appointed by him, and removable at his pleasure. In addition to this, " the king himself often sat in his court, which always attended his person. He there heard causes, and pronounced judgment; and though he was assisted by the advice of other members, it is not to be imagined that a decision could be obtained contrary to his inclination or opinion."[*] Judges were in those days, and afterwards, such abject servants of the king, that " we find that King Edward I. (1272 to 1307) fined and imprisoned his judges, in the same manner as Alfred the Great, among the Saxons, had done before him, by the sole exercise of his authority."[†]

---

[*] 1 Hume, Appendix 2.   [†] Crabbe's History of the English Law, 236.

Parliament, so far as there was a parliament, was a mere *council* of the king.* It assembled only at the pleasure of the king; sat only during his pleasure; and when sitting had no power, so far as *general* legislation was concerned, beyond that of simply *advising* the king. The only legislation to which their assent was constitutionally necessary, was demands for money and military services for *extraordinary* occasions. Even Magna Carta itself makes no provisions whatever for any parliaments, except when the king should want means to carry on war, or to meet some other *extraordinary* necessity.† He had no need of parliaments to raise taxes for the *ordinary* purposes of government; for his revenues from the rents of the crown lands and other sources, were ample for all except extraordinary occasions. Parliaments, too, when assembled, consisted only of bishops, barons, and other great men of the kingdom, unless the king chose to invite others.‡ There was no House of Commons at that time, and the people had no right to be heard, unless as petitioners.§

---

* *Coke* says, " The king of England is armed with divers councils, one whereof is called *commune concilium*, (the common council,) and that is the court of parliament, and so it is *legally* called in writs and judicial proceedings *commune concilium regni Angliæ*, (the common council of the kingdom of England.) And another is called *magnum concilium*, (great council;) this is sometimes applied to the upper house of parliament, and sometimes, out of parliament time, to the peers of the realm, lords of parliament, who are called *magnum concilium regis*, (the great council of the king;) * * Thirdly, (as every man knoweth,) the king hath a privy council for matters of state. * * The fourth council of the king are his judges for law matters."

1 *Coke's Institutes,* 110 a.

† The Great Charter of Henry III., (1216 and 1225,) confirmed by Edward I., (1297,) makes no provision whatever for, or mention of, a parliament, unless the provision, (Ch. 37,) that " Escuage, (a military contribution,) from henceforth shall be taken like as it was wont to be in the time of King Henry our grandfather," mean that a parliament shall be summoned for that purpose.

‡ The Magna Carta of John, (Ch. 17 and 18,) defines those who were entitled to be summoned to parliament, to wit, " The Archbishops, Bishops, Abbots, Earls, and Great Barons of the Realm, * * and all others who hold of us *in chief.*" Those who held land of the king *in chief* included none below the rank of knights.

§ The parliaments of that time were, doubtless, such as Carlyle describes them, when he says, " The parliament was at first a most simple assemblage, quite cognate to the situation; that Red William, or whoever had taken on him the terrible task of being King of England, was wont to invite, oftenest about Christmas time, his subordinate Kinglets, Barons as he called them, to give him the pleasure of their company for a week or two ; there, in earnest conference all morning, in freer talk over Christmas

Even when laws were made at the time of a parliament, they were made in the name of the king alone. Sometimes it was inserted in the laws, that they were made with the *consent* or *advice* of the bishops, barons, and others assembled; but often this was omitted. Their consent or advice was evidently a matter of no legal importance to the enactment or validity of the laws, but only inserted, when inserted at all, with a view of obtaining a more willing submission to them on the part of the people. The style of enactment generally was, either " *The King wills and commands,*" or some other form significant of the sole legislative authority of the king. The king could pass laws at any time when it pleased him. The presence of a parliament was wholly unnecessary. Hume says, "It is asserted by Sir Harry Spelman, as an undoubted fact, that, during the reigns of the Norman princes, every order of the king, issued with the consent of his privy council, had the full force of law." * And other authorities abundantly corroborate this assertion.†

The king was, therefore, constitutionally the government; and the only legal limitation upon his power seems to have been simply the *Common Law*, usually called " *the law of the land,*" which he was bound by oath to maintain; (which oath had about the same practical value as similar oaths have always had.) This "law of the land" seems not to have been regarded at all by many of the kings, except so far as they found it convenient to do so, or were constrained to observe it by the fear of arousing resistance. But as all people are slow in making resistance, oppression and usurpation often reached a great height; and, in the case of John, they had become so intolerable as to enlist the nation almost universally against him; and he was reduced to the necessity of complying with any terms the barons saw fit to dictate to him.

It was under these circumstances, that the Great Charter of

---

cheer all evening, in some big royal hall of Westminster, Winchester, or wherever it might be, with log fires, huge rounds of roast and boiled, not lacking malmsey and other generous liquor, they took counsel concerning the arduous matters of the kingdom."

* Hume, Appendix 2.

† This point will be more fully established hereafter.

English Liberties was granted. The barons of England, sustained by the common people, having their king in their power, compelled him, as the price of his throne, to pledge himself that he would punish no freeman for a violation of any of his laws, unless with the consent of the peers — that is, the equals — of the accused.

The question here arises, Whether the barons and people intended that those peers (the jury) should be mere puppets in the hands of the king, exercising no opinion of their own as to the intrinsic merits of the accusations they should try, or the *justice* of the laws they should be called on to enforce? Whether those haughty and victorious barons, when they had their tyrant king at their feet, gave back to him his throne, with full power to enact any tyrannical laws he might please, reserving only to a jury ("the country") the contemptible and servile privilege of ascertaining, (under the dictation of the king, or his judges, as to the laws of evidence), the simple *fact* whether those laws had been transgressed? Was this the only restraint, which, when they had all power in their hands, they placed upon the tyranny of a king, whose oppressions they had risen in arms to resist? Was it to obtain such a charter as that, that the whole nation had united, as it were, like one man, against their king? Was it on such a charter that they intended to rely, for all future time, for the security of their liberties? No. They were engaged in no such senseless work as that. On the contrary, when they required him to renounce forever the power to punish any freeman, unless by the consent of his peers, they intended those peers should judge of, and try, the whole case on its merits, independently of all arbitrary legislation, or judicial authority, on the part of the king. In this way they took the liberties of each individual — and thus the liberties of the whole people — entirely out of the hands of the king, and out of the power of his laws, and placed them in the keeping of the people themselves. And this it was that made the trial by jury the palladium of their liberties.

The trial by jury, be it observed, was the only real barrier interposed by them against absolute despotism. Could this trial, then, have been such an entire farce as it necessarily must have been, if the jury had had no power to judge of the justice of the laws the people were required to obey? Did it not rather imply that the jury were to judge independently and fearlessly as to everything involved in the charge, and especially as to its intrinsic justice, and thereon give their decision, (unbiased by any legislation of the king,) whether the accused might be punished? The reason of the thing, no less than the historical celebrity of the events, as securing the liberties of the people, and the veneration with which the trial by jury has continued to be regarded, notwithstanding its essence and vitality have been almost entirely extracted from it in practice, would settle the question, if other evidences had left the matter in doubt.

Besides, if his laws were to be authoritative with the jury, why should John indignantly refuse, as at first he did, to grant the charter, (and finally grant it only when brought to the last extremity,) on the ground that it deprived him of all power, and left him only the name of a king? *He* evidently understood that the juries were to veto his laws, and paralyze his power, at discretion, by forming their own opinions as to the true character of the offences they were to try, and the laws they were to be called on to enforce; and that *"the king wills and commands"* was to have no weight with them contrary to their own judgments of what was intrinsically right.*

The barons and people having obtained by the charter all the liberties they had demanded of the king, it was further

---

* It is plain that the king and all his partisans looked upon the charter as utterly prostrating the king's legislative supremacy before the discretion of juries. When the schedule of liberties demanded by the barons was shown to him, (of which the trial by jury was the most important, because it was the only one that protected all the rest,) "the king, falling into a violent passion, asked, *Why the barons did not with these exactions demand his kingdom? * * and with a solemn oath protested, that he would never grant such liberties as would make himself a slave."* * * But afterwards, "seeing himself deserted, and fearing they would seize his castles, he sent the Earl of Pembroke and other faithful messengers to them, to let them know *he would grant them the laws and liberties they desired."* * * But after the charter had been granted, "the king's mercenary soldiers, desiring war more than peace, were by their leaders continually whispering in his ears, *that he was now no longer king, but the scorn of other princes; and that it was more eligible to be no king, than such a one as he."* * * He applied "to the

provided by the charter itself that twenty-five barons should be appointed by the barons, out of their number, to keep special vigilance in the kingdom to see that the charter was observed, with authority to make war upon the king in case of its violation. The king also, by the charter, so far absolved all the people of the kingdom from their allegiance to him, as to authorize and require them to swear to obey the twenty-five barons, in case they should make war upon the king for infringement of the charter. It was then thought by the barons and people, that something substantial had been done for the security of their liberties.

This charter, in its most essential features, and without any abatement as to the trial by jury, has since been confirmed more than thirty times; and the people of England have always had a traditionary idea that it was of some value as a guaranty against oppression. Yet that idea has been an entire delusion, unless the jury have had the right to judge of the justice of the laws they were called on to enforce.

SECTION II.

The Language of Magna Carta.

The language of the Great Charter establishes the same point that is established by its history, viz., that it is the right and duty of the jury to judge of the justice of the laws.

Pope, that he might by his apostolic authority make void what the barons had done. * * At Rome he met with what success he could desire, where all the transactions with the barons were fully represented to the Pope, and the Charter of Liberties shown to him, in writing; which, when he had carefully perused, he, with a furious look, cried out, *What! Do the barons of England endeavor to dethrone a king, who has taken upon him the Holy Cross, and is under the protection of the Apostolic See; and would they force him to transfer the dominions of the Roman Church to others? By St. Peter, this injury must not pass unpunished.* Then debating the matter with the cardinals, he, by a definitive sentence, damned and cassated forever the Charter of Liberties, and sent the king a bull containing that sentence at large." — *Echard's History of England*, p. 106-7.

These things show that the nature and effect of the charter were well understood by the king and his friends; that they all agreed that he was effectually stripped of power. *Yet the legislative power had not been taken from him; but only the power to enforce his laws, unless juries should freely consent to their enforcement.*

The chapter guaranteeing the trial by jury is in these words:

"Nullus liber homo capiatur, vel imprisonetur, aut disseisetur, aut utlagetur, aut exuletur, aut aliquo modo destruatur; nec super eum ibimus, nec super eum mittemus, nisi per legale judicium parium suorum, vel per legem terræ."*

The corresponding chapter in the Great Charter, granted by Henry III., (1225,) and confirmed by Edward I., (1297,) (which charter is now considered the basis of the English laws and constitution,) is in nearly the same words, as follows:

"Nullus liber homo capiatur, vel imprisonetur, aut disseisetur de libero tenemento, vel libertatibus, vel liberis consuetudinibus suis, aut utlagetur, aut exuletur, aut aliquo modo destruatur, nec super eum ibimus, nec super eum mittemus, nisi per legale judicium parium suorum, vel per legem terræ."

The most common translation of these words, at the present day, is as follows:

"No freeman shall be arrested, or imprisoned, or deprived of his freehold, or his liberties, or free customs, or outlawed, or exiled, or in any manner destroyed, *nor will we (the king) pass upon him, nor condemn him,* unless by the judgment of his peers, or the law of the land."

"*Nec super eum ibimus, nec super eum mittemus.*"

There has been much confusion and doubt as to the true meaning of the words, "*nec super eum ibimus, nec super eum mittemus.*" The more common rendering has been, "*nor will we pass upon him, nor condemn him.*" But•some have translated them to mean, "*nor will we pass upon him, nor commit him to prison.*" *Coke* gives still a different rendering, to the effect that "No man shall be condemned at the king's suit, either before the king in his bench, nor before any other commissioner or judge whatsoever."†

But all these translations are clearly erroneous. In the first

---

* The laws were, at that time, all written in Latin.

† "No man shall be condemned at the king's suit, either before the king in his bench, where pleas are *coram rege,* (before the king,) (and so are the words *nec super eum ibimus,* to be understood,) nor before any other commissioner or judge whatsoever, and so are the words *nec super eum mittemus,* to be understood, but by the judgment of his peers, that is, equals, or according to the law of the land."—2 *Coke's Inst.,* 46.

place, "*nor will we pass upon him*," — meaning thereby to decide upon his guilt or innocence *judicially* — is not a correct rendering of the words, "*nec super eum ibimus.*" There is nothing whatever, in these latter words, that indicates *judicial* action or opinion at all. The words, in their common significaton, describe *physical* action alone. And the true translation of them, as will hereafter be seen, is, "*nor will we proceed against him*," *executively.*

In the second place, the rendering, "*nor will we condemn him*," bears little or no analogy to any common, or even uncommon, signification of the words "*nec super eum mittemus.*" There is nothing in these latter words that indicates *judicial* action or decision. Their common signification, like that of the words *nec super eum ibimus*, describes *physical* action alone. "*Nor will we send upon* (*or against*) *him*," would be the most obvious translation, and, as we shall hereafter see, such is the true translation.

But although these words describe *physical* action, on the part of the king, as distinguished from judicial, they nevertheless do not mean, as one of the translations has it, "*nor will we commit him to prison;*" for that would be a mere repetition of what had been already declared by the words "*nec imprisonetur.*" Besides, there is nothing about prisons in the words "*nec super eum mittemus;*" nothing about sending *him* anywhere; but only about sending (something or somebody) *upon* him, or *against* him — that is, *executively.*

Coke's rendering is, if possible, the most absurd and gratuitous of all. What is there in the words, "*nec super eum mittemus*," that can be made to mean "*nor shall he be condemned before any other commissioner or judge whatsoever?*" Clearly there is nothing. The whole rendering is a sheer fabrication. And the whole object of it is to give color for the exercise of a *judicial* power, by the king, or his judges, which is nowhere given them.

Neither the words, "*nec super eum ibimus, nec super eum mittemus*," nor any other words in the whole chapter, authorize, provide for, describe, or suggest, any *judicial* action whatever, on the part either of the king, or of his judges, or of anybody, *except the peers, or jury.* There is nothing about the king's *judges* at all. And there is nothing whatever, in the whole chapter, *so far as relates to the action of the king*, that describes or suggests anything but *executive* action.*

But that all these translations are certainly erroneous, is proved by a temporary charter, granted by John a short time previous to the Great Charter, for the purpose of giving an opportunity for conference, arbitration, and reconciliation between him and his barons. It was to have force until the matters in controversy between them could be submitted to the Pope, and to other persons to be chosen, some by the king, and some by the barons. The words of the charter are as follows:

"Sciatis nos concessisse baronibus nostris qui contra nos sunt quod nec eos nec homines suos capiemus, nec disseisiemus *nec super eos per vim vel per arma ibimus* nisi per legem regni nostri vel per judicium parium suorum in curia nostra donec consideratio facta fuerit," &c., &c.

That is, "Know that we have granted to our barons who are opposed to us, that we will neither arrest them nor their men, nor disseize them, *nor will we proceed against them by force or by arms*, unless by the law of our kingdom, or by the judgment of their peers in our court, until consideration shall be had," &c., &c.

A copy of this charter is given in a note in Blackstone's Introduction to the Charters.†

Mr. Christian speaks of this charter as settling the true meaning of the corresponding clause of Magna Carta, on the principle that laws and charters on the same subject are to be construed with reference to each other. See 3 *Christian's Blackstone*, 41, *note*.

---

* Perhaps the assertion in the text should be made with this qualification — that the words "*per legem terræ*," (according to the law of the land,) and the words "*per legale judicium parium suorum*," (according to the *legal* judgment of his peers,) imply that the king, before proceeding to any *executive* action, will take notice of "the law of the land," and of the *legality* of the judgment of the peers, and will *execute* upon the prisoner nothing except what the law of the land authorizes, and no judgments of the peers, except *legal* ones. With this qualification, the assertion in the text is strictly correct — that there is nothing in the whole chapter that grants to the king, or his judges, any *judicial* power at all. The chapter only describes and *limits* his *executive* power.

† See Blackstone's Law Tracts, page 294, Oxford Edition.

The true meaning of the words, *nec super eum ibimus, nec super eum mittemus,* is also proved by the "*Articles of the Great Charter of Liberties,*" demanded of the king by the barons, and agreed to by the king, under seal, a few days before the date of the Charter, and from which the Charter was framed.* Here the words used are these:

"Ne corpus liberi hominis capiatur nec imprisonetur nec disseisetur nec utlagetur nec exuletur nec aliquo modo destruatur *nec rex eat vel mittat super eum vi* nisi per judicium parium suorum vel per legem terræ."

That is, "The body of a freeman shall not be arrested, nor imprisoned, nor disseized, nor outlawed, nor exiled, nor in any manner destroyed, *nor shall the king proceed or send (any one) against him* WITH FORCE, unless by the judgment of his peers, or the law of the land."

The true translation of the words *nec super eum ibimus, nec super eum mittemus,* in Magna Carta, is thus made certain, as follows, "*nor will we (the king) proceed against him, nor send (any one) against him* WITH FORCE OR ARMS."†

It is evident that the difference between the true and false translations of the words, *nec super eum ibimus, nec super eum mittemus,* is of the highest legal importance, inasmuch as the true translation, *nor will we (the king) proceed against him, nor send (any one) against him by force or arms,* represents the king only in an *executive* character, *carrying the judgment of the peers and "the law of the land" into execution;* whereas the false translation, *nor will we pass upon him, nor condemn him,* gives color for the exercise of a *judicial* power, on the

---

* These Articles of the Charter are given in Blackstone's collection of Charters, and are also printed with the *Statutes of the Realm.* Also in Wilkins' Laws of the Anglo-Saxons, p. 356.

† Lingard says, "The words, '*We will not destroy him, nor will we go upon him, nor will we send upon him,*' have been very differently expounded by different legal authorities. Their real meaning may be learned from John himself, who the next year promised by his letters patent . . . nec super eos *per vim vel per arma* ibimus, nisi per legem regni nostri, vel per judicium parium suorum in curia nostra, (nor will we go upon them *by force or by arms,* unless by the law of our kingdom, or the judgment of their peers in our court.) Pat. 16 Johan, apud Drad. 11, app. no. 124. He had hitherto been in the habit of *going* with an armed force, or *sending* an armed force on the lands, and against the castles, of all whom he knew or suspected to be his secret enemies, without observing any form of law." — 3 Lingard, 47 note.

part of the king, to which the king had no right, but which, according to the true translation, belongs wholly to the jury.

"*Per legale judicium parium suorum.*"

The foregoing interpretation is corroborated, (if it were not already too plain to be susceptible of corroboration,) by the true interpretation of the phrase "*per legale judicium parium suorum.*"

In giving this interpretation, I leave out, for the present, the word *legale,* which will be defined afterwards.

The true meaning of the phrase, *per judicium parium suorum,* is, *according to the sentence of his peers.* The word *judicium, judgment,* has a technical meaning in the law, signifying the decree rendered in the decision of a cause. In civil suits this decision is called a *judgment ;* in chancery proceedings it is called a *decree ;* in criminal actions it is called a *sentence,* or *judgment,* indifferently. Thus, in a criminal suit, "a motion in arrest of *judgment,*" means a motion in arrest of *sentence.**

In cases of sentence, therefore, in criminal suits, the words *sentence* and *judgment* are synonymous terms. They are, to this day, commonly used in law books as synonymous terms. And the phrase *per judicium parium suorum,* therefore, implies that the jury are to fix the sentence.

The word *per* means *according to.* Otherwise there is no sense in the phrase *per judicium parium suorum.* There

---

* "*Judgment, judicium.* * * The sentence of the law, pronounced by the court, upon the matter contained in the record." — 3 *Blackstone,* 395. *Jacob's Law Dictionary. Tomlin's do.*

"*Judgment* is the decision or sentence of the law, given by a court of justice or other competent tribunal, as the result of the proceedings instituted therein, for the redress of an injury." — *Bouvier's Law Dict.*

"*Judgment, judicium.* * * Sentence of a judge against a criminal. * * Determination, decision in general." — *Bailey's Dict.*

"*Judgment.* * * In a legal sense, a sentence or decision pronounced by authority of a king, or other power, either by their own mouth, or by that of their judges and officers, whom they appoint to administer justice in their stead." — *Chambers' Dict.*

"*Judgment.* * * In law, the sentence or doom pronounced in any case, civil or criminal, by the judge or court by which it is tried." — *Webster's Dict.*

Sometimes the punishment itself is called *judicium, judgment ;* or, rather, it *was* at the time of Magna Carta. For example, in a statute passed fifty-one years after

would be no sense in saying that a king might imprison, disseize, outlaw, exile, or otherwise punish a man, or proceed against him, or send any one against him, *by force or arms, by* a judgment of his peers; but there is sense in saying that the king may imprison, disseize, and punish a man, or proceed against him, or send any one against him, by force or arms, *according to* a judgment, or *sentence,* of his peers; because in that case the king would be merely carrying the sentence or judgment of the peers into execution.

The word *per,* in the phrase "*per* judicium parium suorum," of course means precisely what it does in the next phrase, "*per* legem terræ;" where it obviously means *according to,* and not *by,* as it is usually translated. There would be no sense in saying that the king might proceed against a man by force or arms, *by* the law of the land; but there is sense in saying that he may proceed against him, by force or arms, *according to* the law of the land; because the king would then be acting only as an executive officer, carrying the law of the land into execution. Indeed, the true meaning of the word *by,* as used in similar cases now, always is *according to ;* as, for example, when we say a thing was done by the government, or by the executive, *by law,* we mean only that it was done by them *according to law ;* that is, that they merely executed the law.

Or, if we say that the word *by* signifies *by authority of,* the result will still be the same; for nothing can be done *by authority of* law, except what the law itself authorizes or directs

---

Magna Carta, it was said that a baker, for default in the weight of his bread, " debeat amerciari vel subire *judicium* pillorie;" that is, ought to be amerced, or suffer the punishment, or judgment, of the pillory. Also that a brewer, for " selling ale contrary to the assize," "debeat amerciari, vel pati *judicium* tumbrelli "; that is, ought to be amerced, or suffer the punishment, or judgment, of the tumbrel. — 51 *Henry* 3, *St.* 6. (1266.)

Also the "*Statutes of uncertain date,*" (but supposed to be prior to Edward III., or 1326,) provide, in chapters 6, 7, and 10, for "*judgment* of the pillory." — *See* 1 *Ruffhead's Statutes,* 187, 188. 1 *Statutes of the Realm,* 203.

Blackstone, in his chapter " Of *Judgment,* and its Consequences," says,

"*Judgment* (unless any matter be offered in arrest thereof) follows upon conviction; being the pronouncing of that punishment which is expressly ordained by law." — *Blackstone's Analysis of the Laws of England, Book* 4, *Ch.* 29, *Sec.* 1. *Blackstone's Law Tracts,* 126.

Coke says, "*Judicium* . . the judgment is the guide and direction of the execution." **3** *Inst.* 210.

to be done; that is, nothing can be done by authority of law, except simply to carry the law itself into execution. So nothing could be done *by authority of* the sentence of the peers, or *by authority of* "the law of the land," except what the sentence of the peers, or the law of the land, themselves authorized or directed to be done; nothing, in short, but to carry the sentence of the peers, or the law of the land, themselves into execution.

Doing a thing *by* law, or *according to* law, is only carrying the law into execution. And punishing a man *by*, or *according to*, the sentence or judgment of his peers, is only carrying that sentence or judgment into execution.

If these reasons could leave any doubt that the word *per* is to be translated *according to*, that doubt would be removed by the terms of an antecedent guaranty for the trial by jury, granted by the Emperor Conrad, of Germany,* two hundred years before Magna Carta. Blackstone cites it as follows: — (3 *Blackstone*, 350.)

" Nemo beneficium suum perdat, nisi *secundum* consuetudinem antecessorum nostrorum, et judicium parium suorum." That is, No one shall lose his estate,† unless *according to* ("*secundum*") the custom (or law) of our ancestors, and (*according to*) the sentence (or judgment) of his peers.

The evidence is therefore conclusive that the phrase *per judicium parium suorum* means *according to the sentence of his peers ;* thus implying that the jury, and not the government, are to fix the sentence.

If any additional proof were wanted that juries were to fix the sentence, it would be found in the following provisions of Magna Carta, viz. :

" A freeman shall not be amerced for a small crime, (*delicto*,) but according to the degree of the crime; and for a great crime in proportion to the magnitude of it, saving to him his *contene-*

---

* This precedent from Germany is good authority, because the trial by jury was in use, in the northern nations of Europe generally, long before Magna Carta, and probably from time immemorial ; and the Saxons and Normans were familiar with it before they settled in England.

† *Beneficium* was the legal name of an estate held by a feudal tenure. See Spelman's Glossary.

ment; and after the same manner a merchant, saving to him his merchandise. And a villein shall be amerced after the same manner, saving to him his waynage,† if he fall under our mercy; *and none of the aforesaid amercements shall be imposed, (or assessed, ponatur,) but by the oath of honest men of the neighborhood. Earls and Barons shall not be amerced but by their peers,* and according to the degree of their crime." ‡

Pecuniary punishments were the most common punishments at that day, and the foregoing provisions of Magna Carta show that the amount of those punishments was to be fixed by the jury.

Fines went to the king, and were a source of revenue; and if the amounts of the fines had been left to be fixed by the king, he would have had a pecuniary temptation to impose unreasonable and oppressive ones. So, also, in regard to other punishments than fines. If it were left to the king to fix the punishment, he might often have motives to inflict cruel and oppressive ones. As it was the object of the trial by jury to protect the people against all possible oppression from the king, it was necessary that the jury, and not the king, should fix the punishments. §

" Legale."

The word "*legale*," in the phrase "*per legale judicium*

---

* *Contenement* of a freeman was the means of living in the condition of a freeman.

† *Waynage* was a villein's plough-tackle and carts.

‡ Tomlin says, " The ancient practice was, when any such fine was imposed, to inquire by a jury *quantum inde regi dare valeat per annum, salva sustentatione sua et uxoris et liberorum suorum,* (how much is he able to give to the king per annum, saving his own maintenance, and that of his wife and children). And since the disuse of such inquest, it is never usual to assess a larger fine than a man is able to pay, without touching the implements of his livelihood ; but to inflict corporal punishment, or a limited imprisonment, instead of such a fine as might amount to imprisonment for life. And this is the reason why fines in the king's courts are frequently denominated ransoms, because the penalty must otherwise fall upon a man's person, unless it be redeemed or ransomed by a pecuniary fine." — *Tomlin's Law Dict., word Fine.*

§ Because juries were to fix the sentence, it must not be supposed that the king was *obliged* to carry the sentence into execution ; *but only that he could not go beyond the sentence.* He might pardon, or he might acquit on grounds of law, notwithstanding the sentence ; but he could not punish beyond the extent of the sentence. Magna Carta does not prescribe that the king *shall punish* according to the sentence of the peers ; but only that he shall not punish "*unless according to*" that sentence. He may acquit or pardon, notwithstanding their sentence or judgment ; but he cannot punish, except according to their judgment.

parium suorum," doubtless means two things. 1. That the sentence must be given in a legal manner; that is, by the legal number of jurors, legally empanelled and sworn to try the cause; and that they give their judgment or sentence after a legal trial, both in form and substance, has been had. 2. That the sentence shall be for a legal cause or offence. If, therefore, a jury should convict and sentence a man, either without giving him a legal trial, or for an act that was not really and legally criminal, the sentence itself would not be legal; and consequently this clause forbids the king to carry such a sentence into execution; for the clause guarantees that he will execute no judgment or sentence, except it be *legale judicium,* a legal sentence. Whether a sentence be a legal one, would have to be ascertained by the king or his judges, on appeal, or might be judged of informally by the king himself.

The word *"legale"* clearly did not mean that the *judicium parium suorum* (judgment of his peers) should be a sentence which any law (of the king) should *require* the peers to pronounce; for in that case the sentence would not be the sentence of the peers, but only the sentence of the law, (that is, of the king); and the peers would be only a mouthpiece of the law, (that is, of the king,) in uttering it.

" Per legem terræ."

One other phrase remains to be explained, viz., *"per legem terræ," "by the law of the land."*

All writers agree that this means the *common law.* Thus, Sir Matthew Hale says:

" The common law is sometimes called, by way of eminence, *lex terræ,* as in the statute of *Magna Carta,* chap. 29, where certainly the common law is principally intended by those words, *aut per legem terræ;* as appears by the exposition thereof in several subsequent statutes; and particularly in the statute of 28 Edward III., chap. 3, which is but an exposition and explanation of that statute. Sometimes it is called *lex Angliæ,* as in the statute of Merton, cap. 9, " *Nolumus leges Angliæ mutari,"* &c., (We will that the laws of England be not changed). Sometimes it is called *lex et consuetudo regni* (the law and custom of the kingdom); as in all commissions of oyer and terminer; and in the statutes of 18 Edward I., cap. —, and *de quo warranto,* and divers others. But most commonly it is called the Common Law, or the Common Law of England; as in the statute *Articuli super Chartas*, cap. 15, in the statute 25 Edward III., cap. 5, (4,) and infinite more records and statutes." — 1 *Hale's History of the Common Law*, 128.

This common law, or "law of the land," *the king was sworn to maintain.* This fact is recognized by a statute made at Westminster, in 1346, by Edward III., which commences in this manner:

"Edward, by the Grace of God, &c., &c., to the Sheriff of Stafford, Greeting: Because that by divers complaints made to us, we have perceived that *the law of the land, which we by oath are bound to maintain*," &c. — *St. 20 Edward III.*

The foregoing authorities are cited to show to the unprofessional reader, what is well known to the profession, that *legem terræ, the law of the land,* mentioned in Magna Carta, was the common, ancient, fundamental law of the land, which the kings were bound by oath to observe; *and that it did not include any statutes or laws enacted by the king himself, the legislative power of the nation.*

If the term *legem terræ* had included laws enacted by the king himself, the whole chapter of Magna Carta, now under discussion, would have amounted to nothing as a protection to liberty; because it would have imposed no restraint whatever upon the power of the king. The king could make laws at any time, and such ones as he pleased. He could, therefore, have done anything he pleased, *by the law of the land,* as well as in any other way, if his own laws had been "*the law of the land.*" If his own laws had been "the law of the land," within the meaning of that term as used in Magna Carta, this chapter of Magna Carta would have been sheer nonsense, inasmuch as the whole purport of it would have been simply that "no man shall be arrested, imprisoned, or deprived of his freehold, or his liberties, or free customs, or outlawed, or exiled, or in any manner destroyed (by the king); nor shall the king proceed against him, nor send any one against him with force and arms, unless by the judgment of his peers, *or unless the king shall please to do so.*"

This chapter of Magna Carta would, therefore, have imposed not the slightest restraint upon the power of the king, or afforded the slightest protection to the liberties of the people, if the laws of the king had been embraced in the term *legem terræ.* But if *legem terræ* was the common law, which the king was sworn to maintain, then a real restriction was laid upon his power, and a real guaranty given to the people for their liberties.

Such, then, being the meaning of *legem terræ,* the fact is established that Magna Carta took an accused person entirely out of the hands of the legislative power, that is, of the king; and placed him in the power and under the protection of his peers, and the common law alone; that, in short, Magna Carta suffered no man to be punished for violating any enactment of the legislative power, unless the peers or equals of the accused freely consented to it, or the common law authorized it; that the legislative power, *of itself,* was wholly incompetent to *require* the conviction or punishment of a man for any offence whatever.

Whether Magna Carta allowed of any other trial than by jury.

The question here arises, whether "*legem terræ*" did not allow of some other mode of trial than that by jury.

The answer is, that, at the time of Magna Carta, it is not probable, (for the reasons given in the note,) that *legem terræ* authorized, in criminal cases, any other trial than the trial by jury; but, if it did, it certainly authorized none but the trial by battle, the trial by ordeal, and the trial by compurgators. These were the only modes of trial, except by jury, that had been known in England, in criminal cases, for some centuries previous to Magna Carta. All of them had become nearly extinct at the time of Magna Carta, and it is not probable that they were included in "*legem terræ,*" as that term is used in that instrument. But if they were included in it, they have now been long obsolete, and were such as neither this nor any future age will ever return to.* For all practical purposes of

---

* *The trial by battle* was one in which the accused challenged his accuser to single combat, and staked the question of his guilt or innocence on the result of the duel. This trial was introduced into England by the Normans, within one hundred and fifty years before Magna Carta. It was not very often resorted to even by the Normans

the present day, therefore, it may be asserted that **Magna Carta** allows no trial whatever but trial by jury.

Whether Magna Carta allowed sentence to be fixed otherwise than by the jury.

Still another question arises on the words *legem terræ*, viz., whether, in cases where the question of guilt was determined by the jury, the amount of *punishment* may not have been fixed by *legem terræ*, the Common Law, instead of its being fixed by the jury.

I think we have no evidence whatever that, at the time of Magna Carta, or indeed at any other time, *lex terræ*, the com-

---

themselves; probably never by the Anglo-Saxons, unless in their controversies with the Normans. It was strongly discouraged by some of the Norman princes, particularly by Henry II., by whom the trial by jury was especially favored. It is probable that the trial by battle, so far as it prevailed at all in England, was rather tolerated as a matter of chivalry, than authorized as a matter of law. At any rate, it is not likely that it was included in the "*legem terræ*" of Magna Carta, although such duels have occasionally occurred since that time, and have, by some, been supposed to be lawful. I apprehend that nothing can be properly said to be a part of *lex terræ*, unless it can be shown either to have been of Saxon origin, or to have been recognized by **Magna Carta.**

The trial by ordeal was of various kinds. In one ordeal the accused was required to take hot iron in his hand; in another to walk blindfold among red-hot ploughshares ; in another to thrust his arm into boiling water ; in another to be thrown, with his hands and feet bound, into cold water ; in another to swallow the *morsel of execration;* in the confidence that his guilt or innocence would be miraculously made known. This mode of trial was nearly extinct at the time of Magna Carta, and it is not likely that it was included in "*legem terræ*," as that term is used in that instrument. This idea is corroborated by the fact that the trial by ordeal was specially prohibited only four years after Magna Carta, "by act of Parliament in 3 Henry III., according to Sir Edward Coke, or rather by an order of the king in council." — 3 *Blackstone* 345, *note.*

I apprehend that this trial was never forced upon accused persons, but was only allowed to them, *as an appeal to God,* from the judgment of a jury.*

The trial by compurgators was one in which, if the accused could bring twelve of his neighbors, who would make oath that they believed him innocent, he was held to be so. It is probable that this trial was really the trial by jury, or was allowed as an appeal from a jury. It is wholly improbable that two different modes of trial, so nearly resembling each other as this and the trial by jury do, should prevail at the same time, and among a rude people, whose judicial proceedings would naturally be of the simplest kind. But if this trial really were any other than the trial by jury, it must have been nearly or quite extinct at the time of Magna Carta; and there is no probability that it was included in "*legem terræ*."

* Hallam says, " It appears as if the ordeal were permitted to persons already convicted by the verdict of a jury." — 2 *Middle Ages,* 446, *note.*

mon law, fixed the punishment in cases where the question of
guilt was tried by a jury; or, indeed, that it did in any other
case. Doubtless certain punishments were common and usual
for certain offences; but I do not think it can be shown that
the *common law*, the *lex terræ*, which the king was sworn to
maintain, required any one specific punishment, or any precise
amount of punishment, for any one specific offence. If such
a thing be claimed, it must be shown, for it cannot be presumed. In fact, the contrary must be presumed, because, in
the nature of things, the amount of punishment proper to be
inflicted in any particular case, is a matter requiring the exercise of discretion at the time, in order to adapt it to the moral
quality of the offence, which is different in each case, varying
with the mental and moral constitutions of the offenders, and
the circumstances of temptation or provocation. And Magna
Carta recognizes this principle distinctly, as has before been
shown, in providing that freemen, merchants, and villeins,
"shall not be amerced for a small crime, but according to the
degree of the crime; and for a great crime in proportion to the
magnitude of it;" and that "none of the aforesaid amercements shall be imposed (or assessed) but by the oaths of
honest men of the neighborhood;" and that "earls and barons
shall not be amerced but by their peers, and according to the
quality of the offence."

All this implies that the moral quality of the offenee was to
be judged of at the trial, and that the punishment was to be
fixed by the discretion of the peers, or jury, and not by any
such unvarying rule as a common law rule would be.

I think, therefore, it must be conceded that, in all cases,
tried by a jury, Magna Carta intended that the punishment
should be fixed by the jury, and not by the common law, for
these several reasons.

1. It is uncertain whether the *common law* fixed the punishment of any offence whatever.

2. The words "*per judicium parium suorum*," *according
to the sentence of his peers*, imply that the jury fixed the sentence in *some* cases tried by them; and if they fixed the
sentence in some cases, it must be presumed they did in all,
unless the contrary be clearly shown.

3. The express provisions of Magna Carta, before adverted to, that no amercements, or fines, should be imposed upon freemen, merchants, or villeins, "but by the oath of honest men of the neighborhood," and "according to the degree of the crime," and that "earls and barons should not be amerced but by their peers, and according to the quality of the offence," *proves* that, at least, there was no common law fixing the amount of *fines*, or, if there were, that it was to be no longer in force. And if there was no common law fixing the amount of *fines*, or if it was to be no longer in force, it is reasonable to infer, (in the absence of all evidence to the contrary,) either that the common law did not fix the amount of any other punishment, or that it was to be no longer in force for that purpose.*

Under the Saxon laws, fines, payable to the injured party, seem to have been the common punishments for all offences. Even murder was punishable by a fine payable to the relatives of the deceased. The murder of the king even was punishable

---

* Coke attempts to show that there is a distinction between amercements and fines — admitting that amercements must be fixed by one's peers, but claiming that fines may be fixed by the government. (2 *Inst.* 27, 8 *Coke's Reports* 38.) But there seems to have been no ground whatever for supposing that any such distinction existed at the time of Magna Carta. If there were any such distinction in the time of Coke, it had doubtless grown up within the four centuries that had elapsed 'since Magna Carta, and is to be set down as one of the numberless inventions of government for getting rid of the restraints of Magna Carta, and for taking men out of the protection of their peers, and subjecting them to such punishments as the government chooses to inflict.

The first statute of Westminster, passed sixty years after Magna Carta, treats the fine and amercement as synonymous, as follows:

"Forasmuch as *the common fine and amercement* of the whole county in Eyre of the justices for false judgments, or for other trespass, is unjustly assessed by sheriffs and baretors in the shires, * * it is provided, and the king wills, that from henceforth such sums shall be assessed before the justices in Eyre, afore their departure, *by the oath of knights and other honest men,*" &c. — 3 *Edward I., Ch.* 18. (1275.)

And in many other statutes passed after Magna Carta, the terms *fine* and *amercement* seem to be used indifferently, in prescribing the punishments for offences. As late as 1461, (246 years after Magna Carta,) the statute 1 *Edward IV., Ch.* 2, speaks of "*fines, ransoms, and amerciaments*" as being levied upon criminals, as if they were the common punishments of offences.

St. 2 and 3 *Philip and Mary, Ch.* 8, uses the terms, "*fines, forfeitures, and amerciaments*" five times. (1555.)

St. 5 *Elizabeth, Ch.* 13, *Sec.* 10, uses the terms "*fines, forfeitures, and amerciaments.*"

That amercements were fines, or pecuniary punishments, inflicted for offences, is proved by the following statutes, (all supposed to have been passed within one hundred

by fine. When a criminal was unable to pay his fine, his relatives often paid it for him. But if it were not paid, he was put out of the protection of the law, and the injured parties, (or, in the case of murder, the kindred of the deceased,) were allowed to inflict such punishment as they pleased. And if the relatives of the criminal protected him, it was lawful to take vengeance on them also. Afterwards the custom grew up of exacting fines also to the king as a punishment for offences.* And this latter was, doubtless, the usual punishment at the time of Magna Carta, as is evidenced by the fact that for many years immediately following Magna Carta, nearly or quite all statutes that prescribed any punishment at all, prescribed that the offender should "be grievously amerced," or "pay a great fine to the king," or a "grievous ransom," — with the alternative in some cases (perhaps *understood* in all) of imprisonment, banishment, or outlawry, in case of non-payment.†

---

and fifteen years after Magna Carta,) which speak of amercements as a species of "*judgment*," or punishment, and as being inflicted for the same offences as other "judgments."

Thus one statute declares that a baker, for default in the weight of his bread, "ought to be *amerced,* or suffer the *judgment* of the pillory ;" and that a brewer, for "selling ale contrary to the assize," "ought to be *amerced,* or suffer the *judgment* of the tumbrel."—51 *Henry III., St.* 6. (1266.)

Among the "*Statutes of Uncertain Date,*" but supposed to be prior to Edward III., (1326,) are the following:

Chap. 6 provides that "if a brewer break the assize, (fixing the price of ale,) the first, second, and third time, he shall be *amerced ;* but the fourth time he shall suffer *judgment* of the pillory without redemption."

Chap. 7 provides that "a butcher that selleth swine's flesh measled, or flesh dead of the murrain, or that buyeth flesh of Jews, and selleth the same unto Christians, after he shall be convict thereof, for the first time he shall be grievously *amerced ;* the second time he shall suffer *judgment* of the pillory ; and the third time he shall be imprisoned and make *fine ;* and the fourth time he shall forswear the town."

Chap. 10, a statute against *forestalling,* provides that,

"He that is convict thereof, the first time shall be *amerced,* and shall lose the thing so bought, and that according to the custom of the town ; he that is convicted the second time shall have *judgment* of the pillory ; at the third time he shall be imprisoned and make *fine ;* the fourth time he shall abjure the town. And this *judgment* shall be given upon all manner of forestallers, and likewise upon them that have given them counsel, help, or favor."— 1 *Ruffhead's Statutes,* 187, 188. 1 *Statutes of the Realm,* 203.

* 1 Hume, Appendix, 1.

† Blackstone says, "Our ancient Saxon laws nominally punished theft with death, if above the value of twelve pence ; but the criminal was permitted to redeem his life

Judging, therefore, from the special provisions in Magna Carta, requiring *fines*, or amercements, to be imposed only by juries, (without mentioning any other punishments;) judging, also, from the statutes which immediately followed Magna Carta, it is probable that the Saxon custom of punishing all, or nearly all, offences by *fines*, (with the alternative to the criminal of being imprisoned, banished, or outlawed, and exposed to private vengeance, in case of non-payment,) continued until the time of Magna Carta; and that in providing expressly that *fines* should be fixed by the juries, Magna Carta provided for nearly or quite all the punishments that were expected to be inflicted; that if there were to be any others, they were to be fixed by the juries; and consequently that nothing was left to be fixed by "*legem terræ.*"

But whether the common law fixed the punishment of any offences, or not, is a matter of little or no practical importance at this day; because we have no idea of going back to any common law punishments of six hundred years ago, if, indeed, there were any such at that time. It is enough for us to know — *and this is what it is material for us to know* — that the jury fixed the punishments, in all cases, unless they were fixed by the *common law;* that Magna Carta allowed

---

by a pecuniary ransom, as among their ancestors, the Germans, by a stated number of cattle. But in the ninth year of Henry the First, (1109,) this power of redemption was taken away, and all persons guilty of larceny above the value of twelve pence were directed to be hanged, which law continues in force to this day." — 4 *Blackstone,* 238.

I give this statement of Blackstone, because the latter clause may seem to militate with the idea, which the former clause corroborates, viz., that at the time of Magna Carta, fines were the usual punishments of offences. But I think there is no probability that a law so unreasonable in itself, (unreasonable even after making all allowance for the difference in the value of money,) and so contrary to immemorial custom, could or did obtain any general or speedy acquiescence among a people who cared little for the authority of kings.

Maddox, writing of the period from William the Conqueror to John, says :

"The amercements in criminal and common pleas, which were wont to be imposed during this first period and afterwards, were of so many several sorts, that it is not easy to place them under distinct heads. Let them, for method's sake, be reduced to the heads following : Amercements for or by reason of murders and manslaughters, for misdemeanors, for disseisins, for recreancy, for breach of assize, for defaults, for nonappearance, for false judgment, and for not making suit, or hue and cry. To them may be added miscellaneous amercements, for trespasses of divers kinds." — 1 *Maddox' History of the Exchequer,* 542.

no punishments to be prescribed by statute — that is, by the legislative power — nor in any other manner by the king, or his judges, in any case whatever; and, consequently, that all statutes prescribing particular punishments for particular offences, or giving the king's judges any authority to fix punishments, were void.

If the power to fix punishments had been left in the hands of the king, it would have given him a power of oppression, which was liable to be greatly abused; which there was no occasion to leave with him; and which would have been incongruous with the whole object of this chapter of Magna Carta; which object was to take all discretionary or arbitrary power over individuals entirely out of the hands of the king, and his laws, and entrust it only to the common law, and the peers, or jury — that is, the people.

What lex terræ did authorize.

But here the question arises, What then did "*legem terræ*" authorize the king, (that is, the government,) to do in the case of an accused person, if it neither authorized any other trial than that by jury, nor any other punishments than those fixed by juries?

The answer is, that, owing to the darkness of history on the point, it is probably wholly impossible, at this day, to state, *with any certainty or precision*, anything whatever that the *legem terræ* of Magna Carta did authorize the king, (that is, the government,) to do, (if, indeed, it authorized him to do anything,) in the case of criminals, *other than to have them tried and sentenced by their peers, for common law crimes;* and to carry that sentence into execution.

The trial by jury was a part of *legem terræ*, and we have the means of knowing what the trial by jury was. The fact that the jury were to fix the sentence, implies that they were to *try* the accused; otherwise they could not know what sentence, or whether any sentence, ought to be inflicted upon him. Hence it follows that the jury were to judge of everything involved in the trial; that is, they were to judge of the nature of the offence, of the admissibility and weight of testimony, and of everything else whatsoever that was of the essence of the trial. If anything whatever could be dictated to them, either of law or evidence, the sentence would not be theirs, but would be dictated to them by the power that dictated to them the law or evidence. The trial and sentence, then, were wholly in the hands of the jury.

We also have sufficient evidence of the nature of the oath administered to jurors in criminal cases. It was simply, that they *would neither convict the innocent, nor acquit the guilty.* This was the oath in the Saxon times, and probably continued to be until Magna Carta.

We also know that, in case of *conviction*, the sentence of the jury was not necessarily final; that the accused had the right of appeal to the king and his judges, and to demand either a new trial, or an acquittal, if the trial or conviction had been against law.

So much, therefore, of the *legem terræ* of Magna Carta, we know with reasonable certainty.

We also know that Magna Carta provides that "No bailiff (*balivus*) shall hereafter put any man to his law, (put him on trial,) on his single testimony, without credible witnesses brought to support it." Coke thinks "that under this word *balivus*, in this act, is comprehended every justice, minister of the king, steward of the king, steward and bailiff." (2 Inst. 44.) And in support of this idea he quotes from a very ancient law book, called the Mirror of Justices, written in the time of Edward I., within a century after Magna Carta. But whether this were really a common law principle, or whether the provision grew out of that jealousy of the government which, at the time of Magna Carta, had reached its height, cannot perhaps now be determined.

We also know that, by Magna Carta, amercements, or fines, could not be imposed to the ruin of the criminal; that, in the case of a freeman, his *contenement*, or means of subsisting in the condition of a frèeman, must be saved to him; that, in the case of a merchant, his merchandise must be spared; and in the case of a villein, his *waynage*, or plough-tackle and carts. This also is likely to have been a principle of the common law, inasmuch as, in that rude age, when the means of getting employment as laborers were not what they are now, the man and his family would probably have been liable to starvation, if these means of subsistence had been taken from him.

We also know, *generally*, that, at the time of Magna Carta, *all acts intrinsically criminal*, all trespasses against persons and property, were crimes, according to *lex terræ*, or the common law.

Beyond the points now given, we hardly know anything, probably nothing *with certainty*, as to what the "*legem terræ*" of *Magna Carta* did authorize, in regard to crimes. There is hardly anything extant that can give us any real light on the subject.

It would seem, however, that there were, even at that day, some common law principles governing arrests; and some common law forms and rules as to holding a man for trial, (by bail or imprisonment;) putting him on trial, such as by indictment or complaint; summoning and empanelling jurors, &c., &c. Whatever these common law principles were, Magna Carta requires them to be observed; for Magna Carta provides for the whole proceedings, commencing with the arrest, ("no freeman shall be *arrested*," &c.,) and ending with the execution of the sentence. And it provides that nothing shall be done, by the government, from beginning to end, unless according to the sentence of the peers, or "*legem terræ*," the common law. The trial by peers was a part of *legem terræ*, and we have seen that the peers must necessarily have governed the whole proceedings at the trial. But all the proceedings for arresting the man, and bringing him to trial, must have been had before the case could come under the cognizance of the peers, and they must, therefore, have been governed by other rules than the discretion of the peers. We may *conjecture*, although we cannot perhaps know with much certainty, that the *lex terræ*, or common law, governing these other proceedings, was somewhat similar to the common law principles, on the same points, at the present day. Such seem to be the opinions of Coke, who says that the phrase *nisi per legem terræ* means *unless by due process of law*.

Thus, he says:

"*Nisi per legem terræ. But by the law of the land.* For

the true sense and exposition of these words, see the statute of 37 Edw. III., cap. 8, where the words, *by the law of the land,* are rendered *without due process of law ;* for there it is said, though it be contained in the Great Charter, that no man be taken, imprisoned, or put out of his freehold, *without process of the law ; that is, by indictment or presentment of good and lawful men, where such deeds be done in due manner,* or *by writ original of the common law.*

" Without being brought in to answer but by due process of the common law.

" No man be put to answer without presentment before justices, or thing of record, or by due process, or by writ original, *according to the old law of the land.*" — 2 *Inst.* 50.

The foregoing interpretations of the words *nisi per legem terræ* are corroborated by the following statutes, enacted in the next century after Magna Carta.

" That no man, from henceforth, shall be attached by any accusation, nor forejudged of life or limb, nor his land, tenements, goods, nor chattels, seized into the king's hands, against the form of the Great Charter, *and the law of the land.*" — *St.* 5 *Edward III., Ch.* 9. (1331.)

" Whereas it is contained in the Great Charter of the franchises of England, that none shall be imprisoned, nor put out of his freehold, nor of his franchises, nor free customs, *unless it be by the law of the land ;* it is accorded, assented, and established, that from henceforth none shall be taken by petition, or suggestion made to our lord the king, or to his council, *unless it be by indictment or presentment of good and lawful people of the same neighborhood where such deeds be done in due manner, or by process made by writ original at the common law ;* nor that none be put out of his franchises, nor of his freehold, *unless he be duly brought into answer, and forejudged of the same by the course of the law ;* and if anything be done against the same, it shall be redressed and holden for none." — *St.* 25 *Edward III., Ch.* 4. (1350.)

" That no man, of what estate or condition that he be, shall be put out of land or tenement, nor taken, nor imprisoned, nor disinherited, nor put to death, without being brought in answer *by due process of law.*" — *St.* 28 *Edward III., Ch.* 3. (1354.)

" That no man be put to answer without presentment before justices, or matter of record, or by due process and writ original, according to the *old law of the land.* And if anything from henceforth be done to the contrary, it shall be void in law, and holden for error." — *St.* 42 *Edward III., Ch.* 3. (1368.)

The foregoing interpretation of the words *nisi per legem terræ* — that is, *by due process of law* — including indictment, &c., has been adopted as the true one by modern writers and courts; as, for example, by Kent, (2 *Comm.* 13,) Story, (3 *Comm.* 661,) and the Supreme Court of New York, (19 *Wendell*, 676; 4 *Hill*, 146.)

The fifth amendment to the constitution of the United States seems to have been framed on the same idea, inasmuch as it provides that "no person shall be deprived of life, liberty, or property, *without due process of law.*"*

Whether the word VEL *should be rendered by* OR, *or by* AND.

Having thus given the meanings, or rather the applications, which the words *vel per legem terræ* will reasonably, and perhaps must necessarily, bear, it is proper to suggest, that it has been supposed by some that the word *vel*, instead of being rendered by *or*, as it usually is, ought to be rendered by *and*, inasmuch as the word *vel* is often used for *et*, and the whole phrase *nisi per judicium parium suorum, vel per legem terræ*, (which would then read, unless by the sentence of his peers, *and* the law of the land,) would convey a more intelligible and harmonious meaning than it otherwise does.

Blackstone suggests that this may be the true reading. (*Charters*, p. 41.) Also Mr. Hallam, who says:

" Nisi per legale judicium parium suorum, *vel* per legem terræ. Several explanations have been offered of the alternative clause; which some have referred to judgment by default, or demurrer; others to the process of attachment for contempt. Certainly there are many legal procedures besides trial by jury, through which a party's goods or person may be taken. But one may doubt whether these were in contemplation of the framers of Magna Carta. In an entry of the Charter of 1217 by a contemporary hand, preserved in the Town-clerk's office in London, called Liber Custumarum et Regum antiquarum, a various reading, *et* per legem terræ, occurs. *Blackstone's Charters*, p. 42 (41.) And the word *vel* is so frequently used for *et*, that I am not wholly free from a suspicion that it

---

* Coke, in his exposition of the words *legem terræ*, gives quite in detail the principles of the common law governing *arrests ;* and takes it for granted that the words " *nisi per legem terræ*" are applicable to arrests, as well as to the indictment, &c. — 2 *Inst.*, 51, 52.

was so intended in this place. The meaning will be, that no person shall be disseized, &c., except upon a lawful cause of action, found by the verdict of a jury. This really seems as good as any of the disjunctive interpretations; but I do not offer it with much confidence." — 2 *Hallam's Middle Ages,* Ch. 8, Part 2, p. 449, *note.**

---

* I cite the above extract from Mr. Hallam solely for the sake of his authority for rendering the word *vel* by *and;* and not by any means for the purpose of indorsing the opinion he suggests, that *legem terræ* authorized "judgments by default or demurrer," *without the intervention of a jury.* He seems to imagine that *lex terræ,* the common law, at the time of Magna Carta, included everything, even to the practice of courts, that is, *at this day,* called by the name of *Common Law;* whereas much of what is *now* called Common Law has grown up, by usurpation, since the time of Magna Carta, in palpable violation of the authority of that charter. He says, "Certainly there are many legal procedures, besides *trial* by jury, through which a party's goods or person may be taken." Of course there are *now* many such ways, in which a party's goods or person *are* taken, besides by the judgment of a jury ; but the question is, whether such takings are not in violation of Magna Carta.

He seems to think that, in cases of "judgment by default or demurrer," there is no need of a jury, and thence to infer that *legem terræ* may not have required a jury in those cases. But this opinion is founded on the erroneous idea that juries are required only for determining contested *facts,* and not for judging of the law. In case of default, the plaintiff must present a *prima facie* case before he is entitled to a judgment ; and Magna Carta, (supposing it to require a jury trial in civil cases, as Mr. Hallam assumes that it does,) as much requires that this *prima facie* case, both law and fact, be made out to the satisfaction of a jury, as it does that a contested case shall be.

As for a demurrer, the jury must try a demurrer (having the advice and assistance of the court, of course) as much as any other matter of law arising in a case.

Mr. Hallam evidently thinks there is no use for a jury, except where there is a "*trial*" — meaning thereby a contest on matters of *fact.* His language is, that " there are many legal procedures, besides *trial* by jury, through which a party's goods or person may be taken." Now Magna Carta says nothing of *trial* by jury; but only of the *judgment,* or sentence, of a jury. It is only *by inference* that we come to the conclusion that there must be a *trial* by jury. Since the jury alone can give the *judgment,* or *sentence,* we *infer* that they must *try* the case; because otherwise they would be incompetent, and would have no moral right, to give *judgment.* They must, therefore, examine the grounds, (both of law and fact,) or rather *try* the grounds, of every action whatsoever, whether it be decided on "default, demurrer," or otherwise, and render their judgment, or sentence, thereon, before any judgment can be a legal one, on which " to take a party's goods or person." In short, the principle of Magna Carta is, that no judgment can be valid *against a party's goods or person,* (not even a judgment for costs,) except a judgment rendered by a jury. Of course a jury must try every question, both of law and fact, that is involved in the rendering of that judgment. They are to have the assistance and advice of the judges, so far as they desire them; but the judgment itself must be theirs, and not the judgment of the court.

As to "process of attachment for contempt," it is of course lawful for a judge, in his character of a peace officer, to issue a warrant for the arrest of a man guilty of a contempt, as he would for the arrest of any other offender, and hold him to bail, (or, in default of bail, commit him to prison,) to answer for his offence before a jury. Or he

The idea that the word *vel* should be rendered by *and*, is corroborated, if not absolutely confirmed, by the following passage in Blackstone, which has before been cited. Speaking of the trial by jury, as established by Magna Carta, he calls it,

" A privilege which is couched in almost the same words

---

may order him into custody without a warrant when the offence is committed in the judge's presence. But there is no reason why a judge should have the power of *punishing* for contempt, any more than for any other offence. And it is one of the most dangerous powers a judge can have, because it gives him absolute authority in a court of justice, and enables him to tyrannize as he pleases over parties, counsel, witnesses, and jurors. If a judge have power to punish for contempt, and to determine for himself what is a contempt, the whole administration of justice (or injustice, if he choose to make it so) is in his hands. And all the rights of jurors, witnesses, counsel, and parties, are held subject to his pleasure, and can be exercised only agreeably to his will. He can of course control the entire proceedings in, and consequently the decision of, every cause, by restraining and punishing every one, whether party, counsel, witness, or juror, who presumes to offer anything contrary to his pleasure.

This arbitrary power, which has been usurped and exercised by judges to punish for contempt, has undoubtedly had much to do in subduing counsel into those servile, obsequious, and cowardly habits, which so universally prevail among them, and which have not only cost so many clients their rights, but have also cost the people so many of their liberties.

If any *summary* punishment for contempt be ever necessary, (as it probably is not,) beyond exclusion for the time being from the court-room, (which should be done, not as a punishment, but for self-protection, and the preservation of order,) the judgment for it should be given by the jury, (where the trial is before a jury,) and not by the court, for the jury, and not the court, are really the judges. For the same reason, exclusion from the court-room should be ordered only by the jury, in cases when the trial is before a jury, because they, being the real judges and triers of the cause, are entitled, if anybody, to the control of the court-room. In appeal courts, where no juries sit, it may be necessary — not as a punishment, but for self-protection, and the maintenance of order — that the court should exercise the power of excluding a person, for the time being, from the court-room; but there is no reason why they should proceed to sentence him as a criminal, without his being tried by a jury.

If the people wish to have their rights respected and protected in courts of justice, it is manifestly of the last importance that they jealously guard the liberty of parties, counsel, witnesses, and jurors, against all arbitrary power on the part of the court.

Certainly Mr. Hallam may very well say that "one may doubt whether these (the several cases he has mentioned) were in contemplation of the framers of Magna Carta " — that is, as exceptions to the rule requiring that all judgments, that are to be enforced " *against a party's goods or person*," be rendered by a jury.

Again, Mr. Hallam says, if the word *vel* be rendered by *and*, " the meaning will be, that no person shall be disseized, &c., *except upon a lawful cause of action*." This is true ; but it does not follow that any cause of action, founded on *statute only*, is therefore a " *lawful* cause of action," within the meaning of *legem terræ*, or the *Common Law*. Within the meaning of the *legem terræ* of Magna Carta, nothing but a *common law* cause of action is a " *lawful* " one.

with that of the Emperor Conrad two hundred years before:
'nemo beneficium suum perdat, nisi secundum consuetudinem
antecessorum nostrorum, *et* judicium parium suorum.' " (No
one shall lose his estate unless according to the custom of our
ancestors, *and* the judgment of his peers.) — 3 *Blackstone*, 350.

If the word *vel* be rendered by *and*, (as I think it must be,
at least in some cases,) this chapter of Magna Carta will then
read that no freeman shall be arrested or punished, "unless
according to the sentence of his peers, *and* the law of the
land."

The difference between this reading and the other is important. In the one case, there would be, at first view, some color
of ground for saying that a man might be punished in either
of two ways, viz., according to the séntence of his peers, *or*
according to the law of the land. In the other case, it requires
both the sentence of his peers *and* the law of the land (common law) to authorize his punishment.

If this latter reading be adopted, the provision would seem
to exclude all trials except trial by jury, and all causes of
action except those of the *common law*.

But I apprehend the word *vel* must be rendered both by
and, and by *or;* that in cases of a *judgment*, it should be
rendered by *and*, so as to require the concurrence both of " the
judgment of the peers *and* the law of the land," to authorize
the king to make execution upon a party's goods or person;
but that in cases of arrest and imprisonment, simply for the
purpose of bringing a man to trial, *vel* should be rendered by
or, because there can have been no judgment of a jury in
such a case, and " the law of the land " must therefore necessarily be the only guide to, and restraint upon, the king. If this
guide and restraint were taken away, the king would be
invested with an arbitrary and most dangerous power in
making arrests, and confining in prison, under pretence of an
intention to bring to trial.

Having thus examined the language of this chapter of Magna
Carta, so far as it relates to criminal cases, its legal import
may be stated as follows, viz. :

No freeman shall be arrested, or imprisoned, or deprived of
his freehold, or his liberties, or free customs, or be outlawed,

or exiled, or in any manner destroyed, (harmed,) nor will we
(the king) proceed against him, nor send any one against him,
by force or arms, unless according to (that is, in execution
of) the sentence of his peers, *and* (or *or*, as the case may
require) the Common Law of England, (as it was at the time
of Magna Carta, in 1215.)

CHAPTER III.

IF any evidence, extraneous to the history and language
of Magna Carta, were needed to prove that, by that chapter
which guaranties the trial by jury, all was meant that has
now been ascribed to it, *and that the legislation of the king
was to be of no authority with the jury beyond what they chose
to allow to it,* and that the juries were to limit the punishments
to be inflicted, we should find that evidence in various sources,
such as the laws, customs, and characters of their ancestors
on the continent, and of the northern Europeans generally; in
the legislation and customs that immediately succeeded Magna
Carta; in the oaths that have at different times been administered to jurors, &c., &c. This evidence can be exhibited here
but partially. To give it all would require too much space
and labor.

SECTION I.

Weakness of the Regal Authority.

Hughes, in his preface to his translation of Horne's "*Mirror
of Justices,*" (a book written in the time of Edward I., 1272
to 1307,) giving a concise view of the laws of England generally, says:

"Although in the Saxon's time I find the usual words
of the acts then to have been *edictum,* (edict,) *constitutio,*
(statute,) little mention being made of the commons, yet I
further find that, *tam demum leges vim et vigorem habuerunt,
cum fuerunt non modo institutæ sed firmatæ approbatione
communitatis.*" (The laws had force and vigor only when
they were not only enacted, but confirmed by the approval
of the community.)

The *Mirror of Justices* itself also says, (ch. 1, sec. 3,) in speaking " *Of the first Constitutions of the Ancient Kings:*"

" Many ordinances were made by many kings, until the time of the king that now is (Edward I.); the which ordinances were abused, *or not used by many, nor very current,* because they were not put in writing, and certainly published." — *Mirror of Justices,* p. 6.

Hallam says:

" The Franks, Lombards, and Saxons seem alike to have been jealous of judicial authority; and averse to surrendering what concerned every man's private right, out of the hands of his neighbors and equals." — 1 *Middle Ages,* 271.

The " judicial authority," here spoken of, was the authority of the kings, (who at that time united the office of both legislators and judges,) and not of a separate department of government, called the judiciary, like what has existed in more modern times.*

Hume says:

" The government of the Germans, and that of all the northern nations, who established themselves on the ruins of Rome, was always extremely free; and those fierce people, accustomed to independence and inured to arms, *were more guided by persuasion than authority, in the submission which they paid to their princes.* The military despotism, which had taken place in the Roman empire, and which, previously to the irruption of those conquerors, had sunk the genius of men, and destroyed every noble principle of science and virtue, was unable to resist the vigorous efforts of a free people, and Europe, as from a new epoch, rekindled her ancient spirit, and shook off the base servitude to arbitrary will and authority under which she had so long labored. The free constitutions then established, however impaired by the encroachments of succeeding princes, still preserve an air of independence and legal administration, which distinguished the European nations; and if that part of the globe maintain sentiments

---

* Hale says :

" The trial by jury of twelve men was the *usual* trial among the Normans, in most suits ; especially in assizes, *et juris utrum.*" — 1 *Hale's History of the Common Law,* 219. This was in Normandy, *before* the conquest of England by the Normans. *See Ditto,* p. 218.

Crabbe says :

" It cannot be denied that the practice of submitting causes to the decision of twelve men was universal among all the northern tribes (of Europe) from the very remotest antiquity." — *Crabbe's History of the English Law,* p. 32.

of liberty, honor, equity, and valor, superior to the rest of mankind, it owes these advantages chiefly to the seeds implanted by those generous barbarians.

"*The Saxons, who subdued Britain, as they enjoyed great liberty in their own country, obstinately retained that invaluable possession in their new settlement; and they imported into this island the same principles of independence, which they had inherited from their ancestors. The chieftains, (for such they were, more than kings or princes,) who commanded them in those military expeditions, still possessed a very limited authority;* and as the Saxons exterminated, rather than subdued the ancient inhabitants, they were, indeed, transplanted into a new territory, *but preserved unaltered all their civil and military institutions.* The language was pure Saxon; even the names of places, which often remain while the tongue entirely changes, were almost all affixed by the conquerors; the manners and customs were wholly German; and the same picture of a fierce and bold liberty, which is drawn by the masterly pen of Tacitus, will suit those founders of the English government. *The king, so far from being invested with arbitrary power, was only considered as the first among the citizens; his authority depended more on his personal qualities than on his station; he was even so far on a level with the people, that a stated price was fixed for his head, and a legal fine was levied upon his murderer, which though proportionate to his station, and superior to that paid for the life of a subject, was a sensible mark of his subordination to the community.*" — 1 *Hume, Appendix,* 1.

Stuart says :

" The Saxons brought along with them into Britain their own customs, language, and civil institutions. Free in Germany, they renounced not their independence, when they had conquered. Proud from victory, and with their swords in their hands, would they surrender their liberties to a private man? Would temporary leaders, limited in their powers, and unprovided in resources, ever think to usurp an authority over warriors, who considered themselves as their equals, were impatient of control, and attached with devoted zeal to their privileges? Or, would they find leisure to form resolutions, or opportunities to put them in practice, amidst the tumult and confusion of those fierce and bloody wars, which their nations first waged with the Britons, and then engaged in among themselves? Sufficiently flattered in leading the armies of their countrymen, the ambition of commanders could as little suggest such designs, as the liberty of the people could submit to them. The conquerors of Britain retained their independ-

ence; and this island saw itself again in that free state in
which the Roman arms had discovered it.

"The same firmness of character, and generosity of manners,
which, in general, distinguished the Germans, were possessed
in an eminent degree by the Saxons; and while we endeavor
to unfold their political institutions, we must perpetually turn
our observation to that masterly picture in which the Roman
historian has described these nations. In the woods of Germany shall we find the principles which directed the state of
land, in the different kingdoms of Europe; and there shall we
find the foundation of those ranks of men, and of those civil
arrangements, which the barbarians everywhere established;
and which the English alone have had the good fortune, or
the spirit, to preserve." — *Stuart on the Constitution of England*, p. 59–61.

"Kings they (the Germans) respected as the first magistrates of the state; but the authority possessed by them was
narrow and limited." — *Ditto*, p. 134.

"Did he, (the king,) at any time, relax his activity and
martial ardor, did he employ his abilities to the prejudice of
his nation, or fancy he was superior to the laws; the same
power which raised him to honor, humbled and degraded him.
The customs and councils of his country pointed out to him
his duty; and if he infringed on the former, or disobeyed the
latter, a fierce people set aside his authority. * * *

"His long hair was the only ornament he affected, and
to be foremost to attack an enemy was his chief distinction.
Engaged in every hazardous expedition, he was a stranger to
repose; and, rivalled by half the heroes of his tribe, he could
obtain little power. Anxious and watchful for the public interest, he felt every moment his dependence, and gave proofs
of his submission.

"He attended the general assembly of his nation, and was
allowed the privilege to harangue it first; but the arts of persuasion, though known and respected by a rude people, were
unequally opposed to the prejudices and passions of men." —
Ditto, p. 135–6.

"*The authority of a Saxon monarch was not more considerable. The Saxons submitted not to the arbitrary rule of princes.
They administered an oath to their sovereigns, which bound
them to acknowledge the laws, and to defend the rights of the
church and people; and if they forgot this obligation, they
forfeited their office.* In both countries, a price was affixed
on kings, a fine expiated their murder, as well as that of the
meanest citizen; and the smallest violation of ancient usage,

or the least step towards tyranny, was always dangerous, and often fatal to them." — *Ditto*, p. 139–40.

"They were not allowed to impose taxes on the kingdom." — *Ditto*, p. 146.

"Like the German monarchs, they deliberated in the general assembly of the nation ; *but their legislative authority was not much respected;* and their assent was considered in no better light than as a form. This, however, was their chief prerogative; and they employed it to acquire an ascendant in the state. To art and insinuation they turned, as their only resource, and flattered a people whom they could not awe; but address, and the abilities to persuade, were a weak compensation for the absence of real power.

"They declared war, it is said, and made peace. In both cases, however, they acted as the instruments of the state, and put in execution the resolutions which its councils had decreed. If, indeed, an enemy had invaded the kingdom, and its glory and its safety were concerned, the great lords took the field at the call of their sovereign. But had a sovereign declared war against a neighboring state, without requiring their advice, or if he meant to revenge by arms an insult offered to him by a subject, a haughty and independent nobility refused their assistance. These they considered as the quarrels of the king, and not of the nation; and in all such emergencies he could only be assisted by his retainers and dependents." — *Ditto*, p. 147–8.

"Nor must we imagine that the Saxon, any more than the German monarchs, succeeded each other in a lineal descent,* or that they disposed of the crown at their pleasure. In both countries, the free election of the people filled the throne; and their choice was the only rule by which princes reigned. The succession, accordingly, of their kings was often broken and interrupted, and their depositions were frequent and groundless. The will of a prince whom they had long respected, and the favor they naturally transferred to his descendant, made them often advance him to the royal dignity; but the crown of his ancestor he considered as the gift of the people, and neither expected nor claimed it as a right." — *Ditto*, p. 151–3.

In Germany "It was the business of the great to command in war, and in peace they distributed justice. * * *

---

* "The people, who in every general council or assembly could oppose and dethrone their sovereigns, were in little dread of their encroachments on their liberties ; and kings, who found sufficient employment in keeping possession of their crowns, would not likely attack the more important privileges of their subjects."

" The *princes* in Germany were *earls* in England. The great
contended in both countries in the number of their retainers,
and in that splendor and magnificence which are so alluring
to a rude people; and though they joined to set bounds to
regal power, they were often animated against each other
with the fiercest hatred.　To a proud and impatient nobility
it seemed little and unsuiting to give or accept compositions
for the injuries they committed or received; and their vassals
adopting their resentment and ·passions, war and bloodshed
alone could terminate their quarrels.　What necessarily resulted from their situation in society, was continued as a
privilege; and the great, in both countries, made war, of their
private authority, on their enemies.　The Saxon earls even
carried their arms against their sovereigns; and, surrounded
with retainers, or secure in fortresses and castles, they despised
their resentment, and defied their power.

" The judges of the people, they presided in both countries
in courts of law.*　The particular districts over which they
exerted their authority were marked out in Germany by the
council of the state; and in England their jurisdiction extended over the fiefs and other territories they possessed.　All
causes, both civil and criminal, were tried before them; and
they judged, except in cases of the utmost importance, without
appeal.　They were even allowed to grant pardon to criminals, and to correct by their clemency the rigors of justice.
Nor did the sovereign exercise any authority in their lands.
In these his officers formed no courts, and his *writ* was disregarded.　＊　＊　＊

" They had officers, as well as the king, who collected their
revenues, and added to their greatness; and the inhabitants
of their lands they distinguished by the name of *subjects.*

" But to attend the general assembly of their nation was the
chief prerogative of the German and Saxon princes; and as
they consulted the interest of their country, and deliberated
concerning matters of state, so in the *king's court*, of which
also they were members, they assisted to pronounce judgment
in the complaints and appeals which were lodged in it." —
Ditto, p. 158 to 165.

Henry says:

"Nothing can be more evident than this important truth;
that our Anglo-Saxon kings were not absolute monarchs; but

---

* This office was afterwards committed to sheriffs.　But even while the court was
held by the lord, "*the Lord was not judge, but the Pares (peers) only.*" — *Gilbert on the
Court of Exchequer,* 61-2.

that their powers and prerogatives were limited by the laws and customs of the country. Our Saxon ancestors had been governed by limited monarchs in their native seats on the continent; and there is not the least appearance or probability that they relinquished their liberties, and submitted to absolute government in their new settlements in this island. It is not to be imagined that men, whose reigning passion was the love of liberty, would willingly resign it; and their new sovereigns, who had been their fellow-soldiers, had certainly no power to compel them to such a resignation." —3 *Henry's History of Great Britain*, 358.

Mackintosh says : " The Saxon chiefs, who were called kings, originally acquired power by the same natural causes which have gradually, and everywhere, raised a few men above their fellows. They were, doubtless, more experienced, more skilful, more brave, or more beautiful, than those who followed them. * * A king was powerful in war by the lustre of his arms, and the obvious necessity of obedience. His influence in peace fluctuated with his personal character. In the progress of usage his power became more fixed and more limited. * * It would be very unreasonable to suppose that the northern Germans who had conquered England, had so far changed their characteristic habits from the age of Tacitus, that the victors became slaves, and that their generals were converted into tyrants." — *Mackintosh's Hist. of England, Ch. 2. 45 Lardner's Cab. Cyc.,* 73-4.

Rapin, in his discourse on the " Origin and Nature of the English Constitution," says :

" There are but two things the Saxons did not think proper to trust their kings with; for being of like passions with other men, they might very possibly abuse them ; namely, the power of changing the laws enacted by consent of king and people; and the power of raising taxes at pleasure. From these two articles sprung numberless branches concerning the liberty and property of the subject, which the king cannot touch, without breaking the constitution, and they are the distinguishing character of the English monarchy. The prerogatives of the crown, and the rights and privileges of the people, flowing from the two fore-mentioned articles, are the ground of all the laws that from time to time have been made by unanimous consent of king and people. The English government consists in the strict union of the king's prerogatives with the people's liberties. * * But when kings arose, as some there were, that aimed at absolute power, by changing the old, and making new laws, at pleasure; by imposing illegal taxes on the people; this excellent government being, in a manner, dissolved by these destructive measures, confusion and civil wars ensued, which some very wrongfully ascribe to the fickle and restless temper of the English." — *Rapin's Preface to his History of England.*

Hallam says that among the Saxons, "the royal authority was weak." — *2 Middle Ages,* 403.

But although the king himself had so little authority, that it cannot be supposed for a moment that his laws were regarded as imperative by the people, it has nevertheless been claimed, in modern times, by some who seem determined to find or make a precedent for the present legislative authority of parliament, that his laws were authoritative, *when assented to* by the *Witena-gemote,* or assembly of wise men — that is, the bishops and barons. But this assembly evidently had no legislative power whatever. The king would occasionally invite the bishops and barons to meet him for consultation on public affairs, *simply as a council,* and not as a legislative body. Such as saw fit to attend, did so. If they were agreed upon what ought to be done, the king would pass a law accordingly, and the barons and bishops would then return and inform the people orally what laws had been passed, and use their influence with them to induce them to conform to the law of the king, and the recommendation of the council. And the people no doubt were much more likely to accept a law of the king, if it had been approved by this council, than if it had not. But it was still only a law of the king, which they obeyed or disregarded according to their own notions of expediency. The numbers who usually attended this council were too small to admit of the supposition that they had any legislative authority whatever, to impose laws upon the people against their will.

Lingard says :

"It was necessary that the king should obtain the assent of these (the members of the Witena-gemotes) to all legislative enactments; *because, without their acquiescence and support, it was impossible to carry them into execution.* To many charters (laws) we have the signatures of the *Witan. They seldom exceed thirty in number ; they never amount to sixty."* — 1 *Lingard,* 486.

It is ridiculous to suppose that the assent of such an assembly gave any *authority* to the laws of the king, or had any influence in securing obedience to them, otherwise than by way of persuasion. If this body had had any real legislative authority, such as is accorded to legislative bodies of the present day, they would have made themselves at once the most conspicuous portion of the government, and would have left behind them abundant evidence of their power, instead of the evidence simply of their assent to a few laws passed by the king.

More than this. If this body had had any real legislative authority, they would have constituted an aristocracy, having, in conjunction with the king, absolute power over the people. Assembling voluntarily, merely on the invitation of the king; deputed by nobody but themselves; representing nobody but themselves; responsible to nobody but themselves; their legislative authority, if they had had any, would of necessity have made the government the government of an aristocracy merely, *and the people slaves, of course.* And this would necessarily have been the picture that history would have given us of the Anglo-Saxon government, *and of Anglo-Saxon liberty.*

The fact that the people had no representation in this assembly, and the further fact that, through their juries alone, they nevertheless maintained that noble freedom, the very tradition of which (after the substance of the thing itself has ceased to exist) has constituted the greatest pride and glory of the nation to this day, *prove* that this assembly exercised no authority which juries of the people acknowledged, except at their own discretion.*

---

* The opinion expressed in the text, that the Witan had no legislative authority, is corroborated by the following authorities :

"From the fact that the new laws passed by the king and the Witan were laid before the shire-mote, (county court,) we should be almost justified in the inference that a second sanction was necessary before they could have the effect of law in that particular county." — *Dunham's Middle Ages, Sec.* 2, *B.* 2, *Ch.* 1. 57 *Lardner's Cab. Cyc.,* 53.

The "*second sanction*" required to give the legislation of the king and Witan the effect of law, was undoubtedly, I think, *as a general thing, the sanction of a jury.* I know of no evidence whatever that laws were ever submitted to popular vote in the county courts, as this author seems to suppose possible. Another mode, sometimes re-

Theré is not a more palpable truth, in the history of the Anglo-Saxon government, than that stated in the Introduction to Gilbert's History of the Common Pleas,* viz., "*that the County and Hundred Courts,*" (to which should have been added the other courts in which juries sat, the courts-baron and court-leet,) "*in those times were the real and only Parliaments of the kingdom.*" And why were they the real and only parliaments of the kingdom? Solely because, as will be hereafter shown, the juries in those courts tried causes on their intrinsic merits, according to their own ideas of justice, irrespective of the laws agreed upon by kings, priests, and barons; and whatever principles they uniformly, or perhaps generally, enforced, *and none others*, became practically the law of the land as matter of course.†

Finally, on this point. Conclusive proof that the legislation of the king was of little or no authority, is found in the fact *that the kings enacted so few laws.* If their laws had been received as authoritative, in the manner that legislative enactments are at this day, they would have been making laws continually. Yet the codes of the most celebrated kings are very small, and were little more than compilations of immemorial customs. The code of Alfred would not fill twelve

---

sorted to for obtaining the sanction of the people to the laws of the Witan, was, it seems, to persuade the people themselves to swear to observe them. Mackintosh says :

"The preambles of the laws (of the Witan) speak of the infinite number of *liegemen* who attended, as only applauding the measures of the assembly. But this applause was neither so unimportant to the success of the measures, nor so precisely distinguished from a share in legislation, as those who read history with a modern eye might imagine. It appears that under Athelstan expedients were resorted to, to obtain a consent to the law from great bodies of the people in their districts, which their numbers rendered impossible in a national assembly. That monarch appears to have sent commissioners to hold *shire-gemotes* or county meetings, where they proclaimed the laws made by the king and his counsellors, which, being acknowledged and sworn to at these *folk-motes* (meetings of the people) became, by their assent, completely binding on the whole nation." — *Mackintosh's Hist. of England, Ch.* 2. 45 *Lardner's Cab. Cyc.*, 75.

* Page 31.

† Hallam says, "It was, however, to the county court that an English freeman chiefly looked for the maintenance of his civil rights." — 2 *Middle Ages*, 392.

Also, "This (the county court) was the great constitutional judicature in all questions of civil right." — *Ditto*, 395.

Also, "The liberties of these Anglo-Saxon thanes were chiefly secured, next to their swords and their free spirits, by the inestimable right of deciding civil and criminal suits in their own county courts." — *Ditto*, 399.

pages of the statute book of Massachusetts, and was little or nothing else than a compilation of the laws of Moses, and the Saxon customs, evidently collected from considerations of convenience, rather than enacted on the principle of authority. The code of Edward the Confessor would not fill twenty pages of the statute book of Massachusetts, and, says Blackstone, "seems to have been no more than a new edition, or fresh promulgation of Alfred's code, or *dome-book*, with such additions and improvements as the experience of a century and a half suggested." — 1 *Blackstone*, 66.*

---

* " Alfred may, in one sense, be called the founder of these laws, (the Saxon,) for until his time they were an *unwritten* code, but he expressly says, ' *that I, Alfred, collected the good laws of our forefathers into one code, and also I wrote them down* '— which is a decisive fact in the history of our laws well worth noting." — *Introduction to Gilbert's History of the Common Pleas*, p. 2, *note*.

Kelham says, " Let us consult our own lawyers and historians, and they will tell us * * that Alfred, Edgar, and Edward the Confessor, were the great *compilers and restorers* of the English Laws." — *Kelham's Preliminary Discourse to the Laws of William the Conqueror*, p. 12. *Appendix to Kelham's Dictionary of the Norman Language.*

" He (Alfred) also, like another Theodosius, *collected the various customs* that he found dispersed in the kingdom, and reduced and digested them into one uniform system, or code of laws, in his *som-bec*, or *liber judicialis* (judicial book). This he *compiled* for the use of the court baron, hundred and county court, the court-leet and sheriff's tourn, tribunals which he established for the trial of all causes, civil and criminal, in the very districts wherein the complaints arose." — 4 *Blackstone*, 411.

Alfred himself says, " Hence I, King Alfred, gathered these together, and commanded many of those to be written down which our forefathers observed — those which I liked — and those which I did not like, by the advice of my Witan, I threw aside. For I durst not venture to set down in writing over many of my own, since I knew not what among them would please those that should come after us. But those which I met with either of the days of me, my kinsman, or of Offa, King of Mercia, or of Æthelbert, who was the first of the English who received baptism — those which appeared to me the justest — I have here collected, and abandoned the others. Then I, Alfred, King of the West Saxons, showed these to all my Witan, and they then said that they were all willing to observe them." — *Laws of Alfred, translated by R. Price, prefixed to Mackintosh's History of England, vol.* 1. 45 *Lardner's Cab. Cyc.*

" King Edward * * projected and begun what his grandson, King Edward the Confessor, afterwards completed, viz., one uniform digest or body of laws to be observed throughout the whole kingdom, *being probably no more than a revival of King Alfred's code*, with some improvements suggested by necessity and experience, particularly the incorporating some of the British, or, rather, Mercian *customs*, and also *such of the Danish* (customs) as were reasonable and approved, into the *West Saxon Lage*, which was still the ground-work of the whole. And this appears to be the best supported and most plausible conjecture, (for certainty is not to be expected,) of the rise and original of that admirable system of maxims and unwritten customs which is now known by the

The Code of William the Conqueror * would fill less than seven pages of the statute book of Massachusetts; and most of the laws contained in it are taken from the laws of the preceding kings, and especially of Edward the Confessor (whose laws William swore to observe); but few of his own being added.

The codes of the other Saxon and Norman kings were, as a general rule, less voluminous even than these that have been named; and probably did not exceed them in originality.† The Norman princes, from William the Conqueror to John, I think without exception, bound themselves, and, in order to maintain their thrones, were obliged to bind themselves, to observe the ancient laws and customs, in other words, the "*lex terræ*," or "*common law*" of the kingdom. Even Magna Carta contains hardly anything other than this same "*common law*," with some new securities for its observance.

---

name of the *common law*, as extending its authority universally over all the realm, and which is doubtless of Saxon parentage." — 4 *Blackstone*, 412.

" By the *Lex Terræ* and *Lex Regni* is understood the laws of Edward the Confessor, confirmed and enlarged as they were by William the Conqueror; and this Constitution or Code of Laws is what even to this day are called ' *The Common Law of the Land.*' " — *Introduction to Gilbert's History of the Common Pleas*, p. 22, *note*.

* Not the conqueror of the English people, (as the friends of liberty maintain,) but only of Harold the usurper. — *See Hale's History of the Common Law*, ch. 5.

† For all these codes see Wilkins' Laws of the Anglo-Saxons.

" Being regulations adapted to existing institutions, the Anglo-Saxon statutes are concise and technical, alluding to the law which was then living and in vigor, rather than defining it. The same clauses and chapters are often repeated word for word, in the statutes of subsequent kings, showing that enactments which bear the appearance of novelty are merely declaratory. Consequently the appearance of a law, seemingly for the first time, is by no means to be considered as a proof that the matter which it contains is new; nor can we trace the progress of the Anglo-Saxon institutions with any degree of certainty, by following the dates of the statutes in which we find them first noticed. All arguments founded on the apparent chronology of the subjects included in the laws, are liable to great fallacies. Furthermore, a considerable portion of the Anglo-Saxon law was never recorded in writing. There can be no doubt but that the rules of inheritance were well established and defined ; yet we have not a single law, and hardly a single document from which the course of the descent of land can be inferred. * * Positive proof cannot be obtained of the commencement of any institution, because the first written law relating to it may posssibly be merely confirmatory or declaratory; neither can the non-existence of any institution be inferred from the absence of direct evidence. Written laws were modified and controlled by customs of which no trace can be discovered, until after the lapse of centuries, although those usages must have been in constant vigor during the long interval of silence." — 1 *Palgrave's Rise and Progress of the English Commonwealth*, 58-9.

How is this abstinence from legislation, on the part of the ancient kings, to be accounted for, except on the supposition that the people would accept, and juries enforce, few or no new laws enacted by their kings? Plainly it can be accounted for in no other way. In fact, all history informs us that anciently the attempts of the kings to introduce or establish new laws, met with determined resistance from the people, and generally resulted in failure. "*Nolumus Leges Angliæ mutari*," (we will that the laws of England be not changed,) was a determined principle with the Anglo-Saxons, from which they seldom departed, up to the time of Magna Carta, and indeed until long after.*

SECTION II.

The Ancient Common Law Juries were mere Courts of Conscience.

But it is in the administration of justice, or of law, that the freedom or subjection of a people is tested. If this administration be in accordance with the arbitrary will of the legislator — that is, if his will, as it appears in his statutes, be the highest rule of decision known to the judicial tribunals, — the government is a despotism, and the people are slaves. If, on the other hand, the rule of decision be those principles of natural equity and justice, which constitute, or at least are embodied in, the general conscience of mankind, the people are free in just so far as that conscience is enlightened.

That the authority of the king was of little weight with the *judicial tribunals*, must necessarily be inferred from the fact already stated, that his authority over the *people* was but weak. If the authority of his laws had been paramount in the judicial tribunals, it would have been paramount with the people, of course; because they would have had no alternative

---

* Rapin says, "The customs now practised in England are, for the most part, the same as the Anglo-Saxons brought with them from Germany." — *Rapin's Dissertation on the Government of the Anglo-Saxons*, vol. 2, Oct. Ed., p. 138. *See Kelham's Discourse before named.*

but submission. The fact, then, that his laws were *not* authoritative with the people, is proof that they were *not* authoritative with the tribunals — in other words, that they were not, as matter of course, enforced by the tribunals.

But we have additional evidence that, up to the time of Magna Carta, the laws of the king were not binding upon the judicial tribunals; and if they were not binding before that time, they certainly were not afterwards, as has already been shown from Magna Carta itself. It is manifest from all the accounts we have of the courts in which juries sat, prior to Magna Carta, such as the court-baron, the hundred court, the court-leet, and the county court, *that they were mere courts of conscience, and that the juries were the judges, deciding causes according to their own notions of equity, and not according to any laws of the king,, unless they thought them just.*

These courts, it must be considered, were very numerous, and held very frequent sessions. There were probably seven, eight, or nine hundred courts *a month*, in the kingdom; the object being, as Blackstone says, "*to bring justice home to every man's door.*" (3 *Blackstone*, 30.) The number of the *county* courts, of course, corresponded to the number of counties, (36.) The *court-leet* was the criminal court for a district less than a county. The *hundred court* was the court for one of those districts anciently called a *hundred*, because, at the time of their first organization for judicial purposes, they comprised (as is supposed) but a hundred families.* The court-baron was the court for a single manor, and there was a court for every manor in the kingdom. All these courts were holden as often as once in three or five weeks; the county court once a month. The king's judges were present at none of these courts; the only officers in attendance being sheriffs, bailiffs, and stewards, merely ministerial, and not judicial, officers; doubtless incompetent, and, if not incompetent, untrustworthy, for giving the juries any reliable information in matters of law, beyond what was already known to the jurors themselves.

---

* Hallam says, "The county of Sussex contains sixty-five ('hundreds'); that of Dorset forty-three; while Yorkshire has only twenty-six; and Lancashire but six."— 2 *Middle Ages*, 391.

And yet these were the courts, in which was done all the judicial business, both civil and criminal, of the nation, except appeals, and some of the more important and difficult cases.* It is plain that the juries, in these courts, must, of necessity, have been the sole judges of all matters of law whatsoever; because there was no one present, but sheriffs, bailiffs, and stewards, to give them any instructions; and surely it will not be pretended that the jurors were bound to take their law from such sources as these.

In the second place, it is manifest that the principles of law, by which the juries determined causes, were, as a general rule, nothing else than their own ideas of natural equity, *and not any laws of the king ;* because but few laws were enacted, and many of those were not written, but only agreed upon in council.† Of those that were written, few copies only were made, (printing being then unknown,) and not enough to supply all, or any considerable number, of these numerous courts. Beside and beyond all this, few or none of the jurors could have read the laws, if they had been written; because few or none of the common people could, at that time, read. Not only were the common people unable to read their own language, but, at the time of Magna Carta, the laws were written in Latin, a language that could be read by few persons except the priests, who were also the lawyers of the nation. Mackintosh says, "the first act of the House of Commons composed and recorded in the English tongue," was in 1415, two centuries after Magna Carta.‡ Up to this time, and for some seventy years later, the laws were generally written

---

* Excepting also matters pertaining to the collection of the revenue, which were determined in the king's court of exchequer. But even in this court it was the law "*that none be amerced but by his peers.*" — *Mirror of Justices,* 49.

† "For the English laws, *although not written,* may, as it should seem, and that without any absurdity, be termed *laws,* (since this itself is law — that which pleases the prince has the force of law,) I mean those laws which it is evident were promulgated by the advice of the nobles and the authority of the prince, concerning doubts to be settled in their assembly. For if from the mere want of writing only, they should not be considered laws, then, unquestionably, writing would seem to confer more authority upon laws themselves, than either the equity of the persons constituting, or the reason of those framing them." — *Glanville's Preface,* p. 38. (Glanville was chief justice of Henry II., 1180.) 2 *Turner's History of the Anglo-Saxons,* 280.

‡ Mackintosh's History of England, ch. 3. Lardner's Cabinet Cyclopædia, 266.

either in Latin or French; both languages incapable of being read by the common people, as well Normans as Saxons; and one of them, the Latin, not only incapable of being read by them, but of being even understood when it was heard by them.

To suppose that the people were bound to obey, and juries to enforce, laws, many of which were unwritten, none of which *they* could read, and the larger part of which (those written in Latin) they could not translate, or understand when they heard them read, is equivalent to supposing the nation sunk in the most degrading slavery, instead of enjoying a liberty of their own choosing.

Their knowledge of the laws passed by the king was, of course, derived only from oral information; and "*the good laws,*" as some of them were called, in contradistinction to others — those which the people at large esteemed to be good laws — were doubtless enforced by the juries, and the others, as a general thing, disregarded.*

That such was the nature of judicial proceedings, and of the power of juries, up to the time of Magna Carta, is further shown by the following authorities.

"The sheriffs and bailiffs caused the free tenants of their bailiwics to meet at their counties and hundreds; *at which justice was so done, that every one so judged his neighbor by such judgment as a man could not elsewhere receive in the like cases,* until such times as the customs of the realm were put in writing, and certainly published.

"And although a freeman commonly was not to serve (as a juror or judge) without his assent, nevertheless it was assented unto that free tenants should meet together in the counties and hundreds, and lords courts, if they were not specially exempted to do such suits, *and there judged their neighbors.*" — *Mirror of Justices,* p. 7, 8.

---

* If the laws of the king were received as authoritative by the juries, what occasion was there for his appointing special commissioners for the trial of offences, without the intervention of a jury, as he frequently did, in manifest and acknowledged violation of Magna Carta, and "the law of the land?" These appointments were undoubtedly made for no other reason than that the juries were not sufficiently subservient, but judged according to their own notions of right, instead of the will of the king — whether the latter were expressed in his statutes, or by his judges.

Gilbert, in his treatise on the Constitution of England, says:

" In the county courts, if the debt was above forty shillings, there issued a *justicies* (a commission) to the sheriff, to enable him to hold such a plea, *where the suitors (jurors) are judges of the law and fact.*" — *Gilbert's Cases in Law and Equity, &c., &c.*, 456.

All the ancient writs, given in Glanville, for summoning jurors, indicate that the jurors judged of everything, *on their consciences only.* The writs are in this form:

" Summon twelve free and legal men (or sometimes twelve knights) to be in court, *prepared upon their oaths to declare whether A or B have the greater right to the land (or other thing) in question.*" See Writs in Beames' Glanville, p. 54 to 70, and 233–306 to 332.

Crabbe, speaking of the time of Henry I., (1100 to 1135,) recognizes the fact that the jurors were the judges. He says:

" By one law, every one was to be tried by his peers, who were of the same neighborhood as himself. * * By another law, *the judges, for so the jury were called*, were to be chosen by the party impleaded, after the manner of the Danish *nembas ;* by which, probably, is to be understood that the defendant had the liberty of taking exceptions to, or challenging the jury, as it was afterwards called." — *Crabbe's History of the English Law*, p. 55.

Reeve says:

" The great court for *civil* business was the *county court ;* held once every four weeks. Here the sheriff presided; *but the suitors of the court, as they were called, that is, the freemen or landholders of the county, were the judges ;* and the sheriff was to execute the judgment. * * *

" The *hundred court* was held before *some bailiff ;* the *leet* before the lord of the manor's *steward.* † * * *

" Out of the county court was derived an inferior court of *civil* jurisdiction, called the *court-baron.* This was held from three weeks to three weeks, *and was in every respect like the county court ;*" (that is, the jurors were judges in it ;) "only the lord to whom this franchise was granted, *or his steward,*

---

† Of course, Mr. Reeve means to be understood that, in the hundred court, and court-leet, *the jurors were the judges,* as he declares them to have been in the county court ; otherwise the " bailiff" or " steward " must have been judge.

presided instead of the sheriff." — 1 *Reeve's History of the English Law*, p. 7.

Chief Baron Gilbert says:

" Besides the tenants of the king, which held *per baroniam,* (by the right of a baron,) and did suit and service (served as judges) at his own court; and the burghers and tenants in ancient demesne, that did suit and service (served as jurors or judges) in their own court in person, and in the king's by proxy, there was also a set of freeholders, that did suit and service (served as jurors) at the county court. These were such as anciently held of the lord of the county, and by the escheats of earldoms had fallen to the king; or such as were granted out by service to hold of the king, but with particular reservation to do suit and service (serve as jurors) before the king's bailiff; *because it was necessary the sheriff, or bailiff of the king, should have suitors (jurors) at the county court, that the business might be despatched. These suitors are the pares (peers) of the county court, and indeed the judges of it; as the pares (peers) were the judges in every court-baron;* and therefore the king's bailiff having a court before him, there must be *pares or judges, for the sheriff himself is not a judge;* and though the style of the court is *Curia prima Comitatus E. C. Milit.' vicecom' Comitat' præd' Tent' apud B.,* &c. (First Court of the county, E. C. knight, sheriff of the aforesaid county, held at B., &c.); by which it appears that the court was the sheriff's; *yet, by the old feudal constitutions, the lord was not judge, but the pares (peers) only;* so that, even in a *justicies,* which was a commission to the sheriff to hold plea of more than was allowed by the natural jurisdiction of a county court, *the pares (peers, jurors) only were judges, and not the sheriff;* because it was to hold plea in the same manner as they used to do in that (the lord's) court." — *Gilbert on the Court of Exchequer,* ch. 5, p. 61-2.

" It is a distinguishing feature of the feudal system, to make civil jurisdiction necessarily, and criminal jurisdiction ordinarily, coëxtensive with tenure; and accordingly there is inseparably incident to every manor a court-baron (curia baronum), *being a court in which the freeholders of the manor are the sole judges,* but in which the lord, by himself, or more commonly by his steward, presides." — *Political Dictionary,* word *Manor.*

The same work, speaking of the *county* court, says: " *The judges were the freeholders who did suit to the court."* See word *Courts.*

" In the case of freeholders attending as suitors, the county court or court-baron, (as in the case of the ancient tenants *per. baroniam* attending Parliament,) *the suitors are the judges of the court, both for law and for fact*, and the sheriff or the under sheriff in the county court, and the lord or his steward in the court-baron, are only presiding officers, *with no judicial authority.*" — *Political Dictionary*, word *Suit.*

"Court, (curtis, curia aula); the space enclosed by the walls of a feudal residence, in which the followers of a lord used to assemble in the middle ages, to administer justice, and decide respecting affairs of common interest, &c. It was next used for those who stood in immediate connexion with the lord and master, the *pares curiæ*, (peers of the court,) the limited portion of the general assembly, to which was entrusted the pronouncing of judgment," &c.—*Encyclopedia Americana*, word *Court.*

"In court-barons or county courts *the steward was not judge, but the pares (peers, jurors)*; nor was the speaker in the House of Lords judge, but the barons only." — *Gilbert on the Court of Exchequer*, ch. 3, p. 42.

Crabbe, speaking of the Saxon times, says:

"The sheriff presided at the *hundred court*, * * and sometimes sat in the place of the alderman (earl) in the *county court.*" — *Crabbe*, 23.

The sheriff afterwards became the sole presiding officer of the county court.

Sir Thomas Smith, Secretary of State to Queen Elizabeth, writing more than three hundred years after Magna Carta, in describing the difference between the *Civil* Law and the English Law, says:

"*Judex* is of us called Judge, but our fashion is so divers, that they which give the deadly stroke, and either condemn or acquit the man for guilty or not guilty, *are not called judges, but the twelve men. And the same order as well in civil matters and pecuniary, as in matters criminal.*" — *Smith's Commonwealth of England*, ch. 9, p. 53, Edition of 1621.

Court-Leet. "That the *leet* is the most ancient court in the land for *criminal* matters, (the court-baron being of no less antiquity in *civil*,) has been pronounced by the highest legal authority. * * Lord Mansfield states that this court was coeval with the establishment of the Saxons here, and its activity marked very visibly both among the Saxons and Danes. * * The leet is a court of record for the cognizance of criminal matters, or pleas of the crown; and necessarily belongs to the king; though a subject, usually the lord

of the manor, may be, and is, entitled to the profits, consisting
of the essoign pence, fines, and amerciaments.

"*It is held before the steward, or was, in ancient times, before
the bailiff, of the lord.*" — *Tomlin's Law Dict.*, word *Court-
Leet.*

Of course the jury were the judges in this court, where only
a "steward" or "bailiff" of a manor presided.

"No cause of consequence was determined without the
king's writ; for even in the county courts, of the debts, which
were above forty shillings, there issued a *Justicies* (commission)
to the sheriff, to enable him to hold such plea, *where the suitors
are judges of the law and fact.*" — *Gilbert's History of the
Common Pleas, Introduction,* p. 19.

"This position" (that "the matter of law was decided by
the King's Justices, but the matter of fact by the *pares*") "*is
wholly incompatible with the common law, for the Jurata
(jury) were the sole judges both of the law and the fact.*" —
Gilbert's History of the Common Pleas, p. 70, *note.*

"We come now to the challenge; and of old *the suitors in
court, who were judges,* could not be challenged; nor by the
feudal law could the *pares* be even challenged, *Pares qui
ordinariam jurisdictionem habent recusari non possunt;* (the
peers who have ordinary jurisdiction cannot be rejected;) "*but
those suitors who are judges of the court,* could not be challenged; and the reason is, that there are several qualifications
required by the writ, viz., that they be *liberos et legales homines de vincineto* (free and legal men of the neighborhood) of
the place laid in the declaration," &c., &c. — *Ditto,* p. 93.

"*Ad questionem juris non respondent Juratores.*" (To the
question of law the jurors do not answer.) "The Annotist
says, that this is indeed a maxim in the Civil-Law Jurisprudence, *but it does not bind an English jury, for by the common
law of the land the jury are judges as well of the matter of
law, as of the fact,* with this difference only, that the (a Saxon
word) or judge on the bench is to give them no assistance in
determining the matter of *fact,* but if they have any doubt
among themselves relating to matter of *law,* they may then
request him to explain it to them, which when he hath done,
and they are thus become well informed, they, and they only,
become competent judges of the matter of *law.* And this is
the province of the judge on the bench, namely, to show, or
teach the law, but not to take upon him the trial of the delinquent, either in matter of fact or in matter of law." (Here
various Saxon laws are quoted.) "In neither of these funda-

mental laws is there the least word, hint, or idea, that the earl or alderman (that is to say, the *Prepositus* (presiding officer) of the court, which is tantamount to *the judge on the bench*) is to take upon him to judge the delinquent in any sense whatever, the sole purport of his office is to *teach* the secular or worldly law." — *Ditto*, p. 57, *note.*

" The administration of justice was carefully provided for; it was not the caprice of their lord, *but the sentence of their peers, that they obeyed. Each was the judge of his equals, and each by his equals was judged.*" — *Introd. to Gilbert on Tenures*, p. 12.

Hallam says: " A respectable class of free socagers, having, in general, full rights of alienating their lands, and holding them probably at a small certain rent from the lord of the manor, frequently occur in Domes-day Book. * * They undoubtedly were suitors to the court-baron of the lord, to whose *soc*, or right of justice, they belonged. *They were consequently judges in civil causes, determined before the manorial tribunal.*" — 2 *Middle Ages*, 481.

Stephens adopts as correct the following quotations from Blackstone:

" The *Court-Baron* is a court incident to every manor in the kingdom, to be holden by the steward within the said manor." * * It "*is a court of common law, and it is the court before the freeholders who owe suit and service to the manor,*" (are bound to serve as jurors in the courts of the manor,) "*the steward being rather the registrar than the judge.* * * The freeholders' court was composed of the lord's tenants, who were the *pares* (equals) of each other, and were bound by their feudal tenure to assist their lord in the dispensation of domestic justice. This was formerly held every three weeks; *and its most important business was to determine, by writ of right, all controversies relating to the right of lands within the manor.*" — 3 *Stephens' Commentaries*, 392–3. 3 *Blackstone*, 32–3.

" A *Hundred Court* is only a larger court-baron, being held for all the inhabitants of a particular hundred, instead of a manor. *The free suitors (jurors) are here also the judges, and the steward the register.*" — 3 *Stephens*, 394. 3 *Blackstone*, 33.

" The *County Court* is a court incident to the jurisdiction of the sheriff. * * *The freeholders of the county are the real judges in this court, and the sheriff is the ministerial officer.*" — 3 *Stephens*, 395–6. 3 *Blackstone*, 35–6.

Blackstone describes these courts, as courts "*wherein injuries were redressed in an easy and expeditious manner, by the suffrage of neighbors and friends.*" — 3 *Blackstone*, 30.

"When we read of a certain number of *freemen* chosen by the parties to decide in a dispute — all bound by oath to vote *in foro conscientia* — and that *their* decision, *not the will of the judge presiding, ended the suit*, we at once perceive that a great improvement has been made in the old form of compurgation — an improvement which impartial observation can have no hesitation to pronounce as identical in its main features with the trial by jury." — *Dunham's Middle Ages*, Sec. 2, B. 2, Ch. 1. 57 *Lardner's Cab. Cyc.*, 60.

"The bishop and the earl, or, in his absence, the gerefa, (sheriff,) and sometimes both the earl and the gerefa, presided at the *schyre-mote* (county court); the gerefa (sheriff) usually alone presided at the *mote* (meeting or court) of the hundred. In the cities and towns which were not within any peculiar jurisdiction, there was held, at regular stated intervals, a *burgh mote*, (borough court,) for the administration of justice, at which a gerefa, or a magistrate appointed by the king, presided." — *Spence's Origin of the Laws and Political Institutions of Modern Europe*, p. 444.

"The right of the plaintiff and defendant, and of the prosecutor and criminal, *to challenge the judices*, (judges,) *or assessors,** appointed to try the cause in civil matters, and to decide upon the guilt or innocence of the accused in criminal matters*, is recognized in the treatise called the Laws of Henry the First; but I cannot discover, from the Anglo-Saxon laws or histories, that before the Conquest the parties had any general right of challenge; *indeed, had such right existed, the injunctions to all persons standing in the situation of judges (jurors) to do right according to their conscience*, would scarcely have been so frequently and anxiously repeated." — *Spence*, 456.

Hale says:

"The administration of the common justice of the kingdom seems to be wholly dispensed in the county courts, hundred courts, and courts-baron; except some of the greater crimes reformed by the laws of King Henry I., and that part thereof which was sometimes taken up by the *Justitiarius Angliæ*.

---

* The jurors were sometimes called "assessors," because they assessed, or determined the amount of fines and amercements to be imposed.

This doubtless bred great inconvenience, uncertainty, and variety in the laws, viz. :

" *First, by the ignorance of the judges, which were the freeholders of the county.*   *   *

"Thirdly, a third inconvenience was, that all the business of any moment was carried by parties and factions. *For the freeholders being generally the judges,* and conversing one among another, *and being as it were the chief judges, not only of the fact, but of the law;* every man that had a suit there, sped according as he could make parties." — 1 *Hale's History of the Common Law,* p. 246.

" In all these tribunals," (county court, hundred court, &c.,) "*the judges were the free tenants,* owing suit to the court, and afterwards called its peers." — 1 *Lingard's History of England,* 488.

Henry calls the twelve jurors "assessors," and says :

" These assessors, *who were in reality judges,* took a solemn oath, that they would faithfully discharge the duties of their office, and not suffer an innocent man to be condemned, nor any guilty person to be acquitted." — 3 *Henry's History of Great Britain,* 346.

Tyrrell says :

" Alfred cantoned his kingdom, first into *Trihings* and *Lathes,* as they are still called in Kent and other places, consisting of three or four Hundreds; *in which, the freeholders being judges,* such causes were brought as could not be determined in the Hundred court." — *Tyrrell's Introduction to the History of England,* p. 80.

Of the *Hundred Court* he says :

" In this court anciently, *one of the principal inhabitants, called the alderman, together with the barons of the Hundred* * —id est the freeholders — was judge." — *Ditto,* p. 80.

Also he says :

" By a law of Edward the Elder, ' Every sheriff shall con-

---

* "The barons of the Hundred" were the freeholders. Hallam says : "The word *baro,* originally meaning only a man, was of very large significance, and is not unfrequently applied to common freeholders, as in the phrase *court-baron.*" — 3 *Middle Ages,* 14–15.
Blackstone says : "The *court-baron* * * is a court of common law, and it is the court of the barons, by which name the freeholders were sometimes anciently called ; for that it is held before the freeholders who owe suit and service to the manor." — 3 *Blackstone,* 33.

vene the people once a month, and do equal right to all, putting an end to controversies at times appointed.'" — *Ditto,* p. 86.

" A statute, emphatically termed the ' Grand Assize,' enabled the defendant, if he thought proper, to abide by the testimony of the twelve good and lawful knights, chosen by four others of the vicinage, *and whose oaths gave a final decision to the contested claim.*" — 1 *Palgrave's Rise and Progress of the English Commonwealth,* 261.

" From the moment when the crown became accustomed to the ' Inquest,' a restraint was imposed upon every branch of the prerogative. *The king could never be informed of his rights, but through the medium of the people.* Every ' extent ' by which he claimed the profits and advantages resulting from the casualties of tenure, every process by which he repressed the usurpations of the baronage, depended upon the ' good men and true ' who were impanelled to ' pass ' between the subject and the sovereign; and the thunder of the Exchequer at Westminster might be silenced by the honesty, the firmness, or the obstinacy, of one sturdy knight or yeoman in the distant shire.

Taxation was controlled in the same manner by the voice of those who were most liable to oppression. * * A jury was impanelled to adjudge the proportion due to the sovereign; and this course was not essentially varied, even after the right of granting aids to the crown was fully acknowledged to be vested in the parliament of the realm. The people taxed themselves; and the collection of the grants was checked and controlled, and, perhaps, in many instances evaded, by these virtual representatives of the community.

The principle of the jury was, therefore, not confined to its mere application as a mode of trying contested facts, whether in civil or criminal cases; and, both in its form and in its consequences, it had a very material influence upon the general constitution of the realm. * * The main-spring of the machinery of remedial justice existed in the franchise of the lower and lowest orders of the political hierarchy. Without the suffrage of the yeoman, the burgess, and the churl, the sovereign could not exercise the most important and most essential function of royalty; from them he received the power of life and death; he could not wield the sword of justice until the humblest of his subjects placed the weapon in his hand." — 1 *Palgrave's Rise and Progress of the English Constitution,* 274–7.

Coke says, " The court of the county is no court of record,* *and the suitors are the judges thereof.*" — 4 *Inst.*, 266.

Also, " The court of the Hundred is no court of record, *and the suitors be thereof judges.*" — 4 *Inst.*, 267.

Also, " The court-baron is a court incident to every manor, and is not of record, *and the suitors be thereof judges.*" — 4 *Inst.*, 268.

Also, " The court of ancient demesne is in the nature of a court-baron, *wherein the suitors are judges*, and is no court of record." — 4 *Inst.*, 269.

Millar says, " Some authors have thought that jurymen were originally *compurgators*, called by a defendant to swear that they believed him innocent of the facts with which he was charged. . . But . . compurgators were merely witnesses; *jurymen were, in reality, judges.* The former were called to confirm the oath of the party by swearing, according to their belief, that he had told the truth, (in his oath of purgation;) *the latter were appointed to try, by witnesses, and by all other means of proof, whether he was innocent or guilty.* . . Juries were accustomed to ascertain the truth of facts, by the defendant's oath of purgation, together with that of his compurgators. . . Both of them (jurymen and compurgators) were obliged to swear that they would *tell the truth.* . . According to the simple idea of our forefathers, guilt or innocence was regarded as a mere matter of fact; and it was thought that no man, who knew the real circumstances of a case, could be at a loss to determine whether the culprit ought to be condemned or acquitted." — 1 *Millar's Hist. View of Eng. Gov.*, ch. 12, p. 332–4.

Also, " The same form of procedure, which took place in the administration of justice among the vassals of a barony, was gradually extended to the courts held in the *trading towns.*" — *Same*, p. 335.

Also, " The same regulations, concerning the distribution of justice by the intervention of juries, . . *were introduced into the baron courts of the king*, as into those of the nobility, or such of his subjects as retained their allodial property." — *Same*, p. 337.

Also, " This tribunal " (the *aula regis*, or king's court, afterwards divided into the courts of King's Bench, Common

---

* The ancient jury courts kept no records, because those who composed the courts could neither make nor read records. Their decisions were preserved by the memories of the jurors and other persons present.

Pleas, and Exchequer) "was properly the ordinary baron-court of the king; and, being in the same circumstances with the baron courts of the nobility, it was under the same necessity of trying causes by the intervention of a jury." — *Same*, vol. 2, p. 292.

Speaking of the times of Edward the First, (1272 to 1307,) Millar says :

"What is called the petty jury was therefore introduced into these tribunals, (the King's Bench, the Common Pleas, and the *Exchequer*,) as well as into their auxiliary courts employed to distribute justice in the circuits; and was thus rendered essentially necessary in determining causes of every sort, whether civil, criminal, or *fiscal*." — *Same*, vol. 2, p. 293-4.

Also, " That this form of trial (by jury) obtained universally in all the feudal governments, as well as in that of England, there can be no reason to doubt. In France, in Germany, and in other European countries, where we have any accounts of the constitution and procedure of the feudal courts, it appears that lawsuits of every sort concerning the free-men or vassals of a barony, were determined by the *pares curiæ* (peers of the court;) *and that the judge took little more upon him than to regulate the method of proceeding, or to declare the verdict of the jury*." — *Same*, vol. 1, ch. 12, p. 329.

Also, " Among the Gothic nations of modern Europe, the custom of deciding lawsuits by a jury seems to have prevailed universally; first in the allodial courts of the county, or of the hundred, and afterwards in the baron-courts of every feudal superior." — *Same*, vol. 2, p. 296.

Palgrave says that in Germany " The Graff (gerefa, sheriff) placed himself in the seat of judgment, and gave the charge to the assembled free Echevins, warning them to pronounce judgment according to right and justice." — 2 *Palgrave*, 147.

Also, that, in Germany, " The Echevins were composed of the villanage, somewhat obscured in their functions by the learning of the grave civilian who was associated to them, and somewhat limited by the encroachments of modern feudality; *but they were still substantially the judges of the court*." — *Same*, 148.

Palgrave also says, " Scotland, in like manner, had the laws of Burlaw, or Birlaw, which were made and determined by the neighbors, elected by common consent, in the Burlaw or Birlaw courts, wherein knowledge was taken of complaints between neighbor and neighbor, *which men, so chosen, were judges and arbitrators*, and called Birlaw men." — 1 *Palgrave's Rise*, &c., p. 80.

But, in order to understand the common law trial by jury, as it existed prior to Magna Carta, and as it was guaranteed by that instrument, it is perhaps indispensable to understand more fully the nature of the courts in which juries sat, and the extent of the powers exercised by juries in those courts. I therefore give in a note extended extracts, on these points, from Stuart on the Constitution of England, and from Blackstone's Commentaries.*

---

* Stuart says :

" The courts, or civil arrangements, which were modelled in Germany, preserved the independence of the people; and having followed the Saxons into England, and continuing their importance, they supported the envied liberty we boast of. * *

" As a chieftain led out his retainers to the field, and governed them during war; so in peace he summoned them together, and exerted a civil jurisdiction. He was at once their captain and their judge. They constituted his court; and having inquired with him into the guilt of those of their order whom justice had accused, they assisted him to enforce his decrees.

" This court (the court-baron) was imported into England; but the innovation which conquest introduced into the fashion of the times altered somewhat its appearance. * *

" The head or lord of the manor called forth his attendants to his hall. * * He inquired into the breaches of custom, and of justice, which were committed within the precincts of his territory; and with his followers, *who sat with him as judges*, he determined in all matters of debt, and of trespass to a certain amount. He possessed a similar jurisdiction with the chieftain in Germany, and his tenants enjoyed an equal authority with the German retainers.

" But a mode of administration which intrusted so much power to the great could not long be exercised without blame or injustice. The German, guided by the candor of his mind, and entering into all his engagements with the greatest ardor, perceived not, at first, that the chieftain to whom he submitted his disputes might be swayed, in the judgments he pronounced, by partiality, prejudice, or interest ; and that the influence he maintained with his followers was too strong to be restrained by justice. Experience instructed him of his error; he acknowledged the necessity of appealing from his lord; and the court of the Hundred was erected.

" This establishment was formed both in Germany and England, by the inhabitants of a certain division, who extended their jurisdiction over the territory they occupied.* They bound themselves under a penalty to assemble at stated times; *and having elected the wisest to preside over them, they judged, not only all civil and criminal matters*, but of those also which regarded religion and the priesthood. The judicial power thus invested in the people was extensive ; they were able to preserve their rights, and attended this court in arms.

" As the communication, however, and intercourse, of the individuals of a German community began to be wider, and more general, as their dealings enlarged, and as disputes arose among the members of different hundreds, the insufficiency of these

* " It was the freemen in Germany, and the possessors of land in England, who were *suitors* (jurors) in the hundred court. These ranks of men were the same. The alteration which had happened in relation to property had invested the German freemen with land or territory."

That all these courts were mere *courts of conscience, in
which the juries were sole judges, administering justice according to their own ideas of it,* is not only shown by the extracts

---

courts for the preservation of order was gradually perceived. The *shyre mote,* therefore,
or *county court,* was instituted; and it formed the chief source of justice both in Germany and England.

" The powers, accordingly, which had been enjoyed by the court of the *hundred,* were
considerably impaired. It decided no longer concerning capital offences; it decided not
concerning matters of liberty, and the property of estates, or of slaves; its judgments, in every case, became subject to review; and it lost entirely the decision of
causes, when it delayed too long to consider them.

" Every subject of claim or contention was brought, in the first instance, or by appeal,
to the *county court;* and the *earl,* or *eorldorman,* who presided there, was active to put
the laws in execution. He repressed the disorders which fell out within the circuit of
his authority; and the least remission in his duty, or the least fraud he committed, was
complained of and punished. He was elected from among the great, and was above the
temptation of a bribe; but, to encourage his activity, he was presented with a share of
the territory he governed, or was entitled to a proportion of the fines and profits of justice. Every man, in his district, was bound to inform him concerning criminals, and to
assist him to bring them to trial; and, as in rude and violent times the poor and help-
less were ready to be oppressed by the strong, he was instructed particularly to defend
them.

" His court was ambulatory, and assembled only twice a year, unless the distribution
of justice required that its meetings should be oftener. Every freeholder in the county
was obliged to attend it; and should he refuse this service, his possessions were seized,
and he was forced to find surety for his appearance. The neighboring earls held not
their courts on the same day; and, what seems very singular, no judge was allowed,
after meals, to exercise his office.

" The druids also, or priests, in Germany, as we had formerly occasion to remark, and
the clergy in England, exercised a jurisdiction in the *hundred* and *county* courts. They
instructed the people in religious duties, and in matters regarding the priesthood; and
the princes, earls, or *eorldormen,* related to them the laws and customs of the community.
These judges were mutually a check to each other; but it was expected that they
should agree in their judgments, and should willingly unite their efforts for the public
interest.*

" *But the prince or earl performed not, at all times, in person, the obligations of his office.*
The enjoyment of ease and of pleasure, to which in Germany he had delivered himself
over, when disengaged from war, and the mean idea he conceived of the drudgery of
civil affairs, *made him often delegate to an inferior person the distribution of justice in his
district.* The same sentiments were experienced by the Saxon nobility; and the service
which they owed by their tenures, and the high employments they sustained, called
them often from the management of their counties. The progress, too, of commerce,

---

* It would be wholly erroneous, I think, to infer from this statement of Stuart, that either the
"priests, princes, earls, or *eorldormen*" exercised any authority over the jury in the trial of causes,
in the way of dictating the law to them. Henry's account of this matter doubtless gives a much
more accurate representation of the truth. He says that *anciently*

"The meeting (the county court) was opened with a discourse by the bishop, explaining, out of
the Scriptures and ecclesiastical canons, their several duties as good Christians and members of the

already given, but is explicitly acknowledged in the following
one, in which the *modern " courts of conscience "* are compared
with the *ancient hundred and county courts,* and the preference

---

giving an intricacy to cases, and swelling the civil code, added to the difficulty of their
office, and made them averse to its duties. *Sheriffs, therefore, or deputies, were frequently
appointed to transact their business; and though these were at first under some subordination
to the earls, they grew at length to be entirely independent of them. The connection of jurisdiction and territory ceasing to prevail, and the civil being separated from the ecclesiastical
power, they became the sole and proper officers for the direction of justice in the counties.*

"The *hundred,* however, and *county* courts, were not equal of themselves for the
purposes of jurisdiction and order. It was necessary that a court should be erected,
of supreme authority, where the disputes of the great should be decided, where the
disagreeing sentiments of judges should be reconciled, and where protection should be
given to the people against their fraud and injustice.

" The princes accordingly, or chief nobility, in the German communities, assembled
together to judge of such matters. The Saxon nobles continued this prerogative; and
the king, or, in his absence, the chief *justiciary,* watched over their deliberations. But
it was not on every trivial occasion that this court interested itself. In smaller concerns,
justice was refused during three sessions of the *hundred,* and claimed without effect, at
four courts of the county, before there could lie an appeal to it.

" So gradually were these arrangements established, and so naturally did the varying
circumstances in the situation of the Germans and Anglo-Saxons direct those successive improvements which the preservation of order, and the advantage of society,
called them to adopt. The admission of the people into the courts of justice preserved,
among the former, that equality of ranks for which they were remarkable ; and it
helped to overturn, among the latter, those envious distinctions which the feudal system
tended to introduce, and prevented that venality in judges, and those arbitrary proceedings, which the growing attachment to interest, and the influence of the crown,
might otherwise have occasioned." — *Stuart on the Constitution of England,* p. 222
to 245.

" In the Anglo-Saxon period, accordingly, *twelve* only were elected; and these,
together with the judge, or presiding officer of the district, being sworn to regard justice, and the voice of reason, or conscience, all causes were submitted to them." —
Ditto, p. 260.

" Before the orders of men were very nicely distinguished, the jurors were elected
from the same rank. When, however, a regular subordination of orders was established, and when a knowledge of property had inspired the necessitous with envy, and
the rich with contempt, *every man was tried by his equals.* The same spirit of liberty
which gave rise to this regulation attended its progress. Nor could monarchs assume
a more arbitrary method of proceeding. ' I will not ' (said the Earl of Cornwall to his

church. After this, the alderman, or one of his assessors, made a discourse on the laws of the
land, and the duties of good subjects and good citizens. *When these preliminaries were over,
they proceeded to try and determine, first the causes of the church, next the pleas of the
crown, and last of all the controversies of private parties."* — 3 *Henry's History of Great
Britain,* 348.

This view is corroborated by *Tyrrell's Introduction to the History of England,* p. 83–84, and
by *Spence's Origin of the Laws and Political Institutions of Modern Europe,* p. 447, and the
note on the same page. Also by a law of Canute to this effect, *In every county let there be
twice a year an assembly, whereat the bishop and the earl shall be present, the one to instruct
the people in divine, the other in human, laws.* — *Wilkins,* p. 136.

given to the latter, on the ground that the duties of the jurors in the one case, and of the commissioners in the other, are the same, and that the consciences of a jury are a safer and purer

---

sovereign) 'render up my castles, nor depart the kingdom, but by judgment of my peers.' Of this institution, so wisely calculated for the preservation of liberty, all our historians have pronounced the eulogium." — *Ditto*, p. 262–3.

Blackstone says :

" The policy of our ancient constitution, as regulated and established by the great Alfred, was to bring justice home to every man's door, by constituting as many courts of judicature as there are manors and towns in the kingdom; *wherein injuries were redressed in an easy, and expeditious manner, by the suffrage of neighbors and friends.* These little courts, however, communicated with others of a larger jurisdiction, and those with others of a still greater power; ascending gradually from the lowest to the supreme courts, which were respectively constituted to correct the errors of the inferior ones, and to determine such causes as, by reason of their weight and difficulty, demanded a more solemn discussion. The course of justice flowing in large streams from the king, as the fountain, to his superior courts of record ; and being then subdivided into smaller channels, till the whole and every part of the kingdom were plentifully watered and refreshed. An institution that seems highly agreeable to the dictates of natural reason, as well as of more enlightened policy. * * *

" These inferior courts, at least the name and form of them, still continue in our legal constitution ; but as the superior courts of record have, in practice, obtained a concurrent original jurisdiction, and as there is, besides, a power of removing plaints or actions thither from all the inferior jurisdictions ; upon these accounts (among others) it has happened that these petty tribunals have fallen into decay, and almost into oblivion; whether for the better or the worse may be matter of some speculation, when we consider, on the one hand, the increase of expense and delay, and, on the other, the more able and impartial decisions that follow from this change of jurisdiction.

" The order I shall observe in discoursing on these several courts, constituted for the redress of *civil* injuries, (for with those of a jurisdiction merely *criminal* I shall not at present concern myself,*) will be by beginning with the lowest, and those whose jurisdiction, though public and generally dispersed through the kingdom, is yet (with regard to each particular court) confined to very narrow limits; and so ascending gradually to those of the most extensive and transcendent power." — 3 *Blackstone*, 30 to 32.

" The *court-baron* is a court incident to every manor in the kingdom, *to be holden by the steward within the said manor.* This court-baron is of two natures ; the one is a customary court, of which we formerly spoke, appertaining entirely to the copy-holders, in which their estates are transferred by surrender and admittance, and other matters transacted relative to their tenures only. The other, of which we now speak, is a court of common law, and it is a court of the barons, by which name the freeholders were sometimes anciently called ; *for that it is held by the freeholders who owe suit and service to the manor, the steward being rather the registrar than the judge.* These courts, though in their nature distinct, are frequently confounded together. *The court we are now considering, viz., the freeholders court, was composed of the lord's tenants, who were the pares* (equals)

* There was no distinction between the civil and criminal courrts, as to the rights or powers of juries.

tribunal than the consciences of individuals specially appointed, and holding permanent offices.

"But there is one species of courts constituted by act of Parliament, in the city of London, and other trading and populous districts, which, in their proceedings, so vary from the course of the common law, that they deserve a more particular consideration. I mean the court of requests, *or courts of conscience*, for the recovery of small debts. The first of these was established in London so early as the reign of Henry VIII., by an act of their common council; which, however, was certainly insufficient for that purpose, and illegal, till confirmed by statute 3 Jac. I., ch. 15, which has since been explained and amended by statute 14 Geo. II., ch. 10. The constitution is this: two aldermen and four commoners sit twice a week to hear all causes of debt not exceeding the value of forty shillings; which they examine in a summary way, by the oath of the parties or other witnesses, *and make such order therein as is consonant to equity and good conscience.* * * * Divers trading towns and other districts have obtained acts of Parlia-

---

of each other, and were bound by their feudal tenure to assist their lord in the dispensation of domestic justice. This was formerly held every three weeks ; and its most important business is to determine, by writ of right, all controversies relating to the right of lands within the manor. It may also hold plea of any personal actions, of debt, trespass in the case, or the like, where the debt or damages do not amount to forty shillings; which is the same sum, or three marks, that bounded the jurisdiction of the ancient Gothic courts in their lowest instance, or *fierding courts*, so called because four were instituted within every superior district or hundred." — 3 *Blackstone*, 33, 34.

"A *hundred court* is only a larger court-baron, being held for all the inhabitants of a particular hundred, instead of a manor. *The free suitors are here also the judges, and the steward the registrar, as in the case of a court-baron.* It is likewise no court of record, resembling the former at all points, except that in point of territory it is of greater jurisdiction. This is said by Sir Edward Coke to have been derived out of the county court for the ease of the people, that they might have justice done to them at their own doors, without any charge or loss of time ; but its institution was probably coeval with that of hundreds themselves, which were formerly observed to have been introduced, though not invented, by Alfred, being derived from the polity of the ancient Germans. The *centeni*, we may remember, were the principal inhabitants of a district composed of different villages, originally in number a *hundred*, but afterward only called by that name, and who probably gave the same denomination to the district out of which they were chosen. Cæsar speaks positively of the judicial power exercised in *their* hundred courts and courts-baron. '*Princeps regiorum atque pagorum*' (which we may fairly construe the lords of hundreds and manors) '*inter suos jus dicunt, controversias que minuunt.*' (The chiefs of the country and the villages declare the law among them, and abate controversies.) And Tacitus, who had examined their constitution still more attentively, informs us not only of the authority of the lords, but that of the *centeni*, the hunderers, or jury, *who were taken out of the common freeholders, and had themselves a share in the determination.* '*Eliguntur in conciliis et principes, qui jura per pagos vicosque reddunt, centeni*

ment, for establishing in them *courts of conscience* upon nearly
the same plan as that in the city of London.

"The anxious desire that has been shown to obtain these
several acts, proves clearly that the nation, in general, is truly
sensible of the great inconvenience arising from the disuse of
the ancient county and hundred courts, wherein causes of this
small value were always formerly decided with very little
trouble and expense to the parties. But it is to be feared that
the general remedy, which of late hath been principally applied
to this inconvenience, (the erecting these new jurisdictions,)
may itself be attended in time with very ill consequences; as
the method of proceeding therein is entirely in derogation of
the common law; and their large discretionary powers create
a petty tyranny in a set of standing commissioners; and as the
disuse of the trial by jury may tend to estrange the minds of
the people from that valuable prerogative of Englishmen,
which has already been more than sufficiently excluded in
many instances. *How much rather is it to be wished that the
proceedings in the county and hundred courts could be again*

---

singulis, ex plebe comites concilium simul et auctoritas adsunt.' (The princes are chosen in
the assemblies, who administer the laws throughout the towns and villages, and with
each one are associated an hundred companions, taken from the people, for purposes
both of counsel and authority.) This hundred court was denominated *hæreda* in the
Gothic constitution. But this court, as causes are equally liable to removal from hence
as from the common court-baron, and by the same writs, and may also be reviewed by
writ of false judgment, is therefore fallen into equal disuse with regard to the trial of
actions." — 3 *Blackstone*, 34, 35.

"The *county court* is a court incident to the jurisdiction of the *sheriff*. It is not a
court of record, but may hold pleas of debt, or damages, under the value of forty shillings ; over some of which causes these inferior courts have, by the express words of
the statute of Gloucester, (6 Edward I., ch. 8,) a jurisdiction totally exclusive of the
king's superior courts. * * The county court may also hold plea of many real actions,
and of all personal actions to any amount, by virtue of a special writ, called a *justicies*,
which is a writ empowering the sheriff, for the sake of despatch, to do the same justice
in his county court as might otherwise be had at Westminster. *The freeholders of the
county court are the real judges in this court, and the sheriff is the ministerial officer.* * * *
In modern times, as proceedings are removable from hence into the king's superior
courts, by writ of *pone* or *recordari*, in the same manner as from hundred courts and
courts-baron, and as the same writ of false judgment may be had in nature of a writ
of error, this has occasioned the same disuse of bringing actions therein." — 3 *Blackstone*, 36, 37.

"Upon the whole, we cannot but admire the wise economy and admirable provision
of our ancestors in settling the distribution of justice in a method so well calculated for
cheapness, expedition, and ease. By the constitution which they established, all trivial
debts, and injuries of small consequence, were to be recovered or redressed in every
man's own county, hundred, or perhaps parish." — 3 *Blackstone*, 59.

revived, without burdening the freeholders with too frequent and tedious attendances; and at the same time removing the delays that have insensibly crept into their proceedings, and the power that either party has of transferring at pleasure their suits to the courts at Westminster! *And we may, with satisfaction, observe, that this experiment has been actually tried, and has succeeded in the populous county of Middlesex,* which might serve as an example for others. For by statute 23 Geo. II., ch. 33, it is enacted:

1. That a special county court shall be held at least once in a month, in every hundred of the county of Middlesex, *by the county clerk.*

2. *That twelve freeholders of that hundred, qualified to serve on juries, and struck by the sheriff, shall be summoned to appear at such court by rotation;* so as none shall be summoned oftener than once a year.

3. That in all causes not exceeding the value of forty shillings, *the county clerk and twelve suitors (jurors) shall proceed in a summary way,* examining the parties and witnesses on oath, without the formal process anciently used; *and shall make such order therein as they shall judge agreeable to conscience."* — 3 *Blackstone,* 81–83.

What are these but courts of conscience? And yet Blackstone tells us they are a *revival of the ancient hundred and county courts.* And what does this fact prove, but that the ancient common law courts, in which juries sat, were mere courts of conscience?

It is perfectly evident that in all these courts the jurors were the judges, and determined all questions of law for themselves; because the only alternative to that supposition is, *that the jurors took their law from sheriffs, bailiffs, and stewards,* of which there is not the least evidence in history, nor the least probability in reason. It is evident, also, that they judged independently of the laws of the king, for the reasons before given, viz., that the authority of the king was held in very little esteem; and, secondly, that the laws of the king (not being printed, and the people being unable to read them if they had been printed) must have been in a great measure unknown to them, and could have been received by them only on the authority of the sheriff, bailiff, or steward. If laws were to be received by them on the authority of these officers, the latter would have imposed such laws upon the people as they pleased.

These courts, that have now been described, were continued in full power long after Magna Carta, no alteration being made in them by that instrument, *nor in the mode of administering justice in them.*

There is no evidence whatever, so far as I am aware, that the juries had any *less* power in the courts held by the king's justices, than in those held by sheriffs, bailiffs, and stewards; and there is no probability whatever that they had. All the difference between the former courts and the latter undoubtedly was, that, in the former, the juries had the benefit of the advice and assistance of the justices, which would, of course, be considered valuable in difficult cases, on account of the justices being regarded as more learned, not only in the laws of the king, but also in the common law, or "law of the land."

The conclusion, therefore, I think, inevitably must be, that neither the laws of the king, nor the instructions of his justices, had any authority over jurors beyond what the latter saw fit to accord to them. And this view is confirmed by this remark of Hallam, the truth of which all will acknowledge:

"The rules of legal decision, among a rude people, are always very simple; not serving much to guide, far less to control the feelings of natural equity." — 2 *Middle Ages*, ch. 8, part 2, p. 465.

It is evident that it was in this way, *by the free and concurrent judgments of juries, approving and enforcing certain laws and rules of conduct, corresponding to their notions of right and justice*, that the laws and customs, which, for the most part, made up the *common law*, and were called, at that day, "*the good laws, and good customs*," and "*the law of the land*," were established. How otherwise could they ever have become established, as Blackstone says they were, "*by long and immemorial usage, and by their universal reception throughout the kingdom*,"* when, as the Mirror says, "*justice was so done, that every one so judged his neighbor, by such judgment as a man could not elsewhere receive in the like cases, until such*

---

* 1 Blackstone, 63–67.

times as the customs of the realm were put in writing and cer-
tainly published ?"

The fact that, in that dark age, so many of the principles
of natural equity, as those then embraced in the *Common
Law*, should have been so uniformly recognized and enforced
by juries, as to have become established by general consent as
" *the law of the land ;*" and the further fact that this "law of
the land" was held so sacred that even the king could not
lawfully infringe or alter it, but was required to swear to
maintain it, are beautiful and impressive illustrations of the
truth that men's minds, even in the comparative infancy of
other knowledge, have clear and coincident ideas of the elementary principles, and the paramount obligation, of justice.
The same facts also prove that the common mind, and the
general, or, perhaps, rather, the universal conscience, as devel-
oped in the untrammelled judgments of juries, may be safely
relied upon for the preservation of individual rights in civil
society ; and that there is no necessity or excuse for that deluge
of arbitrary legislation, with which the present age is over-
whelmed, under the pretext that unless laws be *made*, the law
will not be known; a pretext, by the way, almost universally
used for overturning, instead of establishing, the principles
of justice.

SECTION III.

The Oaths of Jurors.

The oaths that have been administered to jurors, in England, and which are their *legal* guide to their duty, *all* (so far
as I have ascertained them) corroborate the idea that the jurors
are to try all cases on their intrinsic merits, independently of
any laws that they deem unjust or oppressive.   It is probable
that an oath was never administered to a jury in England,
either in a civil or criminal case, to try it *according to law*.

The earliest oath that I have found prescribed by law to be
administered to jurors is in the laws of Ethelred, (about the
year 1015,) which require that the jurors " *shall swear, with
their hands upon a holy thing, that they will condemn no man*

that is innocent, nor acquit any that is guilty." — 4 *Black-stone,* 302. 2 *Turner's History of the Anglo-Saxons,* 155. *Wilkins' Laws of the Anglo-Saxons,* 117. *Spelman's Glossary,* word *Jurata.*

Blackstone assumes that this was the oath of the *grand* jury (4 *Blackstone,* 302); but there was but one jury at the time this oath was ordained. The institution of two juries, grand and petit, took place after the Norman Conquest.

Hume, speaking of the administration of justice in the time of Alfred, says that, in every hundred,

"Twelve freeholders were chosen, who, having sworn, together with the hundreder, or presiding magistrate of that division, *to administer impartial justice,* proceeded to the examination of that cause which was submitted to their jurisdiction." — *Hume,* ch. 2.

By a law of Henry II., in 1164, it was directed that the sheriff "*faciet jurare duodecim legales homines de vicineto seu de villa, quod inde veritatem secundum conscientiam suam manifestabunt,*" (shall make twelve legal men from the neighborhood *to swear that they will make known the truth according to their conscience.*) — *Crabbe's History of the English Law,* 119. 1 *Reeves,* 87. *Wilkins,* 321–323.

Glanville, who wrote within the half century previous to Magna Carta, says:

"Each of the knights summoned for this purpose (as jurors) ought to swear that he will neither utter that which is false, nor knowingly conceal the truth." — *Beames' Glanville,* 65.

Reeve calls the trial by jury "*the trial by twelve men sworn to speak the truth."* — 1 *Reeve's History of the English Law,* 87.

Henry says that the jurors "took a solemn oath, that they would faithfully discharge the duties of their office, and not suffer an innocent man to be condemned, nor any guilty person to be acquitted." — 3 *Henry's Hist. of Great Britain,* 346.

The *Mirror of Justices,* (written within a century after Magna Carta,) in the chapter on the abuses of the Common Law, says:

"It is abuse to use the words, *to their knowledge,* in their oaths, to make the jurors speak upon thoughts, *since the chief words of their oaths be that they speak the truth."* — p. 249.

Smith, writing in the time of Elizabeth, says that, in *civil* suits, the jury "be sworn to declare the truth of that issue according to the evidence, and their conscience." — *Smith's Commonwealth of England,* edition of 1621, p. 73.

In *criminal* trials, he says:

"The clerk giveth the juror an oath to go uprightly betwixt the prince and the prisoner." — *Ditto,* p. 90.*

---

* This quaint and curious book (Smith's Commonwealth of England) describes the *minutiæ* of trials, giving in detail the mode of impanelling the jury, and then the conduct of the lawyers, witnesses, and court. I give the following extracts, *tending to show that the judges impose no law upon the juries, in either civil or criminal cases, but only require them to determine the causes according to their consciences.*

In civil causes he says:

"When it is thought that it is enough pleaded before them, and the witnesses have said what they can, one of the judges, with a brief and pithy recapitulation, reciteth to the twelve in sum the arguments of the sergeants of either side, that which the witnesses have declared, and the chief points of the evidence showed in writing, and once again putteth them in mind of the issue, and sometime giveth it them in writing, delivering to them the evidence which is showed on either part, if any be, (evidence here is called writings of contracts, authentical after the manner of England, that is to say, written, sealed, and delivered,) and biddeth them go together." — p. 74.

This is the whole account given of the charge to the jury.

In criminal cases, after the witnesses have been heard, and the prisoner has said what he pleases in his defence, the book proceeds :

"When the judge hath heard them say enough, he asketh if they can say any more: If they say no, then he turneth his speech to the inquest. 'Good men, (saith he,) ye of the inquest, ye have heard what these men say against the prisoner. You have also heard what the prisoner can say for himself. *Have an eye to your oath, and to your duty, and do that which God shall put in your minds to the discharge of your consciences,* and mark well what is said.'" — p. 92.

This is the whole account given of the charge in a criminal case.

The following statement goes to confirm the same idea, that jurors in England have formerly understood it to be their right and duty to judge only according to their consciences, and not to submit to any dictation from the court, either as to law or fact.

"If having pregnant evidence, nevertheless, the twelve do acquit the malefactor, which they will do sometime, especially if they perceive either one of the justices or of the judges, or some other man, to pursue too much and too maliciously the death of the prisoner, * * the prisoner escapeth; but the twelve (are) not only rebuked by the judges, but also threatened of punishment; and many times commanded to appear in the Star-Chamber, or before the Privy Council for the matter. But this threatening chanceth oftener than the execution thereof ; *and the twelve answer with most gentle words, they did it according to their consciences,* and pray the judges to be good unto them, *they did as they thought right, and as they accorded all,* and so it passeth away for the most part." — p. 100.

The account given of the trial of a peer of the realm corroborates the same point :

"If any duke, marquis, or any other of the degrees of a baron, or above, lord of the Parliament, be appeached of treason, or any other capital crime, he is judged by his peers and equals; that is, the yeomanry doth not go upon him, but an inquest of the Lords of Parliament, and they give their voice not one for all, but each severally as they do in Parliament, being (beginning) at the youngest lord. And for judge one lord sitteth, who is constable of England for that day. The judgment once given, he breaketh his staff, and abdicateth his office. In the rest there is no difference from that above written," (that is, in the case of a freeman.) — p. 98.

Hale says:

"Then twelve, and no less, of such as are indifferent and are returned upon the principal panel, or the *tales*, are sworn to try the same according to the evidence." — 2 *Hale's History of the Common Law*, 141.

It appears from Blackstone that, even *at this day, neither in civil nor criminal cases*, are jurors in England sworn to try causes *according to law*. He says that in *civil* suits the jury are

"Sworn well and truly to *try the issue* between the parties, and a true verdict to give according to the evidence." — 3 *Blackstone*, 365.

"*The issue*" to be tried is whether A owes B anything; and if so, how much? or whether A has in his possession anything that belongs to B; or whether A has wronged B, and ought to make compensation; and if so, how much?

No statute passed by a legislature, simply as a legislature, can alter either of these "issues" in hardly any conceivable case, perhaps in none. No *unjust* law could ever alter them in any. They are all mere questions of natural justice, which legislatures have no power to alter, and with which they have no right to interfere, further than to provide for having them settled by the most competent and impartial tribunal that it is practicable to have, and then for having all just decisions enforced. And any tribunal, whether judge or jury, that attempts to try these issues, has no more moral right to be swerved from the line of justice, by the will of a legislature, than by the will of any other body of men whatever. And this oath does not require or permit a jury to be so swerved.

In criminal cases, Blackstone says the oath of the jury in England is:

"Well and truly to try, and true deliverance make, between our sovereign lord, the king, and the prisoner whom they have in charge, and a true verdict to give according to the evidence." — 4 *Blackstone*, 355.

"The issue" to be tried, in a criminal case, is "*guilty*," or "*not guilty*." The laws passed by a legislature can rarely, if ever, have anything to do with this issue. "*Guilt*" is an *intrinsic* quality of actions, and can neither be created, destroyed, nor changed by legislation. And no tribunal that attempts to try this issue can have any moral right to declare a man *guilty*, for an act that is intrinsically innocent, at the bidding of a legislature, any more than at the bidding of anybody else. And this oath does not require or permit a jury to do so.

The words, "*according to the evidence*," have doubtless been introduced into the above oaths in modern times. They are unquestionably in violation of the Common Law, and of Magna Carta, if by them be meant such evidence only as the government sees fit to allow to go to the jury. If the government can dictate the evidence, and require the jury to decide according to that evidence, it necessarily dictates the conclusion to which they must arrive. In that case the trial is really a trial by the government, and not by the jury. *The jury* cannot *try an issue*, unless *they* determine what evidence shall be admitted. The ancient oaths, it will be observed, say nothing about "*according to the evidence*." They obviously take it for granted that the jury try the whole case; and of course that *they* decide what evidence shall be admitted. It would be intrinsically an immoral and criminal act for a jury to declare a man guilty, or to declare that one man owed money to another, unless all the evidence were admitted, which *they* thought ought to be admitted, for ascertaining the truth.*

Grand Jury. — If jurors are bound to enforce all laws passed by the legislature, it is a very remarkable fact that the oath of grand juries does not require them to be governed by the laws in finding indictments. There have been various forms of oath administered to grand jurors; but by none of them that I recollect ever to have seen, except those of the States

---

* " The present form of the jurors' oath is that they shall ' give a true verdict *according to the evidence*.' At what time this form was introduced is uncertain; but for several centuries after the Conquest, the jurors, *both in civil and criminal cases*, were sworn merely *to speak the truth*. (Glanville, lib. 2, cap. 17; Bracton, lib. 3, cap. 22; lib. 4, p. 287, 291; Britton, p. 135.) Hence their decision was accurately termed *veredictum*, or verdict, that is, ' a thing truly said '; whereas the phrase ' true verdict ' in the modern oath is not an accurate expression." — *Political Dictionary*, word *Jury*.

of Connecticut and Vermont, are they sworn to present men
according to law. The English form, as given in the essay on
Grand Juries, written near two hundred years ago, and supposed to have been written by *Lord Somers*, is as follows :

" You shall diligently inquire, and true presentment make,
of all such articles, matters, and things, as shall be given you
in charge, and of all other matters and things as shall come to
your knowledge touching this present service. The king's
council, your fellows, and your own, you shall keep secret.
You shall present no person for hatred or malice; neither shall
you leave any one unpresented for favor, or affection, for love
or gain, or any hopes thereof; but in all things you shall present the truth, the whole truth, and nothing but the truth, to
the best of your knowledge. So help you God."

This form of oath is doubtless quite ancient, for the essay
says " our ancestors appointed " it. — *See Essay*, p. 33-34.

On the obligations of this oath, the essay says :

"If it be asked how, or in what manner, the (grand) juries
shall inquire, the answer is ready, *according to the best of their
understandings.* They only, not the judges, are sworn to
search diligently to find out all treasons, &c., within their
charge, and they must and ought to use their own discretion
in the way and manner of their inquiry. *No directions can
legally be imposed upon them by any court or judges;* an
honest jury will thankfully accept good advice from judges, as
their assistants; but they are bound by their oaths to present
the truth, the whole truth, and nothing but the truth, to the
best of their own, not the judge's, knowledge. Neither can
they, without breach of that oath, resign their consciences, or
blindly submit to the dictates of others; and therefore ought
to receive or reject such advices, as they judge them good or
bad.   *   *   Nothing can be more plain and express than
the words of the oath are to this purpose. The jurors need
not search the law books, nor tumble over heaps of old
records, for the explanation of them. Our greatest lawyers
may from hence learn more certainly our ancient law in this
case, than from all the books in their studies. The language
wherein the oath is penned is known and understood by every
man, and the words in it have the same signification as they
have wheresoever else they are used. The judges, without
assuming to themselves a legislative power, cannot put a new
sense upon them, other than according to their genuine, common meaning. They cannot magisterially impose their
opinions upon the jury, and make them forsake the direct

words of their oath, to pursue their glosses. The grand inquest are bound to observe alike strictly every part of their oath, and to use all just and proper ways which may enable them to perform it; otherwise it were to say, that after men had sworn to inquire diligently after the truth, according to the best of their knowledge, they were bound to forsake all the natural and proper means which their understandings suggest for the discovery of it, if it be commanded by the judges." — *Lord Somers' Essay on Grand Juries*, p. 38.

What is here said so plainly and forcibly of the oath and obligations of grand juries, is equally applicable to the oath and obligations of petit juries. In both cases the simple oaths of the jurors, and not the instructions of the judges, nor the statutes of kings nor legislatures, are their legal guides to their duties.*

SECTION IV.

The Right of Juries to fix the Sentence.

The nature of the common law courts existing prior to Magna Carta, such as the county courts, the hundred courts, the court-leet, and the court-baron, all prove, what has already been proved from Magna Carta, that, in jury trials, the juries fixed the sentence; because, in those courts, there was no one but the jury who could fix it, unless it were the sheriff, bailiff, or steward; and no one will pretend that it was fixed by them. The juries unquestionably gave the "judgment" in both civil and criminal cases.

That the juries were to fix the sentence under Magna Carta, is also shown by statutes subsequent to Magna Carta.

A statute passed fifty-one years after Magna Carta, says that a baker, for default in the weight of his bread, "*debeat* amerciari vel subire judicium pillorœ," — that is, "*ought* to be amerced, or suffer the sentence of the pillory." And that a brewer, for "selling ale, contrary to the assize," "*debeat* amerciari, vel pati judicium tumbrelli;" that is, "*ought* to be

---

* Of course, there can be no legal trial by jury, in either civil or criminal cases, where the jury are sworn to try the cases " *according to law.*"

amerced, or suffer judgment of the tumbrel." — 51 *Henry III.*, sт. 6. (1266.)

If the king (the legislative power) had had authority to fix the punishments of these offences imperatively, he would naturally have said these offenders *shall* be amerced, and *shall* suffer judgment of the pillory and tumbrel, instead of thus simply expressing the opinion that they *ought* to be punished in that manner.

The statute of Westminster, passed sixty years after Magna Carta, provides that,

"No city, borough, nor town, *nor any man*, be amerced, without reasonable cause, and according to the quantity of the trespass; that is to say, every freeman saving his freehold, a merchant saving his merchandise, a villein his waynage, *and that by his or their peers.*" — 3 *Edward I.*, ch. 6. (1275.)

The same statute (ch. 18) provides further, that,

"Forasmuch as the *common fine and amercement* of the whole county in Eyre of the justices for false judgments, or for other trespass, is unjustly assessed by sheriffs and baretors in the shires, so that the sum is many times increased, and the parcels otherwise assessed than they ought to be, to the damage of the people, which be many times paid to the sheriffs and baretors, which do not acquit the payers; it is provided, and the king wills, that from henceforth such sums shall be assessed before the justices in Eyre, afore their departure, *by the oath of knights and other honest men*, upon all such as ought to pay; and the justices shall cause the parcels to be put into their estreats, which shall be delivered up unto the exchequer, and not the whole sum." — *St.* 3 *Edward I.*, ch. 18, (1275.)*

The following statute, passed in 1341, one hundred and twenty-five years after Magna Carta, providing for the trial of peers of the realm, and the king's ministers, contains a re-

---

* *Coke*, as late as 1588, admits that amercements must be fixed by the peers (8 Coke's Rep. 38, 2 Inst. 27); but he attempts, wholly without success, as it seems to me, to show a difference between fines and amercements. The statutes are very numerous, running through the three or four hundred years immediately succeeding Magna Carta, in which fines, ransoms, and amercements are spoken of as if they were the common punishments of offences, and as if they all meant the same thing. If, however, any technical difference could be made out between them, there is clearly none in principle; and the word *amercement*, as used in Magna Carta, must be taken in its most comprehensive sense.

cognition of the principle of Magna Carta, that the jury are to fix the sentence.

"Whereas before this time the peers of the land have been arrested and imprisoned, and their temporalities, lands, and tenements, goods and cattels, asseized in the king's hands, and some put to death without judgment of their peers : It is accorded and assented, that no peer of the land, officer, nor other, because of his office, nor of things touching his office, nor by other cause, shall be brought in judgment to lose his temporalities, lands, tenements, goods and cattels, nor to be arrested, nor imprisoned, outlawed, exiled, nor forejudged, nor put to answer, nor be judged, but by *award* (*sentence*) of the said peers in Parliament."— 15 *Edward III.*, st. 1, sec. 2.

Section 4, of the same statute provides,

"That in every Parliament, at the third day of every Parliament, the king shall take in his hands the offices of all the ministers aforesaid," (that is, "the chancellor, treasurer, barons, and chancellor of the exchequer, the justices of the one bench and of the other, justices assigned in the country, steward and chamberlain of the king's house, keeper of the privy seal, treasurer of the wardrobe, controllers, and they that be chief deputed to abide nigh the king's son, Duke of Cornwall,") "and so they shall abide four or five days; except the offices of justices of the one place or the other, justices assigned, barons of exchequer; so always that they and all other ministers be put to answer to every complaint; and if default be found in any of the said ministers, by complaint or other manner, and of that attainted in Parliament, he shall be punished by judgment of the peers, and put out of his office, and another convenient put in his place.   And upon the same our said sovereign lord the king shall do (cause) to be pronounced and made execution without delay, *according to the judgment* (*sentence*) of the said peers in the Parliament."

Here is an admission that the peers were to fix the sentence, or judgment, and the king promises to make execution "*according to*" that sentence.

And this appears to be the law, under which peers of the realm and the great officers of the crown were tried and sentenced, for four hundred years after its passage, and, for aught I know, until this day.

The first case given in Hargrave's collection of English State Trials, is that of *Alexander Nevil*, Archbishop of York,

Robert Vere, Duke of Ireland, *Michael de la Pole,* Earl of
Suffolk, and *Robert Tresilian,* Lord Chief Justice of England,
with several others, convicted of treason, before "the Lords
of Parliament," in 1388. The sentences in these cases were
adjudged by the " Lords of Parliament," in the following terms,
as they are reported.

"Wherefore the said *Lords of Parliament,* there present, as
judges in Parliament, in this case, *by assent of the king, pronounced their sentence,* and did adjudge the said archbishop,
duke, and earl, with Robert Tresilian, so appealed, as aforesaid, to be guilty, and convicted of treason, and to be drawn
and hanged, as traitors and enemies to the king and kingdom;
and that their heirs should be disinherited forever, and their
lands and tenements, goods and chattels, forfeited to the king,
and that the temporalities of the Archbishop of York should
be taken into the king's hands."

Also, in the same case, Sir *John Holt,* Sir *William Burgh,*
Sir *John Cary,* Sir *Roger Fulthorpe,* and *John Locton,* "*were
by the lords temporal, by the assent of the king,* adjudged to
be drawn and hanged, as traitors, their heirs disinherited, and
their lands and tenements, goods and chattels, to be forfeited
to the king."

Also, in the same case, *John Blake,* "of council for the
king," and *Thomas Uske,* under sheriff of Middlesex, having
been convicted of treason,

"*The lords awarded, by assent of the king,* that they should
both be hanged and drawn as traitors, as open enemies to the
king and kingdom, and their heirs disinherited forever, and
their lands and tenements, goods and chattels, forfeited to the
king."

Also, "*Simon Burleigh,* the king's chamberlain," being convicted of treason, "*by joint consent of the king and the lords,*
sentence was pronounced against the said Simon Burleigh, that
he should be drawn from the town to Tyburn, and there be
hanged till he be dead, and then have his head struck from
his body."

Also, "*John Beauchamp,* steward of the household to the
king, *James Beroverse,* and *John Salisbury,* knights, gentle-
men of the privy chamber, *were in like manner condemned.*"
— 1 *Hargrave's State Trials,* first case.

Here the sentences were all fixed by the peers, *with the assent of the king.* But that the king should be consulted, and
his assent obtained to the sentence pronounced by the peers,

does not imply any deficiency of power on their part to fix the sentence independently of the king. There are obvious reasons why they might choose to consult the king, and obtain his approbation of the sentence they were about to impose, without supposing any legal necessity for their so doing.

So far as we can gather from the reports of state trials, peers of the realm were usually sentenced by those who tried them, *with the assent of the king.* But in some instances no mention is made of the assent of the king, as in the case of " Lionel, Earl of Middlesex, Lord High Treasurer of England," in 1624, (four hundred years after Magna Carta,) where the sentence was as follows :

" This High Court of Parliament doth adjudge, that Lionel, Earl of Middlesex, now Lord Treasurer of England, shall lose all his offices which he holds in this kingdom, and shall, hereafter, be made incapable of any office, place, or employment in the state and commonwealth. That he shall be imprisoned in the tower of London, during the king's pleasure. That he shall pay unto our sovereign lord the king a fine of 50,000 pounds. That he shall never sit in Parliament any more, and that he shall never come within the verge of the court." — 2 *Howell's State Trials,* 1250.

Here was a peer of the realm, and a minister of the king, of the highest grade; and if it were ever *necessary* to obtain the assent of the king to sentences pronounced by the peers, it would unquestionably have been obtained in this instance, and his assent would have appeared in the sentence.

Lord Bacon was sentenced by the House of Lords, (1620,) *no mention being made of the assent of the king.* The sentence is in these words :

" And, therefore, this High Court doth adjudge, That the Lord Viscount St. Albans, Lord Chancellor of England, shall undergo fine and ransom of 40,000 pounds. That he shall be imprisoned in the tower during the king's pleasure. That he shall forever be incapable of any office, place, or employment in the state or commonwealth. That he shall never sit in Parliament, nor come within the verge of the court."

And when it was demanded of him, before sentence, whether it were his hand that was subscribed to his confession, and whether he would stand to it; he made the following answer, which implies that the *lords* were the ones to determine his sentence.

"My lords, it is my act, my hand, my heart. *I beseech your lordships to be merciful to a broken reed.*" — 1 *Hargrave's State Trials*, 386–7.

The sentence against Charles the First, (1648,) after reciting the grounds of his condemnation, concludes in this form:

"For all which treasons and crimes, *this court doth adjudge,* that he, the said Charles Stuart, as a tyrant, traitor, murderer, and public enemy to the good people of this nation, shall be put to death by the severing his head from his body."

The report then adds:

"This sentence being read, the president (of the court) spake as followeth: 'This sentence now read and published, is the act, sentence, judgment and resolution of the whole court.'" — 1 *Hargrave's State Trials*, 1037.

Unless it had been the received "*law of the land*" that those who tried a man should fix his sentence, it would have required an act of Parliament to fix the sentence of Charles, and his sentence would have been declared to be "*the sentence of the law,*" instead of "*the act, sentence, judgment, and resolution of the court.*"

But the report of the proceedings in "the trial of Thomas, Earl of Macclesfield, Lord High Chancellor of Great Britain, before the House of Lords, for high crimes and misdemeanors in the execution of his office," in 1725, is so full on this point, and shows so clearly that it rested wholly with the lords to fix the sentence, and that the assent of the king was wholly unnecessary, that I give the report somewhat at length.

After being found guilty, the earl addressed the *lords,* for a *mitigation of sentence,* as follows:

"'I am now to expect your lordships' judgment; and I hope that you will be pleased to consider that I have suffered no small matter already in the trial, in the expense I have been at, the fatigue, and what I have suffered otherways. * * I have paid back 10,800 pounds of the money already; I have lost my office; I have undergone the censure of both houses of Parliament, which is in itself a severe punishment,'" &c., &c.

On being interrupted, he proceeded :

" ' My lords, I submit whether this be not proper in *mitigation of your lordships' sentence ;* but whether it be or not, I leave myself to your lordships' justice and mercy; I am sure neither of them will be wanting, and I entirely submit.' * *

" ' Then the said earl, as also the managers, were directed to withdraw; and the House (of Lords) ordered Thomas, Earl of Macclesfield, to be committed to the custody of the gentleman usher of the black rod; and then proceeded to the consideration of what *judgment,*" (that is, *sentence,* for he had already been found *guilty,*) " to give upon the impeachment against the said earl." * *

" The next day, the Commons, with their speaker, being present at the bar of the House (of Lords), * * the speaker of the House of Commons said as follows :

" ' My Lords, the knights, citizens, and burgesses in Parliament assembled, in the name of themselves, and of all the commons of Great Britain, did at this bar impeach Thomas, Earl of Macclesfield, of high crimes and misdemeanors, and did exhibit articles of impeachment against him, and have made good their charge. I do, therefore, in the name of the knights, citizens, and burgesses, in Parliament assembled, and of all the commons of Great Britain, demand *judgment (sentence)* of your lordships against Thomas, Earl of Macclesfield, for the said high crimes and misdemeanors.'

" Then the Lord Chief Justice King, Speaker of the House of Lords, said : ' Mr. Speaker, the Lords are now ready to proceed to judgment in the case by you mentioned.

" ' Thomas, Earl of Macclesfield, the Lords have unanimously found you guilty of high crimes and misdemeanors, charged on you by the impeachment of the House of Commons, and do now, according to law, proceed to *judgment* against you, which I am ordered to pronounce. Their lordships' *judgment* is, and this high court doth adjudge, that you, Thomas, Earl of Macclesfield, be fined in the sum of thirty thousand pounds unto our sovereign lord the king; and that you shall be imprisoned in the tower of London, and there kept in safe custody, until you shall pay the said fine.' " — 6 *Hargrave's State Trials,* 762–3–4.

This case shows that the principle of Magna Carta, that a man should be *sentenced* only by his peers, was in force, and acted upon as law, in England, so lately as 1725, (five hundred years after Magna Carta,) so far as it applied to a *peer of the realm.*

But the same principle, on this point, that applies to a **peer** of the realm, applies to every freeman. The only difference between the two is, that the peers of the realm have had influence enough to preserve their constitutional rights; while the constitutional rights of the people have been trampled upon and rendered obsolete by the usurpation and corruption of the government and the courts.

SECTION V.

The Oaths of Judges.

As further proof that the legislation of the king, whether enacted with or without the assent and advice of his parliaments, was of no authority unless it were consistent with the *common law*, and unless juries and judges saw fit to enforce it, it may be mentioned that it is probable that no judge in England was ever sworn to observe the laws enacted either by the king alone, or by the king with the advice and assent of parliament.

The judges were sworn to "*do equal law, and execution of right, to all the king's subjects, rich and poor, without having regard to any person;*" and that they will "*deny no man common right;*" * but they were *not* sworn to obey or execute any statutes of the king, or of the king and parliament. Indeed, they are virtually sworn *not* to obey any statutes that are against "*common right,*" or contrary to "*the common law,*" or "*law of the land;*" but to "certify the king thereof" — that is, notify him that his statutes are against the common law; — and then proceed to execute the *common law*, notwithstanding such legislation to the contrary. The words of the oath on this point are these :

"*That ye deny no man common right by (virtue of) the king's letters, nor none other man's, nor for none other cause; and in case any letters come to you contrary to the law,* (that is, the common law, as will be seen on reference to the entire oath given in the note,) *that ye do nothing by such letters, but*

---

* "*Common right*" was the common law. 1 *Coke's Inst.* 142 a. 2 *do.* 55, 6.

certify the king thereof, and proceed to execute the law, (that is, the common law,) *notwithstanding the same letters."*

When it is considered that the king was the sole legislative power, and that he exercised this power, to a great extent, by orders in council, and by writs and "letters" addressed oftentimes to some sheriff, or other person, and that his commands, when communicated to his justices, or any other person, "by letters," or writs, *under seal,* had as much legal authority as laws promulgated in any other form whatever, it will be seen that this oath of the justices *absolutely required* that they disregard any legislation that was contrary to "*common right,*" or "*the common law,*" and notify the king that it was contrary to common right, or the common law, and then proceed to execute the common law, notwithstanding such legislation.*

If there could be any doubt that such was the meaning of this oath, that doubt would be removed by a statute passed by the king two years afterwards, which fully explains this oath, as follows:

"Edward, by the Grace of God, &c., to the Sheriff of *Stafford,* greeting: Because that by divers complaints made to us, we have perceived that *the Law of the Land, which we by our oath are bound to maintain,* is the less well kept, and the execution of the same disturbed many times by maintenance and procurement, as well in the court as in the country; we

---

* The oath of the justices is in these words :

"Ye shall swear, that well and lawfully ye shall serve our lord the king *and his people,* in the office of justice, and that lawfully ye shall counsel the king in his business, and that ye shall not counsel nor assent to anything which may turn him in damage or disherison in any manner, way, or color. And that ye shall not know the damage or disherison of him, whereof ye shall not cause him to be warned by yourself, or by other; *and that ye shall do equal law and execution of right to all his subjects, rich and poor, without having regard to any person.* And that ye take not by yourself, or by other, privily nor apertly, gift nor reward of gold nor silver, nor of any other thing that may turn to your profit, unless it be meat or drink, and that of small value, of any man that shall have any plea or process hanging before you, as long as the same process shall be so hanging, nor after for the same cause. And that ye take no fee, as long as ye shall be justice, nor robe of any man great or small, but of the king himself. And that ye give none advice or counsel to no man great or small, in no case where the king is party. And in case that any, of what estate or condition they be, come before you in your sessions with force and arms, or otherwise against the peace, or against the form of the statute thereof made, *to disturb execution of the common law,*" (mark the term, " *common law,*") " or to menace the people that they may not

greatly moved of conscience in this matter, and for this cause desiring as much for the pleasure of God, and ease and quietness of our subjects, as to save our conscience, and for to save and keep our said oath, by the assent of the great men and other wise men of our council, we have ordained these things following:

"First, we have commanded all our justices, that they shall from henceforth *do equal law and execution of right* to all our subjects, rich and poor, without having regard to any person, *and without omitting to do right for any letters or commandment which may come to them from us, or from any other, or by any other cause. And if that any letters, writs, or commandments come to the justices, or to other deputed to do law and right according to the usage of the realm, in disturbance of the law, or of the execution of the same, or of right to the parties, the justices and other aforesaid shall proceed and hold their courts and processes, where the pleas and matters be depending before them, as if no such letters, writs, or commandments were come to them ; and they shall certify us and our council of such commandments which be contrary to the law,* (that is, " the law of the land," or common law,) *as afore is said.*"* And to the intent that our justices shall do even right to all people in the manner aforesaid, without more favor showing to one than to another, we have ordained and caused our said justices to be sworn, that they shall not from henceforth, as long as they shall be in the office of justice, take fee nor robe of any man, but of ourself, and that they shall take no gift nor reward by themselves, nor by other, privily nor

pursue the law, that ye shall cause their bodies to be arrested and put in prison ; and in case they be such that ye cannot arrest them, that ye certify the king of their names, and of their misprision, hastily, so that he may thereof ordain a convenable remedy. And that ye by yourself, nor by other, privily nor apertly, maintain any plea or quarrel hanging in the king's court, or elsewhere in the country. *And that ye deny no man common right by the king's letters, nor none other man's, nor for none other cause ; and in case any letters come to you contrary to the law,*" (that is, the " common law " before mentioned,) " *that ye do nothing by such letters, but certify the king thereof, and proceed to execute the law,*" (the " common law " before mentioned,) " *notwithstanding the same letters.* And that ye shall do and procure the profit of the king and of his crown, with all things where ye may reasonably do the same. And in case ye be from henceforth found in default in any of the points aforesaid, ye shall be at the king's will of body, lands, and goods, thereof to be done as shall please him, as God you help and all saints." — 18 *Edward III.*, st. 4. (1344.)

* That the terms " *Law* " and " *Right*," as used in this statute, mean the *common law*, is shown by the preamble, which declares the motive of the statute to be that "*the Law of the Land, (the common law,) which we (the king) by our oath are bound to maintain,*" may be the better kept, &c.

apertly, of any man that hath to do before them by any way except meat and drink, and that of small value; and that they shall give no counsel to great men or small, in case where we be party, or which do or may touch us in any point, upon pain to be at our will, body, lands, and goods, to do thereof as shall please us, in case they do contrary. And for this cause we have increased the fees of the same, our justices, in such manner as it ought reasonably to suffice them." — 20 *Edward III.*, ch. 1. (1346.)

Other statutes of similar tenor have been enacted, as follows:

"It is accorded and established, that it shall not be commanded by the great seal, nor the little seal, to disturb or delay *common right;* and though such commandments do come, the justices shall not therefore leave (omit) to do right in any point." — *St.* 2 *Edward III.*, ch. 8. (1328.)

"That by commandment of the great seal, or privy seal, no point of this statute shall be put in delay; nor that the justices of whatsoever place it be shall let (omit) to do the *common law,* by commandment, which shall come to them under the great seal, or the privy seal." — 14 *Edward III.*, st. 1, ch. 14. (1340.)

"It is ordained and established, that neither letters of the signet, nor of the king's privy seal, shall be from henceforth sent in damage or prejudice of the realm, nor in disturbance of the law " (the common law). — 11 *Richard II.*, ch. 10. (1387.)

It is perfectly apparent from these statutes, and from the oath administered to the justices, that it was a matter freely confessed by the king himself, that his statutes were of no validity, if contrary to the common law, or "common right."

The oath of the justices, before given, is, I presume, the same that has been administered to judges in England from the day when it was first prescribed to them, (1344,) until now. I do not find from the English statutes that the oath has ever been changed. The Essay on Grand Juries, before referred to, and supposed to have been written by *Lord Somers,* mentions this oath (page 73) as being still administered to judges, that is, in the time of Charles II., more than three hundred years after the oath was first ordained. If the oath has never been changed, it follows that judges have not only never been sworn to support any statutes whatever of

the king, or of parliament, but that, for five hundred years
past, they actually have been sworn to treat as invalid all
statutes that were contrary to the common law.

SECTION VI.

The Coronation Oath.

That the legislation of the king was of no authority over a
jury, is further proved by the oath taken by the kings at their
coronation.   This oath seems to have been substantially the
same, from the time of the *Saxon* kings, down to the seven-
teenth century, as will be seen from the authorities hereafter
given.

The purport of the oath is, that the king swears *to maintain
the law of the land* — that is, *the common law.*   In other words,
he swears " *to concede and preserve to the English people the
laws and customs conceded to them by the ancient, just, and
pious English kings,* * * *and especially the laws, customs,
and liberties conceded to the clergy and people by the illustrious
king Edward;*" * * *and* " *the just laws and customs which
the common people have chosen,* (*quas vulgus elegit*)."

These are the same laws and customs which were called
by the general name of " *the law of the land,*" or " *the common law,*" and, with some slight additions, were embodied in
Magna Carta.

This oath not only forbids the king to enact any statutes
contrary to the common law, but it proves that his statutes
could be of no authority over the consciences of a jury; since,
as has already been sufficiently shown, it was one part of
this very common law itself, — that is, of the ancient " laws,
customs, and liberties," mentioned in the oath, — that juries
should judge of all questions that came before them, according
to their own consciences, independently of the legislation of
the king.

It was impossible that this right of the jury could subsist
consistently with any right, on the part of the king, to impose
any authoritative legislation upon them.   His oath, therefore,

to maintain the law of the land, or the ancient "laws, customs, and liberties," was equivalent to an oath that he would never *assume* to impose laws upon juries, as imperative rules of decision, or take from them the right to try all cases according to their own consciences. It is also an admission that he had no constitutional power to do so, if he should ever desire it. This oath, then, is conclusive proof that his legislation was of no authority with a jury, and that they were under no obligation whatever to enforce it, unless it coincided with their own ideas of justice.

The ancient coronation oath is printed with the Statutes of the Realm, vol. i., p. 168, and is as follows : *

TRANSLATION.

"*Form of the Oath of the King of England, on his Coronation.*

(The Archbishop of Canterbury, to whom, of right and custom of the Church of Canterbury, ancient and approved, it pertains to anoint and crown the kings of England, on the day of the coronation of the king, and before the king is crowned, shall propound the underwritten questions to the king.)

The laws and customs, conceded to the English people by the ancient, just, and pious English kings, will you concede and preserve to the same people, with the confirmation of an oath ? and especially the laws, customs, and liberties conceded to the clergy and people by the illustrious king Edward ?

---

* The following is a copy of the original :

" *Forma Juramenti Regis Angliæ in Coronacione sua :*

(Archiepiscopus Cantuariæ, ad quo de jure et consuetudine Ecclesiæ Cantuariæ, antiqua et approbata, pertinet Reges Angliæ inungere et coronare, die coronacionis Regis, anteque Rex coronetur, faciet Regi Interrogationes subscriptas.)

Si leges et consuetudines ab antiquis justis et Deo devotis Regibus plebi Anglicano concessas, cum sacramenti confirmacione eidem plebi concedere et servare (volueris :) Et præsertim leges et consuetudines et libertates a glorioso Rege Edwardo clero populoque concessas ?

(Et respondeat Rex,) Concedo et servare volo, et sacramento confirmare.

Servabis Ecclesiæ Dei, Cleroque, et Populo, pacem ex integro et concordiam in Deo secundum vires tuas ?

(Et respondeat Rex,) Servabo.

Facies fieri in omnibus Judiciis tuis equam et rectam justiciam, et discrecionem, in misericordia et veritate, secundum vires tuas ?

(Et respondeat Rex,) Faciam.

Concedis justas, leges et consuetudines esse tenendas, et promittis per te eas esse protegendas, et ad honorem Dei corroborandas, *quas vulgus elegit,* secundum vires tuas ?

(Et respondeat Rex,) Concedo et promitto."

(And the king shall answer,) I do concede, and will preserve them, and confirm them by my oath.

Will you preserve to the church of God, the clergy, and the people, entire peace and harmony in God, according to your powers?

(And the king shall answer,) I will.

In all your judgments, will you cause equal and right justice and discretion to be done, in mercy and truth, according to your powers?

(And the king shall answer,) I will.

Do you concede that the just laws and customs, *which the common people have chosen,* shall be preserved; and do you promise that they shall be protected by you, and strengthened to the honor of God, according to your powers?

(And the king shall answer,) I concede and promise."

The language used in the last of these questions, " Do you concede that the just laws and customs, *which the common people have chosen,* (*quas vulgus elegit,*) shall be preserved?" &c., is worthy of especial notice, as showing that the laws, which were to be preserved, were not necessarily *all* the laws which the kings enacted, *but only such of them as the common people had selected or approved.*

And how had the common people made known their approbation or selection of these laws? Plainly, in no other way than this — *that the juries composed of the common people had voluntarily enforced them.* The common people had no other *legal* form of making known their approbation of particular laws.

The word "concede," too, is an important word. In the English statutes it is usually translated *grant* — as if with an intention to indicate that " the laws, customs, and liberties " of the English people were mere *privileges, granted* to them by the king; whereas it should be translated *concede,* to indicate simply an *acknowledgment,* on the part of the king, that such were the laws, customs, and liberties, which had been chosen and established by the people themselves, and of right belonged to them, and which he was bound to respect.

I will now give some authorities to show that the foregoing oath has, *in substance,* been the coronation oath from the times of William the Conqueror, (1066,) down to the time of James the First, and probably until 1688.

It will be noticed, in the quotation from Kelham, that he says this oath (or the oath of William the Conqueror) is "in sense and substance the very same with that which the *Saxon* kings used to take at their coronations."

Hale says:

" Yet the English were very zealous for them," (that is, for the laws of Edward the Confessor,) " no less or otherwise than they are at this time for the Great Charter; insomuch that they were never satisfied till the said laws were reënforced, and mingled, for the most part, with the coronation oath of king William I., and some of his successors." — 1 *Hale's History of Common Law*, 157.

Also, " William, on his coronation, had sworn to govern by the laws of Edward the Confessor, some of which had been reduced into writing, but the greater part consisted of the immemorial customs of the realm." — *Ditto*, p. 202, note L.

Kelham says:

" Thus stood the laws of England at the entry of William I., and it seems plain that the laws, commonly called the laws of Edward the Confessor, were at that time the standing laws of the kingdom, and considered the great rule of their rights and liberties; and that the English were so zealous for them, ' that they were never satisfied till the said laws were reënforced, and mingled, for the most part, with the coronation oath.' Accordingly, we find that this great conqueror, at his coronation on the Christmas day succeeding his victory, took an oath at the altar of St. Peter, Westminster, *in sense and substance the very same with that which the Saxon kings used to take at their coronations.* * * And at Barkhamstead, in the fourth year of his reign, in the presence of Lanfranc, Archbishop of Canterbury, for the quieting of the people, he swore that he would inviolably observe the good and approved ancient laws which had been made by the devout and pious kings of England, his ancestors, and chiefly by King Edward; and we are told that the people then departed in good humor." — *Kelham's Preliminary Discourse to the Laws of William the Conqueror.* See, also, 1 *Hale's History of the Common Law*, 186.

Crabbe says that William the Conqueror "solemnly swore that he would observe the good and approved laws of Edward the Confessor." — *Crabbe's History of the English Law*, p. 43.

The successors of William, up to the time of Magna Carta,

probably all took the same oath, according to the custom of
the kingdom; although there may be no historical accounts
extant of the oath of each separate king. But history tells us
specially that Henry I., Stephen, and Henry II., confirmed
these ancient laws and customs. It appears, also, that the
barons desired of John (what he afterwards granted by Magna Carta) "*that the laws and liberties of King Edward*,
with other privileges granted to the kingdom and church of
England, might be confirmed, as they were contained in the
charters of Henry the First; further alleging, *that at the time
of his absolution, he promised by his oath to observe these very
laws and liberties.*" — *Echard's History of England*, p. 105–6.

It would appear, from the following authorities, that since
Magna Carta the form of the coronation oath has been "*to
maintain the law of the land*," — meaning that law as embodied in Magna Carta. Or perhaps it is more probable that
the ancient form has been still observed, but that, as its substance and purport were "*to maintain the law of the land*,"
this latter form of expression has been used, in the instances
here cited, from motives of brevity and convenience. This
supposition is the more probable, from the fact that I find no
statute prescribing a change in the form of the oath until 1688.

That Magna Carta was considered as embodying "the law
of the land," or "common law," is shown by a statute passed
by Edward I., wherein he "grants," or concedes,

"That the Charter of Liberties and the Charter of the Forest
* * shall be kept in every point, without breach, * * and
that our justices, sheriffs, mayors, and other ministers, which,
under us, have the *laws of our land* * to guide, shall allow the
said charters pleaded before them in judgment, in all their
points, that is, to wit, *the Great Charter as the Common Law*,
and the Charter of the Forest for the wealth of the realm.

"And we will, that if any judgment be given from henceforth, contrary to the points of the charters aforesaid, by the
justices, or by any other our ministers that hold plea before
them against the points of the charters, it shall be undone,
and holden for naught." — 25 *Edward I.*, ch. 1 and 2. (1297.)

---

* It would appear, from the text, that the Charter of Liberties and the Charter of
the Forest were sometimes called "*laws* of the land."

Blackstone also says:

"It is agreed by all our historians that the Great Charter of King John was, for the most part, *compiled from the ancient customs of the realm, or the laws of Edward the Confessor; by which they usually mean the old common law which was established under our Saxon princes.*" — *Blackstone's Introduction to the Charters.* See *Blackstone's Law Tracts*, 289.

Crabbe says:

"It is admitted, on all hands, that it (Magna Carta) contains nothing but what was confirmatory of the common law, and the ancient usages of the realm, and is, properly speaking, only an enlargement of the charter of Henry I., and his successors." — *Crabbe's History of the English Law*, p. 127.

That the coronation oath of the kings subsequent to Magna Carta was, in substance, if not in form, "*to maintain this law of the land, or common law*," is shown by a statute of Edward Third, commencing as follows:

"Edward, by the Grace of God, &c., &c., to the Sheriff of Stafford, Greeting: Because that by divers complaints made to us, we have perceived that *the law of the land, which we by oath are bound to maintain,*" *&c.* — *St.* 20 *Edward III.* (1346.)

The following extract from Lord Somers' tract on Grand Juries shows that the coronation oath continued the same as late as 1616, (four hundred years after Magna Carta.) He says:

"King James, in his speech to the judges, in the Star Chamber, Anno 1616, told them, 'That he had, after many years, resolved to renew his oath, made at his coronation, concerning justice, and the promise therein contained for *maintaining the law of the land.*' And, in the next page save one, says, '*I was sworn to maintain the law of the land,* and therefore had been perjured if I had broken it. God is my judge, I never intended it.'" — *Somers on Grand Juries*, p. 82.

In 1688, the coronation oath was changed by act of Parliament, and the king was made to swear:

"To govern the people of this kingdom of England, and the dominions thereto belonging, *according to the statutes in Parliament agreed on, and the laws and customs of the same.*" — *St.* 1 *William and Mary*, ch. 6. (1688.)

The effect and legality of this oath will hereafter be considered. For the present it is sufficient to show, as has been already sufficiently done, that from the Saxon times until at least as lately as 1616, the coronation oath has been, in substance, *to maintain the law of the land, or the common law,* meaning thereby the ancient Saxon customs, as embodied in the laws of Alfred, of Edward the Confessor, and finally in Magna Carta.

It may here be repeated that this oath plainly proves that the statutes of the king were of no authority over juries, if inconsistent with their ideas of right; because it was one part of the common law that juries should try all causes according to their own consciences, any legislation of the king to the contrary notwithstanding.*

---

* As the ancient coronation oath, given in the text, has come down from the *Saxon* times, the following remarks of Palgrave will be pertinent, in connection with the oath, as illustrating the fact that, in those times, no special authority attached to the laws of the king :

"The Imperial Witenagemot was not a legislative assembly, in the strict sense of the term, for the whole Anglo-Saxon empire. Promulgating his edicts amidst his peers and prelates, the king uses the language of command; but the theoretical prerogative was modified by usage, and the practice of the constitution required that the law should be accepted by the legislatures (courts) of the several kingdoms. * * The 'Basileus' speaks in the tone of prerogative : Edgar does not merely recommend, he commands that the law shall be adopted by all the people, whether English, Danes, or Britons, in every part of his empire. Let this statute be observed, he continues, by Earl Oslac, and all the host who dwell under his government, and let it be transmitted by *writ* to the ealdormen of the other subordinate states. And yet, in defiance of this positive injunction, the laws of Edgar were not accepted in Mercia until the reign of Canute the Dane. It might be said that the course so adopted may have been an exception to the general rule; but in the scanty and imperfect annals of Anglo-Saxon legislation, we shall be able to find so many examples of similar proceedings, *that this mode of enactment must be considered as dictated by the constitution of the empire.* Edward was the supreme lord of the Northumbrians, but more than a century elapsed before they obeyed his decrees. The laws of the glorious Athelstane had no effect in Kent, (county,) the dependent appanage of his crown, until sanctioned by the *Witan* of the *shire* (county court). And the power of Canute himself, the 'King of all England,' does not seem to have compelled the Northumbrians to receive his code, until the reign of the Confessor, when such acceptance became a part of the compact upon the accession of a new earl.

Legislation constituted but a small portion of the ordinary business transacted by the Imperial Witenagemot. The wisdom of the assembly was shown in avoiding unnecessary change. *Consisting principally of traditionary usages and ancestorial customs, the law was upheld by opinion. The people considered their jurisprudence as a part of their inheritance.* Their privileges and their duties were closely conjoined; *most frequently, the statutes themselves were only affirmances of ancient customs, or declaratory enactments.* In the Anglo-Saxon commonwealth, therefore, the legislative functions of the Witenagemot were of far less importance than the other branches of its authority. * * The members of the Witenagemot were the 'Pares Curiæ' (Peers of Court) of the kingdom. How far, on these occasions, their opinion or their equity controlled the power of the crown, cannot be ascertained. But the form of inserting their names in the 'Testing Clause' was retained under the Anglo-Norman reigns; and the sovereign, who submitted his Charter to the judgment of the *Proceres,* professed to be guided by the opinion which they gave. As the '*Pares*' of the empire, the Witenagemot decided the disputes between the great vassals of the crown. * * The jurisdiction exercised in the Parliament of Edward I., when the barony of a *Lord-Marcher* became the subject of litigation, is entirely analogous to the proceedings thus adopted by the great council of Edward, the son of Alfred, the Anglo-Saxon king.

In this assembly, the king, the prelates, the dukes, the ealdormen, and the optimates passed judgment upon all great offenders. * *

The sovereign could not compel the obedience of the different nations composing the Anglo-Saxon empire. Hence, it became more necessary for him to *conciliate their opinions,* if he solicited any service from a vassal prince or a vassal state beyond the ordinary terms of the compact; still more so, when he needed the support of a free burgh or city. And we may view the assembly (the Witenagemot) as partaking of the character of a political congress, in which the liegemen of the crown, or the communities protected by the ' Basileus,' (sovereign,) were *asked or persuaded* to relieve the exigences of the state, or to consider those measures which might be required for the common weal. The sovereign was compelled to *parley* with his dependents.

It may be doubted whether any one member of the empire had power to legislate for any other member. The Regulus of Cumbria was unaffected by the vote of the Earl of East Angliæ, if he chose to stand out against it. These dignitaries constituted a congress, in which the sovereign could treat more conveniently and effectually with his vassals than by separate negotiations. * * But the determinations of the Witan bound those only who were present, or who concurred in the proposition; and a vassal denying his assent to the grant, might assert that the engagement which he had contracted with his superior did not involve any pecuniary subsidy, but only rendered him liable to perform service in the field." — 1 *Palgrave's Rise and Progress of the English Commonwealth,* 637 to 642.

CHAPTER IV.

THE RIGHTS AND DUTIES OF JURIES IN CIVIL SUITS.

THE evidence already given in the preceding chapters proves that the rights and duties of jurors, in civil suits, were anciently the same as in criminal ones; that the laws of the king were of no obligation upon the consciences of the jurors, any further than the laws were seen by them to be just; that very few laws were enacted applicable to civil suits; that when a new law was enacted, the nature of it could have been known to the jurors only by report, and was very likely not to be known to them at all; that nearly all the law involved in civil suits was *unwritten ;* that there was *usually* no one in attendance upon juries who could possibly enlighten them, unless it were sheriffs, stewards, and bailiffs, who were unquestionably too ignorant and untrustworthy to instruct them authoritatively; that the jurors must therefore necessarily have judged for themselves of the whole case; and that, *as a general rule,* they could judge of it by no law but the law of nature, or the principles of justice as they existed in their own minds.

The ancient oath of jurors in civil suits, viz., that "*they would make known the truth according to their consciences,*" implies that the jurors were above the authority of all legislation. The modern oath, in England, viz., that they "*will well and truly try the issue between the parties, and a true verdict give, according to the evidence,*" implies the same thing. If the laws of the king had been binding upon a jury, they would have been sworn to try the cases *according to law,* or according to the laws.

The ancient writs, in civil suits, as given in Glanville, (within the half century before Magna Carta,) to wit, "Summon twelve free and legal men, (or sometimes twelve knights,) to be in court, *prepared upon their oaths to declare whether A or B have the greater right to the land in question,"* indicate that the jurors judged of the whole matter on their consciences only.

The language of Magna Carta, already discussed, establishes the same point; for, although some of the words, such as "outlawed," and "exiled," would apply only to criminal cases, nearly the whole chapter applies as well to civil as to criminal suits. For example, how could the payment of a debt ever be enforced against an unwilling debtor, if he could neither be " arrested, imprisoned, nor deprived of his freehold," and if the king could neither " proceed against him, nor send any one against him, by force or arms " ? Yet Magna Carta as much forbids that any of these things shall be done against a debtor, as against a criminal, *except according to, or in execution of, " a judgment of his peers, or the law of the land,"* — a provision which, it has been shown, gave the jury the free and absolute right to give or withhold "judgment" according to their consciences, irrespective of all legislation.

The following provisions, in the Magna Carta of John, illustrate the custom of referring the most important matters of a civil nature, even where the king was a party, to the determination of the peers, or of twelve men, acting by no rules but their own consciences. These examples at least show that there is nothing improbable or unnatural in the idea that juries should try all civil suits according to their own judgments, independently of all laws of the king.

Chap. 65. "If we have disseized or dispossessed the Welsh of any lands, liberties, or other things, without the legal judgment of their peers, they shall be immediately restored to them. And if any dispute arises upon this head, the matter shall be determined in the Marches,* *by the judgment of their peers,"* &c.

Chap. 68. " We shall treat with Alexander, king of Scots, concerning the restoring of his sisters, and hostages, and rights and liberties, in the same form and manner as we shall do to the rest of our barons of England ; unless by the engagements, which. his father William. late king of Scots, hath entered into with us, it ought to be otherwise ; *and this shall be left to the determination of his peers in our court."*

---

* *Marches,* the limits, or boundaries, between England and Wales.

Chap. 56. "All evil customs concerning forests, warrens, and foresters, warreners, sheriffs, and their officers, rivers and their keepers, shall forthwith be inquired into in each county, *by twelve knights of the same shire,* chosen by the most creditable persons in the same county, *and upon oath ;* and within forty days after the said inquest, be utterly abolished, so as never to be restored."

There is substantially the same reason why a jury *ought* to judge of the justice of laws, and hold all unjust laws invalid, in civil suits, as in criminal ones. That reason is the necessity of guarding against the tyranny of the government. Nearly the same oppressions can be practised in civil suits as in criminal ones. For example, individuals may be deprived of their liberty, and robbed of their property, by judgments rendered in civil suits, as well as in criminal ones. If the laws of the king were imperative upon a jury in civil suits, the king might enact laws giving one man's property to another, or confiscating it to the king himself, and authorizing civil suits to obtain possession of it. Thus a man might be robbed of his property at the arbitrary pleasure of the king. In fact, all the property of the kingdom would be placed at the arbitrary disposal of the king, through the judgments of juries in civil suits, if the laws of the king were imperative upon a jury in such suits.*

---

* That the kings would have had no scruples to enact laws for the special purpose of plundering the people, by means of the judgments of juries, if they could have got juries to acknowledge the authority of their laws, is evident from the audacity with which they plundered them, without any judgments of juries to authorize them.

It is not necessary to occupy space here to give details as to these robberies ; but only some evidence of the general fact.

Hallam says, that "For the first three reigns (of the Norman kings) * * the intolerable exactions of tribute, the rapine of purveyance, the iniquity of royal courts, are continually in the mouths of the historians. 'God sees the wretched people,' says the Saxon Chronicler, 'most unjustly oppressed ; first they are despoiled of their possessions, and then butchered.' This was a grievous year (1124). Whoever had any property, lost it by heavy taxes and unjust decrees." — 2 *Middle Ages,* 435-6.

"In the succeeding reign of *John,* all the rapacious exactions usual to these Norman kings were not only redoubled, but mingled with outrages of tyranny still more intolerable. * *

"In 1207 John took a seventh of the movables of lay and spiritual persons, all murmuring, but none daring to speak against it." — *Ditto,* 446.

In Hume's account of the extortions of those times, the following paragraph occurs :

"But the most barefaced acts of tyranny and oppression were practised against the

Furthermore, it would be absurd and inconsistent to make a jury paramount to legislation in *criminal* suits, and subordinate to it in *civil* suits; because an individual, by resisting the execution of a *civil* judgment, founded upon an unjust

---

Jews, who were entirely out of the protection of the law, and were abandoned to the immeasurable rapacity of the king and his ministers. Besides many other indignities, to which they were continually exposed, it appears that they were once all thrown into prison, and the sum of 66,000 marks exacted for their liberty. At another time, Isaac, the Jew, paid alone 5100 marks; Brun, 3000 marks; Jurnet, 2000; Bennet, 500. At another, Licorica, widow of David, the Jew of Oxford, was required to pay 6000 marks." — *Hume's Hist. Eng., Appendix* 2.

Further accounts of the extortions and oppressions of the kings may be found in Hume's History, Appendix 2, and in Hallam's Middle Ages, vol. 2, p. 435 to 446.

By Magna Carta John bound himself to make restitution for some of the spoliations he had committed upon individuals " *without the legal judgment of their peers.*" — *See Magna Carta of John,* ch. 60, 61, 65 and 66.

One of the great charges, on account of which the nation rose against John, was, that he plundered individuals of their property, " *without legal judgment of their peers.*" Now it was evidently very weak and short-sighted in John to expose himself to such charges, *if his laws were really obligatory upon the peers ;* because, in that case, he could have enacted any laws that were necessary for his purpose, and then, by civil suits, have brought the cases before juries for their " judgment," and thus have accomplished all his robberies in a perfectly legal manner.

There would evidently have been no sense in these complaints, that he deprived men of their property " *without legal judgment of their peers,*" if his laws had been binding upon the peers; because he could then have made the same spoliations as well with the judgment of the peers as without it. Taking the judgment of the peers in the matter, would have been only a ridiculous and useless formality, if they were to exercise no discretion or conscience of their own, independently of the laws of the king.

It may here be mentioned, in passing, that the same would be true in criminal matters, if the king's laws were obligatory upon juries.

As an illustration of what tyranny the kings would sometimes practise, Hume says :

" It appears from the Great Charter itself, that not only John, a tyrannical prince, and Richard, a violent one, but their father Henry, under whose reign the prevalence of gross abuses is the least to be suspected, were accustomed, from their sole authority, without process of law, to imprison, banish, and attaint the freemen of their kingdom." — *Hume, Appendix* 2.

The provision, also, in the 64th chapter of Magna Carta, that " all unjust and illegal fines, and all amercements, *imposed unjustly, and contrary to the Law of the Land, shall be entirely forgiven,*" &c.; and the provision, in chapter 61, that the king " will cause full justice to be administered " in regard to " all those things, of which any person has, without legal judgment of his peers, been dispossessed or deprived, either by King Henry, our father, or our brother, King Richard," indicate the tyrannical practices that prevailed.

We are told also that John himself "had dispossessed several great men without any judgment of their peers, condemned others to cruel deaths, * * insomuch that his tyrannical will stood instead of a law." — *Echard's History of England,* 106.

Now all these things were very unnecessary and foolish, if his laws were binding

law, could· give rise to a *criminal* suit, in which the jury would be bound to hold the same law invalid. So that, if an unjust law were binding upon a jury in *civil* suits, a defendant, by resisting the execution of the judgment, could, *in effect*, convert the civil action into a criminal one, in which the jury would be paramount to the same legislation, to which, in the *civil* suit, they were subordinate. In other words, in the *criminal* suit, the jury would be obliged to justify the defendant in resisting a law, which, in the *civil* suit, they had said he was bound to submit to.

To make this point plain to the most common mind — suppose a law be enacted that the property of A shall be given to B. B brings a civil action to obtain possession of it. If the jury, in this *civil* suit, are bound to hold the law obligatory, they render a judgment in favor of B, that he be put in possession of the property; *thereby declaring that A is bound to submit to a law depriving him of his property.* But when the execution of that judgment comes to be attempted — that is, when the sheriff comes to take the property for the purpose of delivering it to B — A acting, as he has a *natural* right to do, in defence of his property, resists and kills the sheriff. He is thereupon indicted for murder. On this trial his plea is, that in killing the sheriff, he was simply exercising his *natural* right of defending his property against an unjust law. The jury, not being bound, in a *criminal* case, by the authority of an unjust law, judge the act on its merits, and acquit the defendant — thus declaring that he was *not* bound to submit to the same law which the jury, in the *civil* suit, had, by their judgment, declared that he *was* bound to submit to. Here is a contradiction between the two judgments. In the *civil* suit, the law is declared to be obligatory upon A; in the *criminal* suit, the same law is declared to be of no obligation.

---

upon juries; because, in that case, he could have procured the conviction of these men in a legal manner, and thus have saved the necessity of such usurpation. In short, if the laws of the king had been binding upon juries, there is no robbery, vengeance, or oppression, which he could not have accomplished through the judgments of juries. This consideration is sufficient, of itself, to prove that the laws of the king were of no authority over a jury, in either civil or criminal cases, unless the juries regarded the laws as just in themselves.

It would be a solecism and absurdity in government to allow such consequences as these. Besides, it would be practically impossible to maintain government on such principles; for no government could enforce its *civil* judgments, unless it could support them by *criminal* ones, in case of resistance. A jury must therefore be paramount to legislation in both civil and criminal cases, or in neither. If they are paramount in neither, they are no protection to liberty. If they are paramount in both, then all legislation goes only for what it may chance to be worth in the estimation of a jury.

Another reason why Magna Carta makes the discretion and consciences of juries paramount to all legislation in *civil* suits, is, that if legislation were binding upon a jury, the jurors — (by reason of their being unable to read, as jurors in those days were, and also by reason of many of the statutes being unwritten, or at least not so many copies written as that juries could be supplied with them) — would have been necessitated — at least in those courts in which the king's justices sat — to take the word of those justices as to what the laws of the king really were. In other words, they would have been necessitated *to take the law from the court*, as jurors do now.

Now there were two reasons why, as we may rationally suppose, the people did not wish juries to take their law from the king's judges. One was, that, at that day, the people probably had sense enough to see, (what we, at this day, have not sense enough to see, although we have the evidence of it every day before our eyes,) that those judges, being dependent upon the legislative power, (the king,) being appointed by it, paid by it, and removable by it at pleasure, would be mere tools of that power, and would hold all its legislation obligatory, whether it were just or unjust. This was one reason, doubtless, why Magna Carta made juries, in civil suits, paramount to all instructions of the king's judges. The reason was precisely the same as that for making them paramount to all instructions of judges in criminal suits, viz., that the people did not choose to subject their rights of property, and all other rights involved in civil suits, to the operation of such laws as the king might please to enact. It was seen that to allow the king's judges to dictate the law to the jury would be equiva-

lent to making the legislation of the king imperative upon the
jury.

Another reason why the people did not wish juries, in civil
suits, to take their law from the king's judges, doubtless was,
that, knowing the dependence of the judges upon the king,
and knowing that the king would, of course, tolerate no judges
who were not subservient to his will, they necessarily inferred
that the king's judges would be as corrupt, in the administration of justice, as was the king himself, or as he wished them
to be. And how corrupt that was, may be inferred from the
following historical facts.

Hume says:

"It appears that the ancient kings of England put themselves entirely upon the footing of the barbarous Eastern
princes, whom no man must approach without a present, who
sell all their good offices, and who intrude themselves into
every business that they may have a pretence for extorting
money. Even justice was avowedly bought and sold; the
king's court itself, though the supreme judicature of the kingdom, was open to none that brought not presents to the king;
the bribes given for expedition, delay, suspension, and doubtless for the perversion of justice, were entered in the public
registers of the royal revenue, and remain as monuments of
the perpetual iniquity and tyranny of the times. The barons
of the exchequer, for instance, the first nobility of the kingdom,
were not ashamed to insert, as an article in their records, that
the county of Norfolk paid a sum that they might be fairly
dealt with; the borough of Yarmouth, that the king's charters,
which they have for their liberties, might not be violated;
Richard, son of Gilbert, for the king's helping him to recover
his debt from the Jews; * * Serlo, son of Terlavaston, that
he might be permitted to make his defence, in case he were
accused of a certain homicide; Walter de Burton, for free law,
if accused of wounding another; Robert de Essart, for having
an inquest to find whether Roger, the butcher, and Wace and
Humphrey, accused him of robbery and theft out of envy and
ill-will, or not; William Buhurst, for having an inquest to
find whether he were accused of the death of one Godwin, out
of ill-will, or for just cause. I have selected these few instances from a great number of the like kind, which Madox
had selected from a still greater number, preserved in the
ancient rolls of the exchequer.

Sometimes a party litigant offered the king a certain portion, a half, a third, a fourth, payable out of the debts which he, as the executor of justice, should assist in recovering. Theophania de Westland agreed to pay the half of two hundred and twelve marks, that she might recover that sum against James de Fughleston; Solomon, the Jew, engaged to pay one mark out of every seven that he should recover against Hugh de la Hose; Nicholas Morrel promised to pay sixty pounds, that the Earl of Flanders might be distrained to pay him three hundred and forty-three pounds, which the earl had taken from him; and these sixty pounds were to be paid out of the first money that Nicholas should recover from the earl." — *Hume, Appendix 2.*

"In the reign of Henry II., the best and most just of these (the Norman) princes, * * Peter, of Blois, a judicious and even elegant writer, of that age, gives a pathetic description of *the venality of justice,* and the oppressions of the poor, * * and he scruples not to complain to the king himself of these abuses. We may judge what the case would be under the government of worse princes." — *Hume, Appendix 2.*

Carte says:

"The crown exercised in those days an exorbitant and inconvenient power, ordering the justices of the king's court, in suits about lands, to turn out, put, and keep in possession, which of the litigants they pleased; to send contradictory orders; and take large sums of money from each; to respite proceedings; to direct sentences; and the judges, acting by their commission, conceived themselves bound to observe such orders, to the great delay, interruption, and preventing of justice; at least, this was John's practice." — *Carte's History of England,* vol. 1, p. 832.

Hallam says:

"But of all the abuses that deformed the Anglo-Saxon government, none was so flagitious as the sale of judicial redress. The king, we are often told, is the fountain of justice; but in those ages it was one which gold alone could unseal. Men fined (paid fines) to have right done them; to sue in a certain court; to implead a certain person; to have restitution of land which they had recovered at law. From the sale of that justice which every citizen has a right to demand, it was an easy transition to withhold or deny it. Fines were received for the king's help against the adverse suitor; that is, for perversion of justice, or for delay. Sometimes they were paid by opposite parties, and, of course, for opposite ends." — 2 *Middle Ages,* 438.

In allusion to the provision of Magna Carta on this subject, Hallam says:

"A law which enacts that justice shall neither be sold, denied, nor delayed, stamps with infamy that government under which it had become necessary." — 2 *Middle Ages*, 451.

Lingard, speaking of the times of Henry II., (say 1184,) says:

"It was universally understood that money possessed greater influence than justice in the royal courts, and instances are on record, in which one party has made the king a present to accelerate, and the other by a more valuable offer has succeeded in retarding a decision. * * But besides the fines paid to the sovereigns, *the judges often exacted presents for themselves*, and loud complaints existed against their venality and injustice." — 2 *Lingard*, 231.

In the narrative of "The costs and charges which I, Richard de Anesty, bestowed in recovering the land of William, my uncle," (some fifty years before Magna Carta,) are the following items:

"To Ralph, the king's physician, I gave thirty-six marks and one half; to the king an hundred marks; and to the queen one mark of gold." The result is thus stated. "At last, thanks to our lord the king, and by judgment of his court, my uncle's land was adjudged to me." — 2 *Palgrave's Rise and Progress of the English Commonwealth*, p. 9 and 24.

Palgrave also says:

"The precious ore was cast into the scales of justice, even when held by the most conscientious of our Anglo-Saxon kings. A single case will exemplify the practices which prevailed. Alfric, the heir of 'Aylwin, the black,' seeks to set aside the death-bed bequest, by which his kinsman bestowed four rich and fertile manors upon St. Benedict. Alfric, the claimant, was supported by extensive and powerful connexions; and Abbot Alfwine, the defendant, was well aware that there would be *danger* in the discussion of the dispute in public, or before the Folkmoot, (people's meeting, or county court); or, in other words, that the Thanes of the shire would do their best to give a judgment in favor of their compeer. The plea being removed into the Royal Court, the abbot acted with that prudence which so often calls forth the praises of the monastic scribe. He gladly emptied twenty marks of gold into the sleeve of the Confessor, (Edward,) and five marks of gold presented to Edith, the Fair, encouraged her to aid the bishop, and to exercise her gentle influence in his favor. Alfric, with equal wisdom, withdrew from prosecuting the hopeless cause, in which his opponent might possess an advocate in the royal judge, and a friend in the king's consort. Both parties, therefore, found it desirable to come to an agreement." — 1 *Palgrave's Rise and Progress, &c.*, p. 650.

But Magna Carta has another provision for the trial of *civil* suits, that obviously had its origin in the corruption of the king's judges. The provision is, that four knights, to be chosen in every county, by the people of the county, shall sit with the king's judges, in the Common Pleas, in jury trials, (assizes,) on the trial of three certain kinds of suits, that were among the most important that were tried at all. The reason for this provision undoubtedly was, that the corruption and subserviency of the king's judges were so well known, that the people would not even trust them to sit alone in a jury trial of any considerable importance. The provision is this:

Chap. 22, (of John's Charter.) "Common Pleas shall not follow our court, but shall be holden in some certain place. Trials upon the writ of *novel disseisin*, and of *Mort d'Ancester*, and of *Darrein Presentment*, shall be taken but in their proper counties, and after this manner: We, or, if we should be out of our realm, our chief justiciary, shall send two justiciaries through every county four times a year;* *who, with four knights chosen out of every shire, by the people, shall hold the assizes* (juries) *in the county, on the day and at the place appointed.*"

It would be very unreasonable to suppose that the king's judges were allowed to *dictate* the law to the juries, when the people would not even suffer them to sit alone in jury trials, but themselves chose four men to sit with them, to keep them honest. †

---

* By the Magna Carta of Henry III. this is changed to once a year.

† From the provision of Magna Carta, cited in the text, it must be inferred that there can be no legal trial by jury, in *civil* cases, if only the king's justices preside ; that, to make the trial legal, there must be other persons, chosen by the people, to sit with them; the object being to prevent the jury's being deceived by the justices. I think we must also infer that the king's justices could sit only in the three actions specially mentioned. We cannot go beyond the letter of Magna Carta, in making innovations upon the common law, which required all presiding officers in jury trials to be elected by the people.

This practice of sending the king's judges into the counties to preside at jury trials, was introduced by the Norman kings. Under the Saxons it was not so. *No officer of the king was allowed to preside at a jury trial; but only magistrates chosen by the people.**

But the following chapter of John's charter, which immediately succeeds the one just quoted, and refers to the same suits, affords very strong, not to say conclusive, proof, that juries judged of the law in civil suits — that is, *made the law,* so far as their deciding according to their own notions of justice could make the law.

Chap. 23. "And if, on the county day, the aforesaid assizes cannot be taken, *so many knights and freeholders shall remain, of those who shall have been present on said day, as that the judgments may be rendered by them,* whether the business be more or less."

---

* "The earls, sheriffs, and head-boroughs were annually elected in the full folemote, (people's meeting)." — *Introduction to Gilbert's History of the Common Pleas,* p. 2, *note.*

"It was the especial province of the earldomen or earl to attend the shyre-meeting, (the county court,) twice a year, and there officiate as the county judge in expounding the secular laws, as appears by the fifth of Edgar's laws." — *Same,* p. 2, *note.*

"Every ward had its proper alderman, who was *chosen,* and not imposed by the prince." — *Same,* p. 4, *text.*

"As the aldermen, or earls, were always *chosen*" (by the people) "from among the greatest thanes, who in those times were generally more addicted to arms than to letters, they were but ill-qualified for the administration of justice, and performing the civil duties of their office." — 3 *Henry's History of Great Britain,* 343.

"But none of these thanes were annually elected in the full folemote, (people's meeting,) *as the earls, sheriffs, and head-boroughs were;* nor did King Alfred (as this author suggests) deprive the people of the election of those last mentioned magistrates and nobles, much less did he appoint them himself." — *Introd. to Gilbert's Hist. Com. Pleas,* p. 2, *note.*

"The sheriff was usually not appointed by the lord, but elected by the freeholders of the district." — *Political Dictionary,* word *Sheriff.*

"Among the most remarkable of the Saxon laws we may reckon * * the election of their magistrates by the people, originally even that of their kings, till dear-bought experience evinced the convenience and necessity of establishing an hereditary succession to the crown. But that (the election) of all subordinate magistrates, their military officers or heretochs, their sheriffs, their conservators of the peace, their coroners, their portreeves, (since changed into mayors and bailiffs,) and even their tithing-men and borsholders at the last, continued, some, till the Norman conquest, others for two centuries after, and some remain to this day." — 4 *Blackstone,* 413.

"The election of sheriffs was left to the people, *according to ancient usage.*" — *St. West.* 1, c. 27. — *Crabbe's History of English Law,* 181.

The meaning of this chapter is, that so many of the *civil* suits, as could not be tried on the day when the king's justices were present, should be tried afterwards, *by the four knights before mentioned, and the freeholders, that is, the jury.* It must be admitted, of course, that the juries, in these cases, judged the matters of law, as well as fact, unless it be presumed that the *knights* dictated the law to the jury — a thing of which there is no evidence at all.

As a final proof on this point, there is a statute enacted seventy years after Magna Carta, which, although it is contrary to the common law, and therefore void, is nevertheless good evidence, inasmuch as it contains an acknowledgment, on the part of the king himself, that juries had a right to judge of the whole matter, law and fact, in civil suits. The provision is this:

"It is ordained, that the justices assigned to take the assizes, shall not compel the jurors to say precisely whether it be disseisin, or not, so that they do show the truth of the deed, and seek aid of the justices. But if they will, of their own accord, say that it is disseisin, or not, their verdict shall be admitted at their own peril." — 13 *Edward I.*, st. 1, ch. 3, sec. 2. (1285.)

The question of "disseisin, or not," was a question of law, as well as fact. This statute, therefore, admits that the law, as well as the fact, was in the hands of the jury. The statute is nevertheless void, because the king had no authority to give jurors a dispensation from the obligation imposed upon them by their oaths and the "law of the land," that they should "make known the truth according their (own) consciences." This they were bound to do, and there was no power in the king to absolve them from the duty. And the attempt of the king thus to absolve them, and authorize them to throw the case into the hands of the judges for decision, was simply an illegal and unconstitutional attempt to overturn the "law of the land," which he was sworn to maintain, and gather power into his own hands, through his judges. He had just as much constitutional power to enact that the jurors should not be compelled to declare the *facts*, but that they might leave *them* to be determined by the king's judges, as he had to enact that they should not be compelled to declare the *law*, but might leave *it* to be decided by the king's judges.   It was as much the legal duty of the jury to decide the law as to decide the fact; and no law of the king could affect their obligation to do either. And this statute is only one example of. the numberless contrivances and usurpations which have been resorted to, for the purpose of destroying the original and genuine trial by jury.

CHAPTER V.

OBJECTIONS ANSWERED

THE following objections will be made to the doctrines and the evidence presented in the preceding chapters.

1. That it is a *maxim* of the law, that the judges respond to the question of law, and juries only to the question of fact.

The answer to this objection is, that, since Magna Carta, judges have had more than six centuries in which to invent and promulgate pretended maxims to suit themselves; and this is one of them. Instead of expressing the law, it expresses nothing but the ambitious and lawless will of the judges themselves, and of those whose instruments they are.*

2. It will be asked, Of what use are the justices, if the jurors judge both of law and fact?

The answer is, that they are of use, 1. To assist and enlighten the jurors, if they can, by their advice and information; such advice and information to be received only for what they may chance to be worth in the estimation of the jurors. 2. To do anything that may be necessary in regard to granting appeals and new trials.

3. It is said that it would be absurd that twelve ignorant men should have power to judge of the law, while justices learned in the law should be compelled to sit by and see the law decided erroneously.

One answer to this objection is, that the powers of juries

---

* Judges do not even live up to that part of their own maxim, which requires jurors to try the matter of fact. By dictating to them the laws of evidence, — that is, by dictating what evidence they may hear, and what they may not hear, and also by dictating to them rules for weighing such evidence as they permit them to hear, — they of necessity dictate the conclusion to which they shall arrive. And thus the court really tries the question of fact, as well as the question of law, in every cause. It is clearly impossible, in the nature of things, for a jury to try a question of fact, without trying every question of law on which the fact depends.

are not granted to them on the supposition that they know the
law better than the justices; but on the ground that the justices are untrustworthy, that they are exposed to bribes, are
themselves fond of power and authority, and are also the
dependent and subservient creatures of the legislature; and
that to allow them to dictate the law, would not only expose
the rights of parties to be sold for money, but would be equivalent to surrendering all the property, liberty, and rights of the
people, unreservedly into the hands of arbitrary power, (the
legislature,) to be disposed of at its pleasure. The powers of
juries, therefore, not only place a curb upon the powers of
legislators and judges, but imply also an imputation upon their
integrity and trustworthiness; and *these* are the reasons why
legislators and judges have formerly entertained the intensest
hatred of juries, and, so fast as they could do it without
alarming the people for their liberties, have, by indirection,
denied, undermined, and practically destroyed their power.
And it is only since all the real power of juries has been destroyed, and they have become mere tools in the hands of
legislators and judges, that they have become favorites with
them.

Legislators and judges are necessarily exposed to all the
temptations of money, fame, and power, to induce them to
disregard justice between parties, and sell the rights, and violate the liberties of the people. Jurors, on the other hand,
are exposed to none of these temptations. They are not·liable
to bribery, for they are unknown to the parties until they
come into the jury-box. They can rarely gain either fame,
power, or money, by giving erroneous decisions. Their offices
are temporary, and they know that when they shall have executed them, they must return to the people, to hold all their
own rights in life subject to the liability of such judgments, by
their successors, as they themselves have given an example
for. The laws of human nature do not permit the supposition
that twelve men, taken by lot from the mass of the people,
and acting under such circumstances, will *all* prove dishonest.
It is a supposable case that they may not be sufficiently enlightened to know and do their whole duty, in all cases whatsoever; but that they should *all* prove *dishonest,* is not within

the range of probability. A jury, therefore, insures to us — what no other court does — that first and indispensable requisite in a judicial tribunal, integrity.

4. It is alleged that if juries are allowed to judge of the law, *they decide the law absolutely; that their decision must necessarily stand, be it right or wrong;* and that this power of absolute decision would be dangerous in their hands, by reason of their ignorance of the law.

One answer is, that this power, which juries have of *judging* of the law, is not a power of *absolute decision in all cases.* For example, it is a power to declare imperatively that a man's property, liberty, or life, shall *not* be taken from him; but it is not a power to declare imperatively that they *shall* be taken from him.

Magna Carta does not provide that the judgments of the peers *shall be executed;* but only that *no other than their judgments* shall ever be executed, *so far as to take a party's goods, rights, or person, thereon.*

A judgment of the peers may be reviewed, and invalidated, and a new trial granted. So that practically a jury has no absolute power to take a party's goods, rights, or person. They have only an absolute veto upon their being taken by the government. The government is not bound to do everything that a jury may adjudge. It is only prohibited from doing anything — (that is, from taking a party's goods, rights, or person) — unless a jury have first adjudged it to be done.

But it will, perhaps, be said, that if an erroneous judgment of one jury should be reaffirmed by another, on a new trial, it must *then* be executed. But Magna Carta does not command even this — although it might, perhaps, have been reasonably safe for it to have done so — for if two juries unanimously affirm the same thing, after all the light and aid that judges and lawyers can afford them, that fact probably furnishes as strong a presumption in favor of the correctness of their opinion, as can ordinarily be obtained in favor of a judgment, by any measures of a practical character for the administration of justice. Still, there is nothing in Magna Carta that *compels* the execution of even a second judgment of a jury. The only injunction of Magna Carta upon the government, as to what it *shall do*, on this point, is that it shall "do justice and right," without sale, denial, or delay. But this leaves the government all power of determining what is justice and right, except that it shall not consider anything as justice and right — so far as to carry it into execution against the goods, rights, or person of a party — unless it be something which a jury have sanctioned.

If the government had no alternative but to execute all judgments of a jury indiscriminately, the power of juries would unquestionably be dangerous; for there is no doubt that they may sometimes give hasty and erroneous judgments. But when it is considered that their judgments can be reviewed, and new trials granted, this danger is, for all practical purposes, obviated.

If it be said that juries may *successively* give erroneous judgments, and that new trials cannot be granted indefinitely, the answer is, that so far as Magna Carta is concerned, there is nothing to prevent the granting of new trials indefinitely, if the judgments of juries are contrary to "justice and right." So that Magna Carta does not *require* any judgment whatever to be executed — so far as to take a party's goods, rights, or person, thereon — unless it be concurred in by both court and jury.

Nevertheless, we may, for the sake of the argument, suppose the existence of a *practical*, if not *legal*, necessity, for executing *some* judgment or other, in cases where juries persist in disagreeing with the courts. In such cases, the principle of Magna Carta unquestionably is, that the uniform judgments of *successive* juries shall prevail over the opinion of the court. And the reason of this principle is obvious, viz., that it is the will of the country, and not the will of the court, or the government, that must determine what laws shall be established and enforced; that the concurrent judgments of successive juries, given in opposition to all the reasoning which judges and lawyers can offer to the contrary, must necessarily be presumed to be a truer exposition of the will of the country, than are the opinions of the judges.

But it may be said that, unless jurors submit to the control of the court, in matters of law, they may disagree among themselves, and *never* come to any judgment; and thus justice fail to be done.

Such a case is perhaps possible; but, if possible, it can occur but rarely; because, although one jury may disagree, a succession of juries are not likely to disagree — that is, *on matters of natural law, or abstract justice.** If such a thing should occur, it would almost certainly be owing to the attempt of the court to mislead them. It is hardly possible that any other cause should be adequate to produce such an effect; because justice comes very near to being a self-evident principle. The mind perceives it almost intuitively. If, in addition to this, the court be uniformly on the side of justice, it is not a reasonable supposition that a succession of juries should disagree about it. If, therefore, a succession of juries do disagree on the law of any case, the presumption is, not that justice fails of being done, but that injustice is prevented — *that* injustice, which would be done, if the opinion of the court were suffered to control the jury.

For the sake of the argument, however, it may be admitted to be possible that justice should sometimes fail of being done through the disagreements of jurors, notwithstanding all the light which judges and lawyers can throw upon the question in issue. If it be asked what provision the trial by jury makes for such cases, the answer is, *it makes none; and justice must fail of being done, from the want of its being made sufficiently intelligible.*

Under the trial by jury, justice can never be done — that is, by a judgment that shall take a party's goods, rights, or person — until that justice can be made intelligible or perceptible to the minds of *all* the jurors; or, at least, until it obtain the voluntary assent of all — an assent, which ought not to be given until the justice itself shall have become perceptible to all.

---

* Most disagreements of juries are on matters of fact, which are admitted to be within their province. We have little or no evidence of their disagreements on matters of natural justice. The disagreements of *courts* on matters of law, afford little or no evidence that juries would also disagree on matters of law — that is, *of justice;* because the disagreements of courts are generally on matters of *legislation*, and not on those principles of abstract justice, by which juries would be governed, and in regard to which the minds of men are nearly unanimous.

The principles of the trial by jury, then, are these:

1. That, in criminal cases, the accused is presumed innocent.

2. That, in civil cases, possession is presumptive proof of property; or, in other words, every man is presumed to be the rightful proprietor of whatever he has in his possession.

3. That these presumptions shall be overcome, in a court of justice, only by evidence, the sufficiency of which, and by law, the justice of which, are satisfactory to the understanding and consciences of *all* the jurors.

These are the bases on which the trial by jury places the property, liberty, and rights of every individual.

But some one will say, if these are the principles of the trial by jury, then it is plain that justice must often fail to be done. Admitting, for the sake of the argument, that this may be true, the compensation for it is, that positive *injustice* will also often fail to be done; whereas otherwise it would be done frequently. The very precautions used to prevent *injustice* being done, may often have the effect to prevent *justice* being done. But are we, therefore, to take no precautions against injustice? By no means, all will agree. The question then arises — Does the trial by jury, *as here explained,* involve such extreme and unnecessary precautions against injustice, as to interpose unnecessary obstacles to the doing of justice? Men of different minds may very likely answer this question differently, according as they have more or less confidence in the wisdom and justice of legislators, the integrity and independence of judges, and the intelligence of jurors. This much, however, may be said in favor of these precautions, viz., that the history of the past, as well as our constant present experience, prove how much injustice may, and certainly will, be done, systematically and continually, *for the want of these precautions* — that is, while the law is authoritatively made and expounded by legislators and judges. On the other hand, we have no such evidence of how much justice may fail to be done, *by reason of these precautions* — that is, by reason of the law being left to the judgments and consciences of jurors. We can determine the former point — that is, how much positive injustice is done under the first of these two systems — because the system is in full operation; but we cannot determine how much justice would fail to be done under the latter system, because we have, in modern times, had no experience of the use of the precautions themselves. In ancient times, when these precautions were *nominally* in force, such was the tyranny of kings, and such the poverty, ignorance, and the inability of concert and resistance, on the part of the people, that the system had no full or fair operation. It, nevertheless, under all these disadvantages, impressed itself upon the understandings, and imbedded itself in the hearts, of the people, so as no other system of civil liberty has ever done.

But this view of the two systems compares only the injustice done, and the justice omitted to be done, in the individual cases adjudged, without looking beyond them. And some persons might, on first thought, argue that, if justice failed of being done under the one system, oftener than positive injustice were done under the other, the balance was in favor of the latter system. But such a weighing of the two systems against each other gives no true idea of their comparative merits or demerits; for, possibly, in this view alone, the balance would not be very great in favor of either. To compare, or rather to contrast, the two, we must consider that, under the jury system, the failures to do justice would be only rare and exceptional cases; and would be owing either to the intrinsic difficulty of the questions, or to the fact that the parties had transacted their business in a manner unintelligible to the jury, and the effects would be confined to the individual or individuals interested in the particular suits. No permanent law would be established thereby destructive of the rights of the people in other like cases. And the people at large would continue to enjoy all their natural rights as before. But under the other system, whenever an unjust law is enacted by the legislature, and the judge imposes it upon the jury as authoritative, and they give a judgment in accordance therewith, the authority of the law is thereby established, and the whole people are thus brought under the yoke of that law; because they then understand that the law will be enforced against them in future, if they presume to exercise their rights, or refuse to comply with the exactions of the law.   In this manner all unjust laws are established, and made operative against the rights of the people.

The difference, then, between the two systems is this : Under the one system, a jury, at distant intervals, would (not enforce any positive injustice, but only) fail of enforcing justice, in a dark and difficult case, or in consequence of the parties not having transacted their business in a manner intelligible to a jury; and the plaintiff would thus fail of obtaining what was rightfully due him.   And there the matter would end, *for evil*, though not for good; for thenceforth parties, warned of the danger of losing their rights, would be careful to transact their business in a more clear and intelligible manner.   Under the other system — the system of legislative and judicial authority — positive injustice is not only done in every suit arising under unjust laws, — that is, men's property, liberty, or lives are not only unjustly taken on those particular judgments, — but the rights of the whole people are struck down by the authority of the laws thus enforced, and a wide-sweeping tyranny at once put in operation.

But there is another ample and conclusive answer to the argument that justice would often fail to be done, if jurors were allowed to be governed by their own consciences, instead of the direction of the justices, in matters of law.   That answer is this :

Legitimate government can be formed only by the voluntary association of all who contribute to its support.   As a voluntary association, it can have for its objects only those things in which the members of the association are *all agreed*.   If, therefore, there be any *justice*, in regard to which all the parties to the government *are not agreed*, the objects of the association do not extend to it.*

---

* This is the principle of all voluntary asssociations whatsoever.   No voluntary association was ever formed, and in the nature of things there never can be one formed, for the accomplishment of any objects except those in which *all* the parties to the association are agreed.   Government, therefore, must be kept within these limits, or it is no longer a voluntary association of all who contribute to its support, but a mere tyranny established by a part over the rest.

All, or nearly all, voluntary associations give to a majority, or to some other portion of the members less than the whole, the right to use some *limited* discretion as to the

If any of the members wish more than this, — if they claim to have acquired a more extended knowledge of justice than is common to all, and wish to have their pretended discoveries carried into effect, in reference to themselves, — they must either form a separate association for that purpose, or be content to wait until they can make their views intelligible to the people at large. They cannot claim or expect that the whole people shall practise the folly of taking on trust their pretended superior knowledge, and of committing blindly into their hands all their own interests, liberties, and rights, to be disposed of on principles, the justness of which the people themselves cannot comprehend.

A government of the whole, therefore, must necessarily confine itself to the administration of such principles of law as *all* the people, who contribute to the support of the government, can comprehend and see the justice of. And it can be confined within those limits only by allowing the jurors, who represent all the parties to the compact, to judge of the law, and the justice of the law, in all cases whatsoever. And if any justice be left undone, under these circumstances, it is a justice for which the nature of the association does not provide, which the association does not undertake to do, and which, as an association, it is under no obligation to do.

The people at large, the unlearned and common people, have certainly an indisputable right to associate for the establishment and maintenance of such a government as *they themselves* see the justice of, and feel the need of, for the promotion of their own interests, and the safety of their own rights, without at the same time surrendering all their property, liberty, and rights into the hands of men, who, under the pretence of a superior and incomprehensible knowledge of justice, may dispose of such property, liberties, and rights, in a manner to suit their own selfish and dishonest purposes.

---

means to be used to accomplish the ends in view; but *the ends themselves to be accomplished* are always precisely defined, and are such as every member necessarily agrees to, else he would not voluntarily join the association.

Justice is the object of government, and those who support the government, must be agreed as to the justice to be executed by it, or they cannot rightfully unite in maintaining the government itself.

If a government were to be established and supported *solely* by that portion of the people who lay claim to superior knowledge, there would be some consistency in their saying that the common people should not be received as jurors, with power to judge of the justice of the laws.   But so long as the whole people (or all the male adults) are presumed to be voluntary parties to the government, and voluntary contributors to its support, there is no consistency in refusing to any one of them more than to another the right to sit as juror, with full power to decide for himself whether any law that is proposed to be enforced in any particular case, be within the objects of the association.

The conclusion, therefore, is, that, in a government formed by voluntary association, or on the *theory* of voluntary association, and voluntary support, (as all the North American governments are,) no law can rightfully be enforced by the association in its corporate capacity, against the goods, rights, or person of any individual, except it be such as *all* the members of the association agree that it may enforce.   To enforce any other law, to the extent of taking a man's goods, rights, or person, would be making *some* of the parties to the association accomplices in what they regard as acts of injustice.   It would also be making them consent to what they regard as the destruction of their own rights.   These are things which no legitimate system or theory of government can require of any of the parties to it.

The mode adopted, by the trial by jury, for ascertaining whether all the parties to the government do approve of a particular law, is to take twelve men at random from the whole people, and accept their unanimous decision as representing the opinions of the whole.   Even this mode is not theoretically accurate; for theoretical accuracy would require that every man, who was a party to the government, should individually give his consent to the enforcement of every law in every separate case.   But such a thing would be impossible in practice. The consent of twelve men is therefore taken instead; with the privilege of appeal, and (in case of error found by the the appeal court) a new trial, to guard against possible mistakes.   This system, it is assumed, will ascertain the sense of the whole people — " the country " — with sufficient accuracy for all practical purposes, and with as much accuracy as is practicable without too great inconvenience and expense.

5. Another objection that will perhaps be made to allowing jurors to judge of the law, and the justice of the law, is, that the law would be uncertain.

If, by this objection, it be meant that the law would be un-certain to the minds of the people at large, so that they would not know what the juries would sanction and what condemn, and would not therefore know practically what their own rights and liberties were under the law, the objection is thor-oughly baseless and false. No system of law that was ever devised could be so entirely intelligible and certain to the minds of the people at large as this. Compared with it, the complicated systems of law that are compounded of the law of nature, of constitutional grants, of innumerable and inces-santly changing legislative enactments, and of countless and contradictory judicial decisions, with no uniform principle of reason or justice running through them, are among the blind-est of all the mazes in which unsophisticated minds were ever bewildered and lost. The uncertainty of the law under these systems has become a proverb. So great is this uncertainty, that nearly all men, learned as well as unlearned, shun the law as their enemy, instead of resorting to it for protection. They usually go into courts of justice, so called, only as men go into battle — when there is no alternative left for them. And even then they go into them as men go into dark laby-rinths and caverns — with no knowledge of their own, but trusting wholly to their guides. Yet, less fortunate than other adventurers, they can have little confidence even in their guides, for the reason that the guides themselves know little of the mazes they are threading. They know the mode and place of entrance; but what they will meet with on their way, and what will be the time, mode, place, or condition of their exit; whether they will emerge into a prison, or not; whether *wholly* naked and destitute, or not; whether with their reputations left to them, or not; and whether in time or eternity ; experienced and honest guides rarely venture to pre-dict. Was there ever such fatuity as that of a nation of men

madly bent on building up such labyrinths as these, for no
other purpose than that of exposing all their rights of reputation, property, liberty, and life, to the hazards of being lost in
them, instead of being content to live in the light of the open
day of their own understandings?

What honest, unsophisticated man ever found himself involved in a lawsuit, that he did not desire, of all things, that
his cause might be judged of on principles of natural justice,
as those principles were understood by plain men like himself?
He would then feel that he could foresee the result. These
plain men are the men who pay the taxes, and support the
government. Why should they not have such an administration of justice as they desire, and can understand?

If the jurors were to judge of the law, and the justice of
the law, there would be something like certainty in the administration of justice, and in the popular knowledge of the
law, and men would govern themselves accordingly. There
would be something like certainty, because every man has
himself something like definite and clear opinions, and also
knows something of the opinions of his neighbors, on matters
of justice. And he would know that no statute, unless it were
so clearly just as to command the unanimous assent of twelve
men, who should be taken at random from the whole community, could be enforced so as to take from him his reputation,
property, liberty, or life. What greater certainty can men
require or need, as to the laws under which they are to live?
If a statute were enacted by a legislature, a man, in order to
know what was its true interpretation, whether it were constitutional, and whether it would be enforced, would not be
under the necessity of waiting for years until some suit had
arisen and been carried through all the stages of judicial proceeding, to a final decision. He would need only to use his
own reason as to its meaning and its justice, and then talk
with his neighbors on the same points. Unless he found them
nearly unanimous in their interpretation and approbation of it,
he would conclude that juries would not unite in enforcing it,
and that it would consequently be a dead letter. And he
would be safe in coming to this conclusion.

There would be something like certainty in the administration of justice, and in the popular knowledge of the law, for the further reason that there would be little legislation, and men's rights would be left to stand almost solely upon the law of nature, or what was once called in England "the *common law*," (before so much legislation and usurpation had become incorporated into the common law,) — in other words, upon the principles of natural justice.

Of the certainty of this law of nature, or the ancient English common law, I may be excused for repeating here what I have said on another occasion.

"Natural law, so far from being uncertain, when compared with statutory and constitutional law, is the only thing that gives any certainty at all to a very large portion of our statutory and constitutional law. The reason is this. The words in which statutes and constitutions are written are susceptible of so many different meanings, — meanings widely different from, often directly opposite to, each other, in their bearing upon men's rights, — that, unless there were some rule of interpretation for determining which of these various and opposite meanings are the true ones, there could be no certainty at all as to the meaning of the statutes and constitutions themselves. Judges could make almost anything they should please out of them. Hence the necessity of a rule of interpretation. *And this rule is, that the language of statutes and constitutions shall be construed, as nearly as possible, consistently with natural law.*

The rule assumes, what is true, that natural law is a thing certain in itself; also that it is capable of being learned. It assumes, furthermore, that it actually is understood by the legislators and judges who make and interpret the written law. Of necessity, therefore, it assumes further, that they (the legislators and judges) are *incompetent* to make and interpret the *written* law, unless they previously understand the natural law applicable to the same subject. It also assumes that the *people* must understand the natural law, before they can understand the written law.

It is a principle perfectly familiar to lawyers, and one that must be perfectly obvious to every other man that will reflect a moment, that, as a general rule, *no one can know what the written law is, until he knows what it ought to be;* that men are liable to be constantly misled by the various and conflicting senses of the same words, unless they perceive the true legal sense in which the words *ought to be taken.* And this true legal sense is the sense that is most nearly consistent with

natural law of any that the words can be made to bear, consistently with the laws of language, and appropriately to the
subjects to which they are applied.

Though the words *contain* the law, the *words* themselves
are not the law.   Were the words themselves the law, each
single written law would be liable to embrace many different
laws, to wit, as many different laws as there were different
senses, and different combinations of senses, in which each
and all the words were capable of being taken.

Take, for example, the Constitution of the United States.
By adopting one or another sense of the single word "*free,*"
the whole instrument is changed.   Yet the word *free* is capable
of some ten or twenty different senses.   So that, by changing
the sense of that single word, some ten or twenty different constitutions could be made out of the same written instrument.
But there are, we will suppose, a thousand other words in the
constitution, each of which is capable of from two to ten different senses.   So that, by changing the sense of only a single
word at a time, several thousands of different constitutions
would be made.   But this is not all.   Variations could also be
made by changing the senses of two or more words at a time,
and these variations could be run through all the changes and
combinations of senses that these thousand words are capable
of.   We see, then, that it is no more than a literal truth, that
out of that single instrument, as it now stands, without alter-
ing the location of a single word, might be formed, by construction and interpretation, more different constitutions than
figures can well estimate.

But each written law, in order to be a law, must be taken
only in some *one* definite and distinct sense; and that definite
and distinct sense must be selected from the almost infinite
variety of senses which its words are capable of.   How is this
selection to be made?   It can be only by the aid of that perception of natural law, or natural justice, which men naturally
possess.

Such, then, is the comparative certainty of the natural and
the written law.   Nearly all the certainty there is in the latter,
so far as it relates to principles, is based upon, and derived
from, the still greater certainty of the former.   In fact, nearly
all the uncertainty of the laws under which we live, — which
are a mixture of natural and written laws, — arises from the
difficulty of construing, or, rather, from the facility of miscon-
struing, the *written* law; while natural law has nearly or
quite the same certainty as mathematics.   On this point, Sir
William Jones, one of the most learned judges that have ever
lived, learned in Asiatic as well as European law, says, — and

the fact should be kept forever in mind, as one of the most important of all truths: — "*It is pleasing to remark the similarity, or, rather, the identity of those conclusions which pure, unbiassed reason, in all ages and nations, seldom fails to draw, in such juridical inquiries as are not fettered and manacled by positive institutions.*" * In short, the simple fact that the written law must be interpreted by the natural, is, of itself, a sufficient confession of the superior certainty of the latter.

The written law, then, even where it can be construed consistently with the natural, introduces labor and obscurity, instead of shutting them out. And this must always be the case, because words do not create ideas, but only recall them; and the same word may recall many different ideas. For this reason, nearly all abstract principles can be seen by the single mind more clearly than they can be expressed by words to another. This is owing to the imperfection of language, and the different senses, meanings, and shades of meaning, which different individuals attach to the same words, in the same circumstances.†

Where the written law cannot be construed consistently with the natural, there is no reason why it should ever be enacted at all. It may, indeed, be sufficiently plain and certain to be easily understood; but its certainty and plainness are but a poor compensation for its injustice. Doubtless a law forbidding men to drink water, on pain of death, might be made so intelligible as to cut off all discussion as to its meaning; but would the intelligibleness of such a law be any equivalent for the right to drink water? The principle is the same in regard to all unjust laws. Few persons could

---

* Jones on Bailments, 133.

† Kent, describing the difficulty of construing the written law, says :

"Such is the imperfection of language, and the want of technical skill in the makers of the law, that statutes often give occasion to the most perplexing and distressing doubts and discussions, arising from the ambiguity that attends them. It requires great experience, as well as the command of a perspicuous diction, to frame a law in such clear and precise terms, as to secure it from ambiguous expressions, and from all doubts and criticisms upon its meaning." — *Kent*, 460.

The following extract from a speech of Lord Brougham, in the House of Lords, confesses the same difficulty :

"There was another subject, well worthy of the consideration of government during the recess, — the expediency, *or rather the absolute necessity*, of some arrangement for the preparation of bills, not merely private, but public bills, *in order that legislation might be consistent and systematic, and that the courts might not have so large a portion of their time occupied in endeavoring to construe acts of Parliament, in many cases unconstruable, and in most cases difficult to be construed.*" — *Law Reporter*, 1848, p. 525.

reasonably feel compensated for the arbitary destruction of their rights, by having the order for their destruction made known beforehand, in terms so distinct and unequivocal as to admit of neither mistake nor evasion. Yet this is all the compensation that such laws offer.

Whether, therefore, written laws correspond with, or differ from, the natural, they are to be condemned. In the first case, they are useless repetitions, introducing labor and obscurity. In the latter case, they are positive violations of men's rights.

There would be substantially the same reason in enacting mathematics by statute, that there is in enacting natural law. Whenever the natural law is sufficiently certain to all men's minds to justify its being enacted, it is sufficiently certain to need no enactment. On the other hand, until it be thus certain, there is danger of doing injustice by enacting it; it should, therefore, be left open to be discussed by anybody who may be disposed to question it, and to be judged of by the proper tribunal, the judiciary.*

It is not necessary that legislators should enact natural law in order that it may be known to the *people*, because that would be presuming that the legislators already understand it better than the people, — a fact of which I am not aware that they have ever heretofore given any very satisfactory evidence. The same sources of knowledge on the subject are open to the people that are open to the legislators, and the people must be presumed to know it as well as they.

The objections made to natural law, on the ground of obscurity, are wholly unfounded. It is true, it must be learned, like any other science; but it is equally true that it is very easily learned. Although as illimitable in its applications as the infinite relations of men to each other, it is, nevertheless, made up of simple elementary principles, of the truth and justice of which every ordinary mind has an almost intuitive perception. *It is the science of justice,* — and almost all men have the same perceptions of what constitutes justice, or of what justice requires, when they understand alike the facts from which their inferences are to be drawn. Men living in contact with each other, and having intercourse together, *cannot avoid* learning

---

* This condemnation of written laws must, of course, be understood as applying only to cases where principles and rights are involved, and not as condemning any governmental arrangements, or instrumentalities, that are consistent with natural right, and which must be agreed upon for the purpose of carrying natural law into effect. These things may be varied, as expediency may dictate, so only that they be allowed to infringe no principle of justice. And they must, of course, be written, because they do not exist as fixed principles, or laws in nature.

natural law, to a very great extent, even if they would. The dealings of men with men, their separate possessions, and their individual wants, are continually forcing upon their minds the questions, — Is this act just? or is it unjust? Is this thing mine? or is it his? And these are questions of natural law; questions, which, in regard to the great mass of cases, are answered alike by the human mind everywhere.

Children learn many principles of natural law at a very early age. For example: they learn that when one child has picked up an apple or a flower, it is his, and that his associates must not take it from him against his will. They also learn that if he voluntarily exchange his apple or flower with a playmate, for some other article of desire, he has thereby surrendered his right to it, and must not reclaim it. These are fundamental principles of natural law, which govern most of the greatest interests of individuals and society; yet children learn them earlier than they learn that three and three are six, or five and five, ten. Talk of enacting natural law by statute, that it may be known! It would hardly be extravagant to say, that, in nine cases in ten, men learn it before they have learned the language by which we describe it. Nevertheless, numerous treatises are written on it, as on other sciences. The decisions of courts, containing their opinions upon the almost endless variety of cases that have come before them, are reported; and these reports are condensed, codified, and digested, so as to give, in a small compass, the facts, and the opinions of the courts as to the law resulting from them. And these treatises, codes, and digests are open to be read of all men. And a man has the same excuse for being ignorant of arithmetic, or any other science, that he has for being ignorant of natural law. He can learn it as well, if he will, without its being enacted, as he could if it were.

If our governments would but themselves adhere to natural law, there would be little occasion to complain of the ignorance of the people in regard to it. The popular ignorance of law is attributable mainly to the innovations that have been made upon natural law by legislation; whereby our system has become an incongruous mixture of natural and statute law, with no uniform principle pervading it. To learn such a system, — if system it can be called, and if learned it can be, — is a matter of very similar difficulty to what it would be to learn a system of mathematics, which should consist of the mathematics of nature, interspersed with such other mathematics as might be created by legislation, in violation of all the natural principles of numbers and quantities.

But whether the difficulties of learning natural law be

greater or less than here represented, they exist in the nature
of things, and cannot be removed. Legislation, instead of
removing, only increases them. This it does by innovating
upon natural truths and principles, and introducing jargon and
contradiction, in the place of order, analogy, consistency, and
uniformity.

Further than this; legislation does not 'even profess to
remove the obscurity of natural law. That is no part of its
object. It only professes to substitute something arbitrary in
the place of natural law. Legislators generally have the sense
to see that legislation will not make natural law any clearer
than it is. Neither is it the object of legislation to establish the
authority of natural law. Legislators have the sense to see that
they can add nothing to the authority of natural law, and that
it will stand on its own authority, unless they overturn it.

The whole object of legislation, excepting that legislation
which merely makes regulations, and provides instrumentalities for carrying other laws into effect, is to overturn natural
law, and substitute for it the arbitrary will of power. In other
words, the whole object of it is to destroy men's rights. At
least, such is its only effect ; and its designs must be inferred
from its effect. Taking all the statutes in the country, there
probably is not one in a hundred, — except the auxiliary ones
just mentioned, — that does not violate natural law ; that does
not invade some right or other.

Yet the advocates of arbitrary legislation are continually
practising the fraud of pretending that unless the legislature
make the laws, the laws will not be known. The whole object
of the fraud is to secure to the government the authority of
making laws that never ought to be known."

In addition to the authority already cited, of Sir William
Jones, as to the certainty of natural law, and the uniformity
of men's opinions in regard to it, I may add the following:

"There is that great simplicity and plainness in the Common Law, that Lord Coke has gone so far as to assert, (and
Lord Bacon nearly seconds him in observing,) that ' he never
knew two questions arise merely upon common law ; but that
they were mostly owing to statutes ill-penned and overladen
with provisos.' " — 3 *Eunomus*, 157–8.

If it still be said that juries would disagree, as to what was
natural justice, and that one jury would decide one way, and
another jury another ; the answer is, that such a thing is hardly
credible, as that twelve men, taken at random from the people

at large, should *unanimously* decide a question of natural justice one way, and that twelve other men, selected in the same manner, should *unanimously* decide the same question the other way, *unless they were misled by the justices.* If, however, such things should sometimes happen, from any cause whatever, the remedy is by appeal, and new trial.

CHAPTER VI.

IT may probably be safely asserted that there are, at this day, no legal juries, either in England or America. And if there are no legal juries, there is, of course, no legal trial, nor "judgment," by jury.

In saying that there are probably no legal juries, I mean that there are probably no juries appointed in conformity with the principles of the *common law*.

The term *jury* is a technical one, derived from the common law; and when the American constitutions provide for the trial by jury, they provide for the *common law* trial by jury; and not merely for any trial by jury that the government itself may chance to invent, and call by that name. It is the *thing*, and not merely the *name*, that is guarantied. Any legislation, therefore, that infringes any *essential principle* of the *common law*, in the selection of jurors, is unconstitutional; and the juries selected in accordance with such legislation are, of course, illegal, and their judgments void.

It will also be shown, in a subsequent chapter,* that since Magna Carta, the legislative power in England (whether king or parliament) has never had any constitutional authority to infringe, by legislation, any essential principle of the common law in the selection of jurors. All such legislation is as much unconstitutional and void, as though it abolished the trial by jury altogether. In reality it does abolish it.

What, then, are the *essential principles* of the common law, controlling the selection of jurors?

They are two.

---

* On the English Constitution.

1. That *all* the freemen, or adult male members of the state, shall be eligible as jurors.*

Any legislation which requires the selection of jurors to be made from a less number of freemen than the whole, makes the jury selected an illegal one.

If a part only of the freemen, or members of the state, are eligible as jurors, the jury no longer represent "the country," but only a part of "the country."

If the selection of jurors can be restricted to any less number of freemen than the whole, it can be restricted to a very small proportion of the whole; and thus the government be taken out of the hands of "the country," or the whole people, and be thrown into the hands of a few.

That, at common law, the whole body of freemen were eligible as jurors, is sufficiently proved, not only by the reason of the thing, but by the following evidence:

1. Everybody must be presumed eligible, until the contrary be shown. We have no evidence, that I am aware of, of a prior date to Magna Carta, to *disprove* that all freemen were eligible as jurors, unless it be the law of Ethelred, which requires that they be *elderly* † men. Since no specific age is given, it is probable, I think, that this statute meant nothing more than that they be more than twenty-one years old. If it meant anything more, it was probably contrary to the common law, and therefore void.

2. Since Magna Carta, we have evidence showing quite conclusively that all freemen, above the age of twenty-one years, were eligible as jurors.

The *Mirror of Justices*, (written within a century after Magna Carta,) in the section " *Of Judges* " — that is, *jurors* — says:

"All those who are not forbidden by law may be judges

---

* Although all the freemen are legally eligible as jurors, any one may nevertheless be challenged and set aside, at the trial, for any special *personal* disqualification ; such as mental or physical inability to perform the duties; having been convicted, or being under charge, of crime; interest, bias, &c. But it is clear that the common law allows none of these points to be determined by the court, but only by " *triers*."

† What was the precise meaning of the Saxon word, which I have here called *elderly*, I do not know. In the Latin translations it is rendered by *seniores*, which may perhaps mean simply those who have attained their majority.

(jurors). To women it is forbidden by law that they be judges; and thence it is, that feme coverts are exempted to do suit in inferior courts. On the other part, a villein cannot be a judge, by reason of the two estates, which are repugnants; persons attainted of false judgments cannot be judges, nor infants, nor any under the age of twenty-one years, nor infected persons, nor idiots, nor madmen, nor deaf, nor dumb, nor parties in the pleas, nor men excommunicated by the bishop, nor criminal persons. * * And those who are not of the Christian faith cannot be judges, nor those who are out of the king's allegiance." — *Mirror of Justices*, 59–60.

In the section " *Of Inferior Courts*," it is said:

" From the first assemblies came consistories, which we now call courts, and that in divers places, and in divers manners; whereof the sheriffs held one monthly, or every five weeks, according to the greatness or largeness of the shires. And these courts are called county courts, *where the judgment is by the suitors*, if there be no writ, and is by warrant of jurisdiction ordinary. The other inferior courts are the courts of every lord of the fee, to the likeness of the hundred courts. * * There are other inferior courts which the bailiffs hold in every hundred, from three weeks to three weeks, *by the suitors of the freeholders of the hundred. All the tenants within the fees are bounden to do their suit there*, and that not for the service of their persons, but for the service of their fees. But women, infants within the age of twenty-one years, deaf, dumb, idiots, those who are indicted or appealed of mortal felony, before they be acquitted, diseased persons, and excommunicated persons are exempted from doing suit." — *Mirror of Justices*, 50–51.

In the section " *Of the Sheriff's Turns*," it is said:

" The sheriffs by ancient ordinances hold several meetings twice in the year in every hundred; *where all the freeholders within the hundred* are bound to appear for the service of their fees." — *Mirror of Justices*, 50.

The following statute was passed by Edward I., seventy years after Magna Carta:

"Forasmuch also as sheriffs, hundreders, and bailiffs of liberties, have used to grieve those which be placed under them, putting in assizes and juries men diseased and decrepit, and having continual or sudden disease; and men also that dwelled not in the country at the time of the summons; and summon also an unreasonable number of jurors, for to extort money from some of them, for letting them go in peace, and so the assizes and juries pass many times by poor men, and the rich abide at home by reason of their bribes; it is ordained that from henceforth in one assize no more shall be summoned than four and twenty; and old men above three score and ten years, being continually sick, or being diseased at the time of the summons, or not dwelling in that country, shall not be put in juries of petit assizes." — *St.* 13 *Edward I.*, ch. 38. (1285.)

Although this command to the sheriffs and other officers, not to summon, as jurors, those who, from age .and disease, were physically incapable of performing the duties, may not, of itself, afford any absolute or legal implication, by which we can determine precisely who were, and who were not, eligible as jurors at common law, yet the exceptions here made nevertheless carry a seeming confession with them that, at common law, all male adults were eligible as jurors.

But the main principle of the feudal system itself shows that *all* the full and free adult male members of the state — that is, all who were free born, and had not lost their civil rights by crime, or otherwise — *must*, at common law, have been eligible as jurors. What was that principle? It was, that the state rested for support upon the land, and not upon taxation levied upon the people personally. The lands of the country were considered the property of the state, and were made to support the state *in this way.* A portion of them was set apart to the king, the rents of which went to pay his personal and official expenditures, not including the maintenance of armies, or the administration of justice. War and the administration of justice were provided for in the following manner. The freemen, or the free-born adult male members of the state — who had not forfeited their political rights — were entitled to land *of right,* (until all the land was taken up,) on condition of their rendering certain military and civil services to the state. The military services consisted in serving personally as soldiers, or contributing an equivalent in horses, provisions, or other military supplies. The civil services consisted, among other things, in serving as jurors (and, it would appear, as witnesses) in the courts of justice. For these services

they received no compensation other than the use of their
lands. In this way the state was sustained; and the king
had no power to levy additional burdens or taxes upon the
people. The persons holding lands on these terms were called
freeholders — in later times *freemen* — meaning free and full
members of the state.

Now, as the principle of the system was that the freeholders
held their lands of the state, on the condition of rendering
these military and civil services as *rents* for their lands, the
principle implies that *all* the freeholders were liable to these
rents, and were therefore eligible as jurors. Indeed, I do not
know that it has ever been doubted that, at common law, *all*
the freeholders were eligible as jurors. If all had not been
eligible, we unquestionably should have had abundant evidence of the exceptions. And if anybody, at this day, allege
any exceptions, the burden will be on him to prove them. The
presumption clearly is that *all* were eligible.

The first invasion, which I find made, by the English statutes, upon this common law principle, was made in 1285,
seventy years after Magna Carta. It was then enacted as
follows:

"Nor shall any be put in assizes or juries, though they
ought to be taken in their own shire, that hold a tenement of
less than the value of *twenty shillings yearly*. And if such
assizes and juries be taken out of the shire, no one shall be
placed in them who holds a tenement of less value than forty
shillings yearly at the least, except such as be witnesses in deeds
or other writings, whose presence is necessary, so that they be
able to travel." — *St.* 13 *Edward I.*, ch. 38. (1285.)

The next invasion of the common law, in this particular,
was made in 1414, about two hundred years after Magna
Carta, when it was enacted:

"That no person shall be admitted to pass in any inquest
upon trial of the death of a man, nor in any inquest betwixt
party and party in plea real, nor in plea personal, whereof the
debt or the damage declared amount to forty marks, if the
same person have not lands or tenements of the yearly value
of *forty shillings above all charges of the same.*"—2 *Henry V.*,
st. 2, ch. 3. (1414.)

Other statutes on this subject of the property qualifications of jurors, are given in the note.*

---

* In 1483 it was enacted, by a statute entitled " Of what credit and estate those jurors must be which shall be impanelled in the Sheriff's Turn."

" That no bailiff nor other officer from henceforth return or impanel any such person in any shire of England, to be taken or put in or upon any inquiry in any of the said Turns, but such as be of good name and fame, and having lands and tenements of freehold within the same shires, to the yearly value of *twenty shillings* at the least, or else lands and tenements holden by custom of manor, commonly called *copy-hold*, within the said shires, to the yearly value of twenty-six shillings eight pence over all charges at the least." — 1 *Richard III.*, ch. 4. (1483.)

In 1486 it was enacted, " That the justices of the peace of every shire of this realm for the time being may take, by their discretion, an inquest, whereof every man shall have lands and tenements to the yearly value of *forty shillings* at the least, to inquire of the concealments of others," &c., &c. — 3 *Henry VII.*, ch. 1. (1486.)

A statute passed in 1494, in regard to jurors in the city of London, enacts:

" That no person nor persons hereafter be impanelled, summoned, or sworn in any jury or inquest in courts within the same city, (of London,) except he be of lands, tenements, *or goods and chattels*, to the value of *forty marks;* * and that no person or persons hereafter be impanelled, summoned, nor sworn in any jury or inquest in any court within the said city, for lands or tenements, or action personal, wherein the debt or damage amounteth to the sum of forty marks, or above, except he be in lands, tenements, goods, or chattels, to the value of *one hundred marks*." — 11 *Henry VII.*, ch. 21. (1494.)

The statute 4 *Henry VIII.*, ch. 3, sec. 4, (1512) requires jurors in London to have " goods to the value of one hundred marks."

In 1494 it was enacted that " It shall be lawful to every sheriff of the counties of *Southampton, Surry, and Sussex*, to impanel and summons twenty-four lawful men of such, inhabiting within the precinct of his or their turns, as owe suit to the same turn, whereof every one hath lands or freehold to the yearly value of *ten* shillings, or copyhold lands to the yearly value of *thirteen shillings four pence*, above all charges within any of the said counties, or men of less livelihood, if there be not so many there, notwithstanding the statute of 1 *Richard III.*, ch. 4. To endure to the next parliament." — 11 *Henry VII.*, ch. 26. (1494.)

This statute was continued in force by 19 *Henry VII.*, ch. 16. (1503.)

In 1531 it was enacted, " That every person or persons, being the king's natural subject born, which either by the name of citizen, or of a freeman, or any other name, doth enjoy and use the liberties and privileges of any city, borough, or town corporate, where he dwelleth and maketh his abode, being worth in *movable goods and substance* to the clear value of *forty pounds*, be henceforth admitted in trials of murders and felonies in every sessions and gaol delivery, to be kept and holden in and for the liberty of such cities, boroughs, and towns corporate, albeit they have no freehold; any act, statute, use, custom, or ordinance to the contrary hereof notwithstanding." — 23 *Henry VIII.*, ch. 13. (1531.)

In 1585 it was enacted, " That in all cases where any jurors to be returned for trial of any issue or issues joined in any of the Queen's majesty's courts of King's Bench, Common Pleas, and the Exchequer, or before justices of assize, by the laws of this realm now in force, ought to have estate of freehold in lands, tenements, or hereditaments, of the clear yearly value of *forty shillings*, that in every such case the jurors that shall be returned from and after the end of this present session of parliament, shall every of them have estate of freehold in lands, tenements, or hereditaments, to the clear yearly value of *four pounds* at the least." — 27 *Elizabeth*, ch. 6. (1585.)

In 1664–5 it was enacted, " That all jurors (other than strangers upon trials *per medictatem linguæ*) who are to be returned for the trials of issues joined in any of (his)

* A mark was thirteen shillings and four pence.

From these statutes it will be seen that, since 1285, seventy
years after Magna Carta, the common law right of all free
British subjects to eligibility as jurors has been abolished, and
the qualifications of jurors have been made a subject of arbitrary legislation.   In other words, the government has usurped
the authority of *selecting* the jurors that were to sit in judgment
upon its own acts.   This is destroying the vital principle of
the trial by jury itself, which is that the legislation of the government shall be subjected to the judgment of a tribunal, taken
indiscriminately from the whole people, without any choice by
the government, and over which the government can exercise
no control.   If the government can select the jurors, it will, of
course, select those whom it supposes will be favorable to its
enactments.   And an exclusion of *any* of the freemen from
eligibility is a *selection* of those not excluded.

It will be seen, from the statutes cited, that the most absolute authority over the jury box — that is, over the right of
the people to sit in juries — has been usurped by the govern-

---

majesty's courts of king's bench, common pleas, or the exchequer, or before justices of
assize, or nisi prius, oyer and terminer, gaol delivery, or general or quarter sessions
of the peace, from and after the twentieth day of April, which shall be in the year of
our Lord one thousand six hundred and sixty-five, in any county of this realm of England,
shall every of them then have, in their own name, or in trust for them, within the same
county, *twenty pounds by the year*, at least, above reprises, in their own or their wives'
right, of freehold lands, or of ancient demesne, or of rents in fee, fee-tail, or for life.
And that in every county within the dominion of Wales every such juror shall then
have, within the same, *eight pounds by the year*, at the least, above reprises, in manner
aforesaid.   All which persons having such estate as aforesaid are hereby enabled and
made liable to be returned and serve as jurors for the trial of issues before the justices
aforesaid, any law or statute to the contrary in any wise notwithstanding." — 16 *and*
17 *Charles II.*, ch. 3.   (1664–5.)

By a statute passed in 1692, jurors in England are to have landed estates of the
value of *ten pounds a year;* and jurors in Wales to have similar estates of the realm of
six pounds a year. — 4 *and* 5 *William and Mary*, ch. 24, sec. 14.   (1692.)

By the same statute, (sec. 18,) persons may be returned to serve upon the *tales* in
any county of England, who shall have, within the same county, *five pounds by the year*,
above reprises, in the manner aforesaid.

By *St.* 3 *George II.*, ch. 25, sec. 19, 20, no one is to be a juror in London, who shall
not be " an householder within the said city, and have lands, tenements, or personal
estate, to the value of *one hundred pounds.*"

By another statute, applicable only to the county of *Middlesex*, it is enacted,

" That all leaseholders, upon leases where the improved rents or value shall amount
to *fifty pounds or upwards per annum*, over and above all ground rents or other reserva-
tions payable by virtue of the said leases, shall be liable and obliged to serve upon
juries when they shall be legally summoned for that purpose." — 4 *George II.*,
ch. 7, sec. 3.   (1731.)

ment; that the qualifications of jurors have been repeatedly changed, and made to vary from a freehold of *ten shillings yearly*, to one of "*twenty pounds by the year at least above reprises.*" They have also been made different, in the counties of Southampton, Surrey, and Sussex, from what they were in the other counties; different in Wales from what they were in England; and different in the city of London, and in the county of Middlesex, from what they were in any other part of the kingdom.

But this is not all. The government has not only assumed arbitrarily to classify the people, on the basis of property, but it has even assumed to give to some of its judges entire and absolute personal discretion in the selection of the jurors to be impanelled *in criminal cases*, as the following statutes show.

" Be it also ordained and enacted by the same authority, that all panels hereafter to be returned, which be not at the suit of any party, that shall be made and put in afore any justice of gaol delivery or justices of peace in their open sessions *to inquire for the king, shall hereafter be reformed by additions and taking out of names of persons by discretion of the same justices before whom such panel shall be returned; and the same justices shall hereafter command the sheriff, or his ministers in his absence, to put other persons in the same panel by their discretions; and that panel so hereafter to be made, to be good and lawful.* This act to endure only to the next Parliament." —11 *Henry VII.*, ch. 24, sec. 6. (1495.)

This act was continued in force by 1 Henry VIII., ch. 11, (1509,) to the end of the then next Parliament.

It was reënacted, and made perpetual, by 3 Henry VIII., ch. 12. (1511.)

These acts gave unlimited authority to the king's justices to pack juries at their discretion; and abolished the last vestige of the common law right of the people to sit as jurors, and judge of their own liberties, in the courts to which the acts applied.

Yet, as matters of law, these statutes were no more clear violations of the common law, the fundamental and paramount "law of the land," than were those statutes which affixed the property qualifications before named; because, if the king, or the government, can select the jurors on the ground of property, it can select them on any other ground whatever.

Any infringement or restriction of the common law right of the whole body of the freemen of the kingdom to eligibility as jurors, was legally an abolition of the trial by jury itself. The juries no longer represented "the country," but only a part of the country; that part, too, on whose favor the government chose to rely for the maintenance of its power, and which it therefore saw fit to select as being the most reliable instruments for its purposes of oppression towards the rest. And the selection was made on the same principle, on which tyrannical governments generally select their supporters, viz., that of conciliating those who would be most dangerous as enemies, and most powerful as friends — that is, the wealthy.*

These restrictions, or indeed any one of them, of the right of eligibility as jurors, was, in principle, a complete abolition of the English constitution; or, at least, of its most vital and valuable part. It was, in principle, an assertion of a right, on the part of the government, to *select* the individuals who were to determine the authority of its own laws, and the extent of its own powers. It was, therefore, *in effect*, the assertion of a right, on the part of the government itself, to determine its own powers, and the authority of its own legislation, over the people; and a denial of all right, on the part of the people, to judge of or determine their own liberties against the government. It was, therefore, in reality, a declaration of entire absolutism on the part of the government. It was an act as purely despotic, *in principle*, as would have been the express abolition of all juries whatsoever. By "the law of the land," which the kings were sworn to maintain, every free adult male British subject was eligible to the jury box, with full power to exercise his own judgment as to the authority and obligation of every statute of the king, which might come

---

* Suppose these statutes, instead of disfranchising all whose freeholds were of less than the standard value fixed by the statutes, had disfranchised all whose freeholds were of greater value than the same standard — would anybody ever have doubted that such legislation was inconsistent with the English constitution; or that it amounted to an entire abolition of the trial by jury? Certainly not. Yet it was as clearly inconsistent with the common law, or the English constitution, to disfranchise those whose freeholds fell below any arbitrary standard fixed by the government, as it would have been to disfranchise all whose freeholds rose above that standard.

before him. But the principle of these statutes (fixing the qualifications of jurors) is, that nobody is to sit in judgment upon the acts or legislation of the king, or the government, except those whom the government itself shall select for that purpose. A more complete subversion of the essential principles of the English constitution could not be devised.

The juries of England are illegal for another reason, viz., that the statutes cited require the jurors (except in London and a few other places) to be *freeholders*. All the other free British subjects are excluded; whereas, at common law, all such subjects are eligible to sit in juries, whether they be freeholders or not.

It is true, the ancient common law required the jurors to be freeholders; but the term *freeholder* no longer expresses the same idea that it did in the ancient common law; because no land is now holden in England on the same principle, or by the same tenure, as that on which all the land was held in the early times of the common law.

As has heretofore been mentioned, in the early times of the common law the land was considered the property of the state; and was all holden by the *tenants*, so called, (that is, *holders*,) on the condition of their rendering certain military and civil services to the state, (or to the king as the representative of the state,) under the name of *rents*. Those who held lands on these terms were called free *tenants*, that is, *free holders* — meaning free persons, or members of the state, holding lands — to distinguish them from villeins, or serfs, who were not members of the state, but held their lands by a more servile tenure, and also to distinguish them from persons of foreign birth, outlaws, and all other persons, who were not members of the state.

Every freeborn adult male Englishman (who had not lost his civil rights by crime or otherwise) was entitled to land *of right ;* that is, by virtue of his civil freedom, or membership of the body politic. Every member of the state was therefore a freeholder; and every freeholder was a member of the state. And the members of the state were therefore called freeholders. But what is material to be observed, is, that a man's right to

land was an incident to his *civil freedom ;* not his civil freedom
an incident to his right to land.   He was a freeholder because
he was a *freeborn* member of the state ; and not a freeborn
member of the state because he was a freeholder; for this last
would be an absurdity.

As the tenures of lands changed, the term *freeholder* lost its
original significance, and no longer described a man who held
land of the state by virtue of his civil freedom, but only one
who held it in fee-simple — that is, free of any liability to
military or civil services.   But the government, in fixing the
qualifications of jurors, has adhered to the term *freeholder*
after that term has ceased to express the *thing* originally
designated by it.

The principle, then, of the common law, was, that every
freeman, or freeborn male Englishman, of adult age, &c., was
eligible to sit in juries, by virtue of his civil freedom, or his
being a member of the state, or body politic.   But the principle
of the present English statutes is, that a man shall have a right
to sit in juries because he owns lands in fee-simple.   At the
common law a man was *born* to the right to sit in juries.   By
the present statutes he *buys* that right when he buys his land.
And thus this, the greatest of all the political rights of an Englishman, has become a mere article of merchandise ; a thing
that is bought and sold in the market for what it will bring.

Of course, there can be no legality in such juries as these;
but only in juries to which every free or natural born adult
male Englishman is eligible.

The second essential principle of the common law, controlling
the selection of jurors, is, that when the selection of the actual
jurors comes to be made, (from the whole body of male adults,)
that selection shall be made in some mode that excludes the
possibility of choice *on the part of the government.*

Of course, this principle forbids the selection to be made *by
any officer of the government.*

There seem to have been at least three modes of selecting
the jurors, at the common law. 1. By lot.* 2. Two knights,
or other freeholders, were appointed, (probably by the sheriff,)

---

* *Lingard* says : "These compurgators or jurors * * were sometimes * * *drawn
by lot.*" — 1 *Lingard's History of England,* p. 300.

to select the jurors. 3. By the sheriff, bailiff, or other person, who held the court, or rather acted as its ministerial officer. Probably the latter mode may have been the most common, although there may be some doubt on this point.

At the common law the sheriffs, bailiffs, and other officers *were chosen by the people, instead of being appointed by the king*. (4 *Blackstone*, 413. *Introduction to Gilbert's History of the Common Pleas*, p. 2, *note*, and p. 4.) This has been shown in a former chapter.* At common law, therefore, jurors selected by these officers were legally selected, so far as the principle now under discussion is concerned; that is, they were not selected by any officer who was dependent on the government.

But in the year 1315, one hundred years after Magna Carta, the choice of sheriffs was taken from the people, and it was enacted:

" That the sheriffs shall henceforth be assigned by the chancellor, treasurer, barons of the exchequer, and by the justices. And in the absence of the chancellor, by the treasurer, barons and justices." — 9 *Edward II.*, st. 2. (1315.)

These officers, who appointed the sheriffs, were themselves appointed by the king, and held their offices during his pleasure. Their appointment of sheriffs was, therefore, equivalent to an appointment by the king himself. And the sheriffs, thus appointed, held their offices only during the pleasure of the king, and were of course mere tools of the king; and their selection of jurors was really a selection by the king himself. In this manner the king usurped the selection of the jurors who were to sit in judgment upon his own laws.

Here, then, was another usurpation, by which the common law trial by jury was destroyed, so far as related to the *county* courts, in which the sheriffs presided, and which were the most important courts of the kingdom. From this cause alone, if there were no other, there has not been a legal jury in a *county* court in England, for more than five hundred years.

In nearly or quite all the States of the United States the juries are illegal, for one or the other of the same reasons that make the juries in England illegal.

---

* Chapter 4, p. 120, note.

In order that the juries in the United States may be legal —
that is, in accordance with the principles of the common law
— it is necessary that every adult male member of the state
should have his name in the jury box, or be eligible as a juror.
Yet this is the case in hardly a single state.

In New Jersey, Maryland, North Carolina, Tennessee, and
Mississippi, the jurors are required to be *freeholders.* But this
requirement is illegal, for the reason that the term *freeholder*,
in this country, has no meaning analogous to the meaning it
had in the ancient common law.

In Arkansas, Missouri, Indiana, and Alabama, jurors are
required to be " freeholders or householders."   Each of these
requirements is illegal.

In Florida, they are required to be " householders."

In Connecticut, Maine, Ohio, and Georgia, jurors are required to have the qualifications of " electors."

In Virginia, they are required to have a property qualification of one hundred dollars.

In Maine, Massachusetts, Vermont, Connecticut, New York,
Ohio, Indiana, Michigan, and Wisconsin, certain civil authorities of the towns, cities, and counties are authorized to select,
once in one, two, or three years, a certain number of the people — a small number compared with the whole — from whom
jurors are to be taken when wanted; thus disfranchising all
except the few thus selected.

In Maine and Vermont, the inhabitants, by vote in town
meeting, have a veto upon the jurors selected by the authorities
of the town.

In Massachusetts, the inhabitants, by vote in town meeting,
can strike out any names inserted by the authorities, and insert others; thus making jurors elective by the people, and, of
course, representatives only of a majority of the people.

In Illinois, the jurors are selected, for each term of court, by
the county commissioners.

In North Carolina, "*the courts of pleas and quarter sessions
* * shall select the names of such persons only as are freeholders, and as are well qualified to act as jurors, &c.*; thus
giving the courts power to pack the juries." — (*Revised Statutes,* 147.)

In Arkansas, too, "It shall be the duty of the *county court* of each county * * to make out and cause to be delivered to the sheriff a list of not less than sixteen, nor more than twenty-three persons, qualified to serve as *grand* jurors;" and the sheriff is to summon such persons to serve as *grand* jurors.

In Tennessee, also, the jurors are to be selected by the *county courts.*

In Georgia, the jurors are to be selected by "the justices of the inferior courts of each county, together with the sheriff and clerk, or a majority of them."

In Alabama, "the sheriff, judge of the county court, and clerks of the circuit and county courts," or "a majority of" them, select the jurors.

In Virginia, the jurors are selected by the sheriffs; but the sheriffs are appointed by the governor of the state, and that is enough to make the juries illegal. Probably the same objection lies against the legality of the juries in some other states.

How jurors are appointed, and what are their qualifications, in New Hampshire, Rhode Island, Pennsylvania, Delaware, South Carolina, Kentucky, Iowa, Texas, and California, I know not. There is little doubt that there is some valid objection to them, of the kinds already suggested, in all these states.

In regard to jurors in the courts of the United States, it is enacted, by act of Congress :

"That jurors to serve in the courts of the United States, in each state respectively, shall have the like qualifications, and be entitled to the like exemptions, as jurors of the highest court of law of such state now have and are entitled to, and shall hereafter, from time to time, have and be entitled to, and shall be designated by ballot, lot, or otherwise, according to the mode of forming such juries now practised and hereafter to be practised therein, in so far as such mode may be practicable by the courts of the United States, or the officers thereof; and for this purpose, the said courts shall have power to make all necessary rules and regulations for conforming the designation and empanelling of jurors, in substance, to the laws and usages now in force in such state ; and, further, shall have power, by rule or order, from time to time, to conform the same to any change in these respects which may be hereafter adopted by the legislatures of the respective states for the state courts." — *St.* 1840, ch. 47, *Statutes at Large*, vol. 5, p. 394.

In this corrupt and lawless manner, Congress, instead of taking care to preserve the trial by jury, so far as they might, by providing for the appointment of legal juries — incomparably the most important of all our judicial tribunals, and the only ones on which the least reliance can be placed for the preservation of liberty — have given the selection of them over entirely to the control of an indefinite number of state legislatures, and thus authorized each state legislature to adapt the juries of the United States to the maintenance of any and every system of tyranny that may prevail in such state.

Congress have as much constitutional right to give over all the functions of the United States government into the hands of the state legislatures, to be exercised within each state in such manner as the legislature of such state shall please to exercise them, as they have to thus give up to these legislatures the selection of juries for the courts of the United States.

There has, probably, never been a legal jury, nor a legal trial by jury, in a single court of the United States, since the adoption of the constitution.

These facts show how much reliance can be placed in written constitutions, to control the action of the government, and preserve the liberties of the people.

If the real trial by jury had been preserved in the courts of the United States — that is, if we had had legal juries, and the jurors had known their rights — it is hardly probable that one tenth of the past legislation of Congress would ever have been enacted, or, at least, that, if enacted, it could have been enforced.

Probably the best mode of appointing jurors would be this: Let the names of *all* the adult male members of the state, in each township, be kept in a jury box, by the officers of the township; and when a court is to be held for a county or other district, let the officers of a sufficient number of townships be required (without seeing the names) to draw out a name from their boxes respectively, to be returned to the court as a juror. This mode of appointment would guard against collusion and selection; and juries so appointed would be likely to be a fair epitome of "the country."

CHAPTER VII.

ILLEGAL JUDGES.

It is a principle of Magna Carta, and therefore of the trial by jury, (for all parts of Magna Carta must be construed together,) that no judge or other officer *appointed by the king*, shall preside in jury trials, *in criminal cases*, or "pleas of the crown."

This provision is contained in the great charters of both John and Henry, and is second in importance only to the provision guaranteeing the trial by jury, of which it is really a part. Consequently, without the observance of this prohibition, there can be no genuine or *legal* — that is, *common law* — trial by jury.

At the common law, all officers who held jury trials, whether in civil or criminal cases, were chosen by the people.*

---

* The proofs of this principle of the common law have already been given on page 120, *note.*

There is much confusion and contradiction among authors as to the manner in which sheriffs and other officers were appointed; some maintaining that they were appointed by the king, others that they were elected by the people. I imagine that both these opinions are correct, and that several of the king's officers bore the same official names as those chosen by the people; and that this is the cause of the confusion that has arisen on the subject.

It seems to be a perfectly well established fact that, at common law, several magistrates, bearing the names of aldermen, sheriffs, stewards, coroners and bailiffs, were chosen by the people; and yet it appears, from Magna Carta itself, that some of the *king's* officers (of whom he must have had many) were also called "sheriffs, constables, coroners, and bailiffs."

But Magna Carta, in various instances, speaks of sheriffs and bailiffs as "*our* sheriffs and bailiffs;" thus apparently intending to recognize the distinction between officers *of the king*, bearing those names, and other officers, bearing the same official names, but chosen by the people. Thus it says that "no sheriff or bailiff *of ours*, or any other (officer), shall take horses or carts of any freeman for carriage, unless with the consent of the freeman himself." — *John's Charter*, ch. 36.

In a kingdom subdivided into so many counties, hundreds, tithings, manors, cities

But previous to Magna Carta, the kings had adopted the practice of sending officers of their own appointment, called justices, into the counties, to hold jury trials in some cases; and Magna Carta authorizes this practice to be continued so far as it relates to *three* kinds of *civil* actions, to wit: " novel disseisin, mort de ancestor, and darrein presentment;" * but specially forbids its being extended to criminal cases, or pleas of the crown.

This prohibition is in these words:

" Nullus vicecomes, constabularius, coronator, *vel alii balivi nostri*, teneant placita coronæ nostræ." (No sheriff, constable, coroner, *or other our bailiffs*, shall hold pleas of our crown.) — *John's Charter*, ch. 53. *Henry's ditto*, ch. 17.

Some persons seem to have supposed that this was a prohibition merely upon officers *bearing the specific names of* " *sheriffs, constables, coroners and bailiffs,*" to hold criminal trials. But such is not the meaning. If it were, the *name*

---

and boroughs, each having a judicial or police organization of its own, it is evident that many of the officers must have been chosen by the people, else the government could not have maintained its popular character. On the other hand, it is evident that the king, the executive power of the nation, must have had large numbers of officers of his own in every part of the kingdom. And it is perfectly natural that these different sets of officers should, in many instances, bear the same official names; and, consequently that the king, when speaking of his own officers, as distinguished from those chosen by the people, should call them " *our* sheriffs, bailiffs," &c., as he does in Magna Carta.

I apprehend that inattention to these considerations has been the cause of all the confusion of ideas that has arisen on this subject, — a confusion very evident in the following paragraph from Dunham, which may be given as an illustration of that which is exhibited by others on the same points.

" Subordinate to the ealdormen were the *gerefas*, the sheriffs, or reeves, *of whom there were several in every shire, or county. There was one in every borough, as a judge.* There was one at every gate, who witnessed purchases outside the walls; and there was one, higher than either, — the high sheriff, — who was probably the reeve of the shire. This last *appears* to have been appointed by the king. Their functions were to execute the decrees of the king, or ealdormen, to arrest prisoners, to require bail for their appearance at the sessions, to collect fines or penalties levied by the court of the shire, to preserve the public peace, *and to preside in a subordinate tribunal of their own.*" — *Dunham's Middle Ages*, sec. 2, B. 2, ch. 1. 57 *Lardner's Cab. Cyc.*, p. 41.

The confusion of *duties* attributed to these officers indicates clearly enough that different officers, bearing the same official names, must have had different duties, and have derived their authority from different sources, — to wit, the king, and the people.

* *Darrein presentment* was an inquest to discover who presented the last person to a church; *mort de ancestor*, whether the last possessor was seized of land in demesne of his own fee; and *novel disseisin*, whether the claimant had been unjustly disseized of his freehold.

could be changed, and the *thing* retained; and thus the prohibition be evaded. The prohibition applies (as will pres-
ently be seen) to all officers of the king whatsoever; and it
sets up a distinction between officers *of the king*, ("*our* bailiffs,") and officers chosen by the people.

The prohibition upon the king's *justices* sitting in criminal
trials, is included in the words "*vel alii balivi nostri*," (or
other our bailiffs.) The word *bailiff* was anciently a sort of
general name for *judicial officers* and persons employed in and
about the administration of justice. In modern times its use,
as applied to the higher grades of judicial officers, has been
superseded by other words; and it therefore now, more generally, if not universally, signifies an executive or police officer,
a servant of courts, rather than one whose functions are purely
judicial.

The word is a French word, brought into England by the
Normans.

Coke says, "*Baylife* is a French word, and signifies an officer concerned in the administration of justice of a certain province; and because a sheriff hath an office concerning the
administration of justice within his county, or bailiwick, therefore he called his county *baliva sua*, (his bailiwick.)

"I have heard great question made what the true exposition
of this word *balivus* is. In the statute of Magna Carta, cap.
28, the letter of that statute is, *nullus balivus de cætero ponat
aliquem ad legem manifestam nec ad juramentum simplici
loquela sua sine testibus fidelibus ad hoc inductis*." (No bailiff
from henceforth shall put any one to his open law, nor to an
oath (of self-exculpation) upon his own simple accusation, or
complaint, without faithful witnesses brought in for the same.)
"And some have said that *balivus* in this statute signifieth *any
judge*; for the law must be waged and made before the judge.
And this statute (say they) extends to *the courts of common
pleas, king's bench*, &c., for they must bring with them *fideles
testes*, (faithful witnesses,) &c., *and so hath been the usage to
this day*." — 1 *Coke's Inst.*, 168 b.

Coke makes various references, in his margin to Bracton,
Fleta, and other authorities, which I have not examined, but
which, I presume, support the opinion expressed in this quotation.

Coke also, in another place, under the head of the chapter

just cited from Magna Carta, that "*no bailiff shall put any man to his open law,*" &c., gives the following commentary upon it, from the *Mirror of Justices*, from which it appears that in the time of Edward I., (1272 to 1307,) this word *balivus* was understood to include *all judicial,* as well as all other, officers of the king.

The Mirror says: "The point which forbiddeth that no *bailiff* put a freeman to his oath without suit, is to be understood in this manner, — *that no justice, no minister of the king,* nor other steward, nor bailiff, have power to make a freeman make oath, (of self-exculpation,) *without the king's command,** nor receive any plaint, without witnesses present who testify the plaint to be true." — *Mirror of Justices,* ch. 5, sec. 2, p. 257.

Coke quotes this commentary, (in the original French,) and then endorses it in these words :

" By this it appeareth, that under this word *balivus,* in this act, is comprehended *every justice, minister of the king,* steward, and bailiff." — 2 *Inst.,* 44.

Coke also, in his commentary upon this very chapter of Magna Carta, that provides that "*no sheriff, constable, coroner, or other our bailiffs, shall hold pleas of our crown,*" expresses the opinion that it "*is a general law,*" (that is, applicable to all officers of the king,) " by reason of the words *vel alii balivi nostri,* (or other our bailiffs,) *under which words are comprehended all judges or justices of any courts of justice.*" And he cites a decision in the king's bench, in the 17th year of Edward I., (1289,) as authority; which decision he calls " a notable and leading judgment." — 2 *Inst.,* 30—1.

And yet Coke, in flat contradiction of this decision, which he quotes with such emphasis and approbation, and in flat contradiction also of the definition he repeatedly gives of the word *balivus,* showing that it embraced *all ministers of the king whatsoever,* whether high or low, judicial or executive, fabricates an entirely gratuitous interpretation of this chapter

---

* He has no power to do it, *either with, or without, the king's command.* The prohibition is absolute, containing no such qualification as is here interpolated, viz., " *without the king's command.*" If it could be done *with* the king's command, the king would be invested with arbitrary power in the matter.

of Magna Carta, and pretends that after all it only required that *felonies* should be tried before the king's *justices, on account of their superior learning;* and that it permitted all lesser offences to be tried before inferior officers, (meaning of course the *king's* inferior officers.) — 2 *Inst.*, 30.

And thus this chapter of Magna Carta, which, according to his own definition of the word *balivus*, applies to all officers of the king; and which, according to the common and true definition of the term "pleas of the crown," applies to all criminal cases without distinction, and which, therefore, forbids any officer or minister of the king to preside in a jury trial in any criminal case whatsoever, he coolly and gratuitously interprets into a mere senseless provision for simply restricting the discretion of the king in giving *names* to his own officers who should preside at the trials of particular offences; as if the king, who made and unmade all his officers by a word, could not defeat the whole object of the prohibition, by appointing such individuals as he pleased, to try such causes as he pleased, and calling them by such names as he pleased, *if he were but permitted to appoint and name such officers at all;* and as if it were of the least importance what *name* an officer bore, whom the king might appoint to a particular duty.*

---

* The absurdity of this doctrine of Coke is made more apparent by the fact that, at that time, the "justices" and other persons appointed by the king to hold courts were not only dependent upon the king for their offices, and removable at his pleasure, *but that the usual custom was, not to appoint them with any view to permanency, but only to give them special commissions for trying a single cause, or for holding a single term of a court, or for making a single circuit; which, being done, their commissions expired.* The king, therefore, could, *and undoubtedly did, appoint any individual he pleased, to try any cause he pleased, with a special view to the verdicts he desired to obtain in the particular cases.*

This custom of commissioning particular persons to hold jury trials, in *criminal* cases, (and probably also in *civil* ones,) was of course a usurpation upon the common law, but had been practised more or less from the time of William the Conqueror. Palgrave says :

"The frequent absence of William from his insular dominions occasioned another mode of administration, *which ultimately produced still greater changes in the law.* It was the practice of appointing justiciars to represent the king's person, to hold his court, to decide his pleas, to dispense justice on his behalf, to command the military levies, and to act as conservators of the peace in the king's name.* . . The justices who were

* In this extract, Palgrave seems to assume that the king himself had a right to sit as judge, in *jury* trials, in the *county* courts, in both civil and criminal cases. I apprehend he had no such power at the *common law*, but only to sit in the trial of appeals, and in the trial of peers, and of civil suits in which peers were parties, and possibly in the courts of ancient demesne.

Coke evidently gives this interpretation solely because, as he
was giving a general commentary on Magna Carta, he was
bound to give some interpretation or other to every chapter of
it; and for this chapter he could invent, or fabricate, (for it is

---

assigned in the name of the sovereign, and whose powers were revocable at his pleasure, derived their authority merely from their grant. . . Some of those judges were
usually deputed for the purpose of relieving the king from the burden of his judicial
functions. . . The number as well as the variety of names of the justices appear-
ing in the early chirographs of 'Concords,' leave reason for doubting whether, anterior
to the reign of Henry III., (1216 to 1272,) *a court, whose members were changing at
almost every session, can be said to have been permanently constituted. It seems more probable that the individuals who composed the tribunal were selected as suited the pleasure of the
sovereign, and the convenience of the clerks and barons;* and the history of our legal
administration will be much simplified, if we consider all those courts which were afterwards denominated the Exchequer, the King's Bench, the Common Pleas, and the
Chancery, *as being originally committees, selected by the king when occasion required,* out
of a large body, for the despatch of peculiar branches of business, *and which committees,
by degrees, assumed an independent and permanent existence.* . . Justices itinerant,
who, despatched throughout the land, decided the 'Pleas of the Crown,' may be
obscurely traced in the reign of the Conqueror; *not, perhaps, appointed with much regu-
larity, but despatched upon peculiar occasions and emergencies."* — 1 *Palgrave's Rise and
Progress,* &c., p. 289 to 293.

The following statute, passed in 1354, (139 years after Magna Carta,) shows that
even after this usurpation of appointing "justices" of his own, to try criminal cases,
had probably become somewhat established in practice, in defiance of Magna Carta,
the king was in the habit of granting special commissions to still other persons, (especially to sheriffs, — *his* sheriffs, no doubt,) to try particular cases :

"Because that the people of the realm have suffered many evils and mischiefs, for
that sheriffs of divers counties, by virtue of commissions and general writs granted to
them at their own suit, for their singular profit to gain of the people, have made and
taken divers inquests to cause to indict the people at their will, and have taken fine and
ransom of them to their own use, and have delivered them; whereas such persons
indicted were not brought before the king's justices to have their deliverance, it is
accorded and established, for to eschew all such evils and mischiefs, that such commissions and writs before this time made shall be utterly repealed, and that from henceforth no such commissions shall be granted." — *St.* 28 *Edward III.,* ch. 9, (1354.)

How silly to suppose that the illegality of these commissions to try criminal cases,
could have been avoided by simply granting them to persons under the title of "*justices,*" instead of granting them to "*sheriffs.*" The statute was evidently a cheat, or at
least designed as such, inasmuch as it virtually asserts the right of the king to appoint
his tools, under the name of "justices," to try criminal cases, while it *disavows* his
right to appoint them under the name of "sheriffs."

Millar says : " When the king's bench came to have its usual residence at Westminster, the sovereign was induced to *grant special commissions, for trying particular crimes,*
in such parts of the country as were found most convenient; and this practice was
gradually modelled into a regular appointment of certain commissioners, empowered, at
stated seasons, to perform circuits over the kingdom, and to hold courts in particular
towns, for the trial of all sorts of crimes. These judges of the circuit, however, *never
obtained an ordinary jurisdiction, but continued, on every occasion, to derive their authority
from two special commissions :* that of *oyer and terminer,* by which they were appointed to
hear and determine all treasons, felonies and misdemeanors, within certain districts;
and that of *gaol delivery,* by which they were directed to try every prisoner confined in
the gaols of the several towns falling under their inspection." — *Millar's Hist. View of
Eng. Gov.,* vol. 2, ch. 7, p. 282.

The following extract from Gilbert shows to what lengths of usurpation the kings

a sheer fabrication,) no interpretation better suited to his purpose than this. It seems never to have entered his mind, (or if it did, he intended that it should never enter the mind of anybody else,) that the object of the chapter could be to deprive the king of the power of putting his creatures into criminal courts, to pack, cheat, and browbeat juries, and thus maintain his authority by procuring the conviction of those who should transgress his laws, or incur his displeasure.

This example of Coke tends to show how utterly blind, or how utterly corrupt, English judges, (dependent upon the crown and the legislature), have been in regard to everything in Magna Carta, that went to secure the liberties of the people, or limit the power of the government.

Coke's interpretation of this chapter of Magna Carta is of a piece with his absurd and gratuitous interpretation of the words "*nec super eum ibimus, nec super eum mittemus,*" which was pointed out in a former article, and by which he attempted to give a *judicial* power to the king and his judges, where Magna Carta had given it only to a jury. It is also of a piece with his pretence that there was a difference between

---

would sometimes go, in their attempts to get the judicial power out of the hands of the people, and entrust it to instruments of their own choosing :

"From the time of the *Saxons*," (that is, from the commencement of the reign of William the Conqueror,) "till the reign of Edward the first, (1272 to 1307,) the several county courts and sheriffs courts did decline in their interest and authority. The methods by which they were broken were two-fold. *First, by granting commissions to the sheriffs by writ of* JUSTICIES, *whereby the sheriff had a particular jurisdiction granted him to be judge of a particular cause, independent of the suitors of the county court,*" (that is, *without a jury;*) "*and these commissions were after the Norman form, by which (according to which) all power of judicature was immediately derived from the king.*" —*Gilbert on the Court of Chancery,* p. 1.

The several authorities now given show that it was the custom of the *Norman* kings, not only to appoint persons to sit as judges in jury trials, in criminal cases, but that they also commissioned individuals to sit in singular and particular cases, as occasion required ; and that they therefore readily *could*, and naturally *would*, and therefore undoubtedly *did*, commission individuals with a special view to their adaptation or capacity to procure such judgments as the kings desired.

The extract from Gilbert suggests also the usurpation of the *Norman* kings, in their assumption that *they*, (and *not the people*, as by the *common law*,) were the fountains of justice. It was only by virtue of this illegal assumption that they could claim to appoint their tools to hold courts.

All these things show how perfectly lawless and arbitrary the kings were, both before and after Magna Carta, and how necessary to liberty was the principle of Magna Carta and the common law, that no person appointed by the king should hold jury trials in criminal cases.

fine and *amercement,* and that *fines* might be imposed by the king, and that juries were required only for fixing *amercements.*

These are some of the innumerable frauds by which the English people have been cheated out of the trial by jury.

Ex uno disce omnes. From one judge learn the characters of all.*

I give in the note additional and abundant authorities for

---

* The opinions and decisions of judges and courts are undeserving of the least reliance, (beyond the intrinsic merit of the arguments offered to sustain them,) and are unworthy even to be quoted as evidence of the law, *when those opinions or decisions are favorable to the power of the government, or unfavorable to the liberties of the people.* The only reasons that their opinions, *when in favor of liberty,* are entitled to any confidence, are, first, that all presumptions of law are in favor of liberty; and, second, that the admissions of all men, the innocent and the criminal alike, *when made against their own interests,* are entitled to be received as true, because it is contrary to human nature for a man to confess anything but truth against himself.

More solemn farces, or more gross impostures, were never practised upon mankind, than are all, or very nearly all, those oracular responses by which courts assume to determine that certain statutes, in restraint of individual liberty, are within the constitutional power of the government, and are therefore valid and binding upon the people.

The reason why these courts are so intensely servile and corrupt, is, that they are not only parts of, but the veriest creatures of, the very governments whose oppressions they are thus seeking to uphold. They receive their offices and salaries from, and are impeachable and removable by, the very governments upon whose acts they affect to sit in judgment. Of course, no one with his eyes open ever places himself in a position so incompatible with the liberty of declaring his honest opinion, unless he do it with the intention of becoming a mere instrument in the hands of the government for the execution of all its oppressions.

As proof of this, look at the judicial history of England for the last five hundred years, and of America from its settlement. In all that time (so far as I know, or presume) no bench of judges, (probably not even any single judge,) dependent upon the legislature that passed the statute, has ever declared a single *penal* statute invalid, on account of its being in conflict either with the common law, which the judges in England have been sworn to preserve, or with the written constitutions, (recognizing men's natural rights,) which the American judges were under oath to maintain. Every oppression, every atrocity even, that has ever been enacted in either country, by the legislative power, in the shape of a criminal law, (or, indeed, in almost any other shape,) has been as sure of a sanction from the judiciary that was dependent upon, and impeachable by, the legislature that enacted the law, as if there were a physical necessity that the legislative enactment and the judicial sanction should go together. Practically speaking, the sum of their decisions, all and singular, has been, that there are no limits to the power of the government, and that the people have no rights except what the government pleases to allow to them.

It is extreme folly for a people to allow such dependent, servile, and perjured creatures to sit either in civil or criminal trials; but to allow them to sit in criminal trials, and judge of the people's liberties, is not merely fatuity, — it is suicide.

the meaning ascribed to the word *bailiff.* The importance of the principle involved will be a sufficient excuse for such an accumulation of authorities as would otherwise be tedious and perhaps unnecessary.*

The foregoing interpretation of the chapter of Magna Carta now under discussion, is corroborated by another chapter of

---

* Coke, speaking of the word *bailiffs,* as used in the statute of 1 *Westminster,* ch. 35, (1275,) says :

"Here *bailiffs* are taken for the *judges of the court,* as manifestly appeareth hereby." — 2 *Inst.,* 229.

Coke also says, "It is a maxim in law, *aliquis non debet esse judex in propria causa,* (no one ought to be judge in his own cause;) and therefore a fine levied before the *bay- lifes* of *Salop* was reversed, because one of the *baylifes* was party to the fine, *quia non potest esse judex et pars,*" (because one cannot be *judge* and party.) — 1 *Inst.,* 141 a.

In the statute of Gloucester, ch. 11 and 12, (1278,) "the mayor and *bailiffs* of Lon- don (undoubtedly chosen by the people, or at any rate not appointed by the king) are manifestly spoken of as *judges,* or magistrates, holding *jury* trials, as follows :

Ch. II. "It is provided, also, that if any man lease his tenement in the city of Lon- don, for a term of years, and he to whom the freehold belongeth causeth himself to be impleaded by collusion, and maketh default after default, or cometh into court and giveth it up, for to make the termor (lessee) lose his term, (lease,) and the demandant hath his suit, so that the termor may recover by writ of covenant; *the mayor and bailiffs may inquire by a good inquest,* (*jury,*) in the presence of the termor and the demandant, whether the demandant moved his plea upon good right that he had, or by collusion, or fraud, to make the termor lose his term; and if it be found by the inquest (*jury,* that the demandant moved his plea upon good right that he had, the judgment shall be given forthwith; and if it be found by the inquest (jury) that he impleaded him (self) by fraud, to put the termor from his term, then shall the termor enjoy his term, and the execution of judgment for the demandant shall be suspended until the term be expired." — 6 *Edward I.,* ch. 11, (1278.)

Coke, in his commentary on this chapter, calls this court of "the mayor and *bailiffs*" of London, "*the court of the hustings, the greatest and highest court in London;*" and adds, "other cities have the like court, and so called, as York, Lincoln, Winchester, &c. Here the city of London is named; but it appeareth by that which hath been said out of Fleta, that this act extends to such cities and boroughs privileged, — that is, such as have such privilege to hold plea as London hath." — 2 *Inst.,* 322.

The 12th chapter of the same statute is in the following words, which plainly recog- nize the fact that "the mayor and *bailiffs* of London" are *judicial* officers holding courts in London.

"It is provided, also, that if a man, impleaded for a tenement in the same city, (London,) doth vouch a foreigner to warranty, that he shall come into the chancery, and have a writ to summon his warrantor at a certain day before the justices of the bench, *and another writ to the mayor and bailiffs of London, that they shall surcease* (sus- pend proceedings) *in the matter that is before them by writ,* until the plea of the warrantee be determined before the justices of the bench; and when the plea at the bench shall be determined, then shall he that is vouched be commanded to go into the city," (that is, before "the mayor and *bailiffs'*" court,) "to answer unto the chief plea; and a writ shall be awarded at the suit of the demandant by the justices *unto the mayor and bailiffs, that they shall proceed in the plea,*" &c. — 6 *Edward I.,* ch. 12, (1278.)

Coke, in his commentary on this chapter, also speaks repeatedly of "the mayor and *bailiffs*" *as judges holding courts;* and also speaks of this chapter as applicable not only to "the citie of London, specially named for the cause aforesaid, but extended by equity to all other privileged places," (that is, privileged to have a court of "mayor and bail-

Magna Carta, which specially provides that the king's justices shall "go through every county" to "take the assizes" (hold jury trials) in three kinds of *civil* actions, to wit, "novel disseisin, mort de ancestor, and darrein presentment;" but makes no mention whatever of their holding jury trials in *criminal* cases, — an omission wholly unlikely to be made, if it were

---

iffs,") "where foreign voucher is made, as to Chester, Durham, Salop," &c. — 2 *Inst.*, 325–7.

BAILIE. — In Scotch law, a municipal magistrate, corresponding with the English *alderman.** — *Burrill's Law Dictionary.*

BAILIFFE. — *Baillif.* Fr. A bailiff : a ministerial officer with duties similar to those of a sheriff. . . *The judge of a court.* A municipal magistrate, &c. — *Burrill's Law Dict.*

BAILIFF. . . The word *bailiff* is of Norman origin, and was applied in England, at an early period, (after the example, it is said, of the French,) to the chief magistrates of counties, or shires, such as the alderman, the reeve, or sheriff, and also of inferior jurisdictions, such as hundreds and wapentakes. — *Spelman, voc. Balivus;* 1 *Bl. Com.*, 344. *See Bailli, Ballivus.* The Latin *ballivus* occurs, indeed, in the laws of Edward the Confessor, but Spelman thinks it was introduced by a later hand. *Balliva* (bailiwick) was the word formed from *ballivus*, to denote the extent of territory comprised within a bailiff's jurisdiction; and *bailiwick* is still retained in writs and other proceedings, as the name of a sheriff's county. — 1 *Bl. Com.*, 344. *See Balliva. The office of bailiff was at first strictly, though not exclusively, a judicial one.* In France, the word had the sense of what Spelman calls *justitia tutelaris.* *Ballivus* occurs frequently in the *Regiam Majestatem,* in the sense of a *judge.* — *Spelman.* In its sense of a *deputy,* it was formerly applied, in England, to those officers who, by virtue of a deputation, either from the sheriff or the lords of private jurisdictions, exercised within the hundred, or whatever might be the limits of their bailiwick, certain *judicial* and ministerial functions. With the disuse of private and local jurisdictions, the meaning of the term became commonly restricted to such persons as were deputed by the sheriff to assist him in the merely ministerial portion of his duty; such as the summoning of juries, and the execution of writs. — *Brande.* . . The word *bailiff* is also applied in England to the chief magistrates of certain towns and jurisdictions, to the keepers of castles, forests and other places, and to the stewards or agents of lords of manors. — *Burrill's Law Dict.*

" BAILIFF, (from the Lat. *ballivus;* Fr. *baillif,* i. e., *Præfectus provinciæ,*) signifies an officer appointed for the administration of justice within a certain district. The office, as well as the name, appears to have been derived from the French," &c. — *Brewster's Encyclopedia.*

Millar says, " The French monarchs, about this period, were not content with the power of receiving appeals from the several courts of their barons. An expedient was devised of sending royal *bailiffs* into different parts of the kingdom, with a commission to take cognizance of all those causes in which the sovereign was interested, and in reality for the purpose of abridging and limiting the subordinate jurisdiction of the

---

* *Alderman* was a title anciently given to various *judicial* officers, as the Alderman of all England, Alderman of the King, Alderman of the County, Alderman of the City or Borough, alderman of the Hundred or Wapentake. These were all *judicial* officers. See Law Dictionaries.

designed they should attend the trial of such causes. Besides, the chapter here spoken of (in John's charter) does not allow these justices to sit *alone* in jury trials, even in *civil* actions; but provides that four knights, chosen by the county, shall sit

---

neighboring feudal superiors. By an edict of Phillip Augustus, in the year 1190, those *bailiffs* were appointed in all the principal towns of the kingdom." — *Millar's Hist. View of the Eng. Gov.*, vol. ii., ch. 3, p. 126.

" BAILIFF-*office.* — Magistrates who formerly administered justice in the parliaments or courts of France, answering to the English sheriffs, as mentioned by Bracton." — *Bouvier's Law Dict.*

"There be several officers called *bailiffs*, whose offices and employments seem quite different from each other. . . The chief magistrate, in divers ancient corporations, are called *bailiffs*, as in Ipswich, Yarmouth, Colchester, &c. There are, likewise, officers of the forest, who are termed bailiffs." — 1 *Bacon's Abridgment*, 498–9.

" BAILIFF signifies a keeper or superintendent, and is directly derived from the French word *bailli*, which appears to come from the word *balivus*, and that from *bagalus*, a Latin word signifying generally a governor, tutor, or superintendent. . . The French word *bailli* is thus explained by Richelet, (*Dictionaire*, &c.:) *Bailli.— He who in a province has the superintendence of justice, who is the ordinary judge of the nobles*, who is their head for the *ban* and *arriere ban*,* and who maintains the right and property of others against those who attack them. . . All the various officers who are called by this name, though differing as to the nature of their employments, seem to have some kind of superintendence intrusted to them by their superior." — *Political Dictionary.*

" BAILIFF, *balivus.* From the French word *bayliff*, that is, *præfectus provinciæ*, and as the name, so the office itself was answerable to that of France, where there were eight parliaments, which were high courts from whence there lay no appeal, and within the precincts of the several parts of that kingdom which belonged to each parliament, *there were several provinces to which justice was administered by certain officers called bailiffs;* and in England we have several counties in which justice hath been, and still is, in small suits, administered to the inhabitants by the officer whom we now call *sheriff*, or *viscount;* (one of which names descends from the Saxons, the other from the Normans.) And, though the sheriff is not called *bailiff*, yet it was probable that was one of his names also, because the county is often called *balliva;* as in the return of a writ, where the person is not arrested, the sheriff saith, *infra-nominatus, A. B. non est inventus in balliva mea*, &c.; (the within named A. B. is not found in my bailiwick, &c.) And in the statute of Magna Carta, ch. 28, and 14 Ed. 3, ch. 9, the word *bailiff* seems to comprise as well sheriffs, as bailiffs of hundreds.

" *Bailies*, in Scotland, are magistrates of burghs, possessed of certain jurisdictions, having the same power within their territory as sheriffs in the county. . .

" As England is divided into counties, so every county is divided into hundreds; within which, in ancient times, the people had justice administered to them by the several officers of every hundred, which were the *bailiffs*. And it appears by Bracton, (*lib.* 3, *tract.* 2, ch. 34,) that *bailiffs* of hundreds might anciently hold plea of appeal and approvers; but since that time the hundred courts, except certain franchises, are swallowed in the county courts; and now the *bailiff's* name and office is grown into contempt, they being

---

* " *Ban* and *arriere ban*, a proclamation, whereby all that hold lands of the crown, (except some privileged officers and citizens,) are summoned to meet at a certain place in order to serve the king in his wars, either personally, or by proxy." — *Boyer.*

with them to keep them honest.   When the king's justices
were known to be so corrupt and servile that the people would
not even trust them to sit alone, in jury trials, in *civil* actions,

generally officers to serve writs, &c., within their liberties; though, in other respects,
the name is still in good esteem, for the chief magistrates in divers towns are called
bailiffs; and sometimes the persons to whom the king's castles are committed are
termed *bailiffs,* as the *bailiff* of Dover Castle, &c.

" Of the ordinary *bailiffs* there are several sorts, viz., *bailiffs* of liberties; sheriffs'
bailiffs; bailiffs of lords of manors; *bailiffs* of husbandry, &c.   . .

" *Bailiffs* of liberties or franchises are to be sworn to take distresses, *truly impanel
jurors,* make returns by indenture between them and sheriffs, &c.   . .

" *Bailiffs of courts baron* summon those courts, and execute the process thereof.   . .

" Besides these, there are also *bailiffs of the forest.* . . " — *Jacob's Law Dict. Tomlin's do.*

" BAILIWICK, *balliva,* — is not only taken for the county, but signifies generally that
liberty which is exempted from the sheriff of the county, over which the lord of the
liberty appointeth a *bailiff,* with such powers within his precinct as an under-sheriff
exerciseth under the sheriff of the county; such as the *bailiff* of Westminster." —
Jacob's Law Dict. Tomlin's do.

"*A bailiff of a Leet, Court-baron, Manor, Balivus Letæ, Baronis, Manerii.* — He is one
that is appointed by the lord, or his steward, within every manor, to do such offices as
appertain thereunto, as to summon the court, warn the tenants and resiants; also, to
summon the Leet and Homage, levy fines, and make distresses, &c., of which you may
read at large in *Kitchen's Court-leet and Court-baron.*" — *A Law Dictionary, anonymous,
(in Suffolk Law Library.)*

" BAILIFF. — In England an officer appointed by the sheriff. Bailiffs are either
special, and appointed, for their adroitness, to arrest persons; or bailiffs of hundreds,
who collect fines, summon juries, attend the assizes, and execute writs and processes.
The sheriff in England is the king's bailiff.   . .

" *The office of bailiff formerly was high and honorable in England, and officers under that
title on the continent are still invested with important functions.*" — *Webster.*

" BAILLI, (Scotland.) — An alderman; a magistrate who is second in rank in a royal
burgh." — *Worcester.*

" *Baili, or Bailiff.* — (Sorte d'officier de justice.) A bailiff ; a sort of magistrate."
— *Boyer's French Dict.*

" By some opinions, a *bailiff,* in Magna Carta, ch. 28, signifies *any judge.*" — *Cunning-
ham's Law Dict.*

" BAILIFF. — In the court of the Greek emperors there was a grand *bajulos,* first tutor
of the emperor's children. The superintendent of foreign merchants seems also to have
been called *bajulos;* and, as he was appointed by the Venetians, this title (balio) was
transferred to the Venetian ambassador. From Greece, the official *bajulos* (*ballivus,
bailli,* in France; *bailiff,* in England,) was introduced into the south of Europe, and
denoted a superintendent; hence the eight *ballivi* of the knights of St. John, which
constitute its supreme council. In France, the royal bailiffs were commanders of the
militia, administrators or stewards of the domains, *and judges of their districts.*   In the
course of time, only the first duty remained to the bailiff; hence he was *bailli d'épée,
and laws were administered in his name by a lawyer, as his deputy, lieutenant de robe.* The
seigniories, with which high courts were connected, employed bailiffs, who thus consti-

how preposterous is it to suppose that they would not only suffer them to sit, but to sit alone, in *criminal* ones.

It is entirely incredible that Magna Carta, which makes such careful provision in regard to the king's justices sitting in *civil* actions, should make no provision whatever as to their sitting in *criminal* trials, if they were to be allowed to sit in them at all. Yet Magna Carta has no provision whatever on the subject.*

---

tuted, almost everywhere, *the lowest order of judges.* From the courts of the nobility, the appellation passed to the royal courts; from thence to the parliaments. In the greater bailiwicks of cities of importance, Henry II. established a collegial constitution under the name of *presidial courts.* . . *The name of bailiff was introduced into England with William I.* The counties were also called *bailiwicks,* (*ballivæ,*) while the subdivisions were called *hundreds;* but, as the courts of the hundreds have long since ceased, the English bailiffs are only a kind of subordinate officers of justice, like the French *huissiers.* These correspond very nearly to the officers called *constables* in the United States. Every sheriff has some of them under him, for whom he is answerable. In some cities the highest municipal officer yet bears this name, as the high bailiff of Westminster. In London, the Lord Mayor is at the same time bailiff, (which title he bore before the present became usual,) *and administers, in this quality, the criminal jurisdiction of the city, in the court of old Bailey,* where there are, annually, eight sittings of the court, for the city of London and the county of Middlesex. *Usually, the recorder of London supplies his place as judge.* In some instances the term *bailiff,* in England, is applied to the chief magistrates of towns, or to the commanders of particular castles, as that of Dover. The term *baillie,* in Scotland, is applied to a judicial police-officer, having powers very similar to those of justices of peace in the United States." — *Encyclopædia Americana.*

* Perhaps it may be said (and such, it has already been seen, is the opinion of Coke and others) that the chapter of Magna Carta, that " no *bailiff* from henceforth shall put any man to his open law, (put him on trial,) nor to an oath (that is, an oath of self-exculpation) upon his (the bailiff's) own accusation or testimony, without credible witnesses brought in to prove the charge," *is itself* a " provision in regard to the king's justices sitting in criminal trials," and therefore implies that they *are to sit* in such trials.

But, although the word *bailiff* includes all *judicial,* as well as other, officers, and would therefore in this case apply to the king's justices, *if* they were to sit in criminal trials; yet this particular chapter of Magna Carta evidently does not contemplate " *bailiffs* " while acting in their *judicial* capacity, (for they were not allowed to sit in criminal trials at all,) but only in the character of *witnesses;* and that the meaning of the chapter is, that the simple testimony (simplici loquela) of " no bailiff," (of whatever kind,) unsupported by other and " credible witnesses," shall be sufficient to put any man on trial, or to his oath of self-exculpation.*

It will be noticed that the words of this chapter are *not,* " no bailiff *of ours,*" — that is, *of the king,* — as in some other chapters of Magna Carta; but simply " no bailiff," &c. The prohibition, therefore, applies to all " bailiffs," — to those chosen by the peo-

* At the common law, parties, in both civil and criminal cases, were allowed to swear in their own behalf; and it will be so again, if the true trial by jury should be reëstablished.

But what would appear to make this matter absolutely certain is, that unless the prohibition that "no bailiff, &c., *of ours* shall hold pleas of our crown," apply to all officers of the king, justices as well as others, it would be wholly nugatory for any practical or useful purpose, because the prohibition could be evaded by the king, at any time, by simply changing the titles of his officers. Instead of calling them "sheriffs, coroners, constables and bailiffs," he could call them "*justices*," or anything else he pleased; and this prohibition, so important to the liberty of the people, would then be entirely defeated. The king also could make and unmake "justices" at his pleasure; and if he could appoint any officers whatever to preside over juries in criminal trials, he could appoint any tool that he might at any time find adapted to his purpose. It was as easy to make justices of Jeffreys and Scroggs, as of any other material; and to have prohibited all the king's officers, *except his justices*, from presiding in criminal trials, would therefore have been mere fool's play.

We can all perhaps form some idea, though few of us will be likely to form any adequate idea, of what a different thing

---

ple, as well as those appointed by the king. And the prohibition is obviously founded upon the idea (a very sound one in that age certainly, and probably also in this) that public officers (whether appointed by king or people) have generally, or at least frequently, too many interests and animosities against accused persons, to make it safe to convict any man on their testimony alone.

The idea of Coke and others, that the object of this chapter was simply to forbid *magistrates* to put a man on trial, when there were no witnesses against him, but only the simple accusation or testimony of the magistrates themselves, before whom he was to be tried, is preposterous; for that would be equivalent to supposing that magistrates acted in the triple character of judge, jury and witnesses, *in the same trial;* and that, therefore, *in such cases,* they needed to be prohibited from condemning a man on their own accusation or testimony alone. But such a provision would have been unnecessary and senseless, for two reasons; first, because the bailiffs or magistrates had no power to "hold pleas of the crown," still less to try or condemn a man; that power resting wholly with the juries; second, because if bailiffs or magistrates *could* try and condemn a man, without a jury, the prohibition upon their doing so upon their own accusation or testimony alone, would give no additional protection to the accused, so long as these same bailiffs or magistrates were allowed to decide what weight should be given, *both to their own testimony and that of other witnesses;* for, if they wished to convict, they would of course decide that *any* testimony, however frivolous or irrelevant, *in addition to their own,* was sufficient. Certainly a magistrate could always procure witnesses enough to testify to something or other, which *he himself* could decide to be corroborative of his own testimony. And thus the prohibition would be defeated in fact, though observed in form.

the trial by jury would have been *in practice*, and of what would have been the difference to the liberties of England, for five hundred years last past, had this prohibition of Magna Carta, upon the king's officers sitting in the trial of criminal cases, been observed.

The principle of this chapter of Magna Carta, as applicable to the governments of the United States of America, forbids that any officer appointed either by the executive or *legislative* power, or dependent upon them for their salaries, or responsible to them by impeachment, should preside over a jury in criminal trials. To have the trial a legal (that is, a *common law*) and true trial by jury, the presiding officers must be chosen by the people, and be entirely free from all dependence upon, and all accountability to, the executive and legislative branches of the government.*

---

* In this chapter I have called the justices "*presiding* officers," solely for the want of a better term. They are not "*presiding* officers," in the sense of having any authority over the jury; but are only assistants to, and teachers and servants of, the jury. The foreman of the jury is properly the "presiding officer," so far as there is such an officer at all. The sheriff has no authority except over other persons than the jury.

CHAPTER VIII.

THE FREE ADMINISTRATION OF JUSTICE.

THE free administration of justice was a principle of the common law; and it must necessarily be a part of every system of government which is not designed to be an engine in the hands of the rich for the oppression of the poor.

In saying that the free administration of justice was a principle of the common law, I mean only that parties were subjected to no costs for jurors, witnesses, writs, or other necessaries for the trial, *preliminary to the trial itself.* Consequently, no one could lose the benefit of a trial, for the want of means to defray expenses. *But after the trial,* the plaintiff or defendant was liable to be amerced, (by the jury, of course,) for having troubled the court with the prosecution or defence of an unjust suit.* But it is not likely that the losing party was subjected to an amercement as a matter of course, but only in those cases where the injustice of his cause was so evident as to make him inexcusable in bringing it before the courts.

All the freeholders were required to attend the courts, that they might serve as jurors and witnesses, and do any other service that could legally be required of them; and their attendance was paid for by the state. In other words, their attendance and service at the courts were part of the rents which they paid the state for their lands.

The freeholders, who were thus required always to attend

---

* 2 *Sullivan Lectures,* 234–5. 3 *Blackstone,* 274–5, 376. Sullivan says that both plaintiffs and defendants were liable to amercement. Blackstone speaks of plaintiffs being liable, without saying whether defendants were so or not. What the rule really was I do not know. There would seem to be some reason in allowing defendants to defend themselves, *at their own charges,* without exposing themselves to amercement in case of failure.

the courts, were doubtless the only witnesses who were *usually* required in *civil* causes.   This was owing to the fact that, in those days, when the people at large could neither write nor read, few contracts were put in writing.   The expedient adopted for proving contracts, was that of making them in the presence of witnesses, who could afterwards testify to the transactions.   Most contracts in regard to lands were made at the courts, in the presence of the freeholders there assembled.*

In the king's courts it was specially provided by Magna Carta that "justice and right" should not be "sold;" that is, that the king should take nothing from the parties for administering justice.

The oath of a party to the justice of his cause was all that was necessary to entitle him to the benefit of the courts free of all expense; (except the risk of being amerced after the trial, in case the jury should think he deserved it.†)

This principle of the free administration of justice connects itself necessarily with the trial by jury, because a jury could not rightfully give judgment against any man, in either a civil or criminal case, if they had any reason to suppose he had been unable to procure his witnesses.

The true trial by jury would also compel the free administration of justice from another necessity, viz., that of preventing private quarrels ; because, unless the government enforced a man's rights and redressed his wrongs, *free of expense to him*, a jury would be bound to protect him in taking the law into his own hands.   A man has a natural right to enforce his own rights and redress his own wrongs.   If one man owe another a debt, and refuse to pay it, the creditor has a natural right to seize sufficient property of the debtor, wherever he

---

* When any other witnesses than freeholders were required in a civil suit, I am not aware of the manner in which their attendance was procured; but it was doubtless done at the expense either of the state or of the witnesses themselves.   And it was doubtless the same in criminal cases.

† "All claims were established in the first stage by the oath of the plaintiff, except when otherwise specially directed by the law.   The oath, by which any claim was supported, was called the fore-oath, or 'Præjuramentum,' and it was the foundation of his suit.   One of the cases which did not require this initiatory confirmation, was when cattle could be tracked into another man's land, and then the foot-mark stood for the fore-oath." — 2 *Palgrave's Rise and Progress*, &c., 114.

can find it, to satisfy the debt.   If one man commit a trespass upon the person, property or character of another, the injured party has a natural right, either to chastise the aggressor, or to take compensation for the injury out of his property.   But as the government is an impartial party as between these individuals, it is more likely to do *exact* justice between them than the injured individual himself would do.   The government, also, having more power at its command, is likely to right a man's wrongs more peacefully than the injured party himself could do it.   If, therefore, the government will do the work of enforcing a man's rights, and redressing his wrongs, *promptly, and free of expense to him,* he is under a moral obligation to leave the work in the hands of the government; but not otherwise.   When the government forbids him to enforce his own rights or redress his own wrongs, and deprives him of all means of obtaining justice, except on the condition of his employing the government to obtain it for him, *and of paying the government for doing it,* the government becomes itself the protector and accomplice of the wrong-doer.   If the government will forbid a man to protect his own rights, it is bound to do it for him, *free of expense to him.*   And so long as government refuses to do this, juries, if they knew their duties, would protect a man in defending his own rights.

Under the prevailing system, probably one half of the community are virtually deprived of all protection for their rights, except what the criminal law affords them.   Courts of justice, for all civil suits, are as effectually shut against them, as though it were done by bolts and bars.   Being forbidden to maintain their own rights by force, — as, for instance, to compel the payment of debts, — and being unable to pay the expenses of civil suits, they have no alternative but submission to many acts of injustice, against which the government is bound either to protect them, *free of expense,* or allow them to protect themselves.

There would be the same reason in compelling a party to pay the judge and jury for their services, that there is in compelling him to pay the witnesses, or any other *necessary* charges.*

---

* Among the necessary expenses of suits, should be reckoned reasonable compensation to counsel, for they are nearly or quite as important to the administration of justice,

This compelling parties to pay the expenses of civil suits is one of the many cases in which government is false to the fundamental principles on which free government is based. What is the object of government, but to protect men's rights? On what principle does a man pay his taxes to the government, except on that of contributing his proportion towards the necessary cost of protecting the rights of all? Yet, when his own rights are actually invaded, the government, which he contributes to support, instead of fulfilling its implied contract, becomes his enemy, and not only refuses to protect his rights, (except at his own cost,) but even forbids him to do it himself.

All free government is founded on the theory of voluntary association; and on the theory that all the parties to it *voluntarily* pay their taxes for its support, on the condition of receiving protection in return. But the idea that any *poor* man would voluntarily pay taxes to build up a government, which will neither protect his rights, (except at a cost which he cannot meet,) nor suffer himself to protect them by such means as may be in his power, is absurd.

Under the prevailing system, a large portion of the lawsuits determined in courts, are mere contests of purses rather than of rights. And a jury, sworn to decide causes "according to the evidence" produced, are quite likely, *for aught they themselves can know*, to be deciding merely the comparative length of the parties' purses, rather than the intrinsic strength of their respective rights. Jurors ought to refuse to decide a cause at all, except upon the assurance that all the evidence, necessary

---

as are judges, jurors, or witnesses; and the universal practice of employing them, both on the part of governments and of private persons, shows that their importance is generally understood. As a mere matter of economy, too, it would be wise for the government to pay them, rather than they should not be employed; because they collect and arrange the testimony and the law beforehand, so as to be able to present the whole case to the court and jury intelligibly, and in a short space of time. Whereas, if they were not employed, the court and jury would be under the necessity either of spending much more time than now in the investigation of causes, or of despatching them in haste, and with little regard to justice. They would be very likely to do the latter, thus defeating the whole object of the people in establishing courts.

To prevent the abuse of this right, it should perhaps be left discretionary with the jury in each case to determine whether the counsel should receive any pay — and, if any, how much — from the government.

to a full knowledge of the cause, is produced. This assurance they can seldom have, unless the government itself produces all the witnesses the parties desire.

In criminal cases, the atrocity of accusing a man of crime, and then condemning him unless he prove his innocence at his own charges, is so evident that a jury could rarely, if ever, be justified in convicting a man under such circumstances.

But the free administration of justice is not only indispensable to the maintenance of right between man and man; it would also promote simplicity and stability in the laws. The mania for legislation would be, in an important degree, restrained, if the government were compelled to pay the expenses of all the suits that grew out of it.

The free administration of justice would diminish and nearly extinguish another great evil, — that of malicious *civil* suits. It is an old saying, that "*multi litigant in foro, non ut aliquid lucrentur, sed ut vexant alios.*" (Many litigate in court, not that they may gain anything, but that they may harass others.) Many men, from motives of revenge and oppression, are willing to spend their own money in prosecuting a groundless suit, if they can thereby compel their victims, who are less able than themselves to bear the loss, to spend money in the defence. Under the prevailing system, in which the parties pay the expenses of their suits, nothing but money is necessary to enable any malicious man to commence and prosecute a groundless suit, to the terror, injury, and perhaps ruin, of another man. In this way, a court of justice, into which none but a conscientious *plaintiff* certainly should ever be allowed to enter, becomes an arena into which any rich and revengeful oppressor may drag any man poorer than himself, and harass, terrify, and impoverish him, to almost any extent. It is a scandal and an outrage, that government should suffer itself to be made an instrument, in this way, for the gratification of private malice. We might nearly as well have no courts of justice, as to throw them open, as we do, for such flagitious uses. Yet the evil probably admits of no remedy except a free administration of justice. Under a free system, plaintiffs could rarely be influenced by motives of this kind; because **they could put their victim to little or no expense, *neither*** *pending the suit*, (which it is the object of the oppressor to do,) nor at its termination. Besides, if the ancient common law practice should be adopted, of amercing a party for troubling the courts with groundless suits, the prosecutor himself would, in the end, be likely to be amerced by the jury, in such a manner as to make courts of justice a very unprofitable place for a man to go to seek revenge.

In estimating the evils of this kind, resulting from the present system, we are to consider that they are not, by any means, confined to the actual suits in which this kind of oppression is practised; but we are to include all those cases in which the fear of such oppression is used as a weapon to compel men into a surrender of their rights.

CHAPTER IX.

THE CRIMINAL INTENT.

It is a maxim of the common law that there can be no crime without a criminal intent. And it is a perfectly clear principle, although one which judges have in a great measure overthrown in practice, that *jurors* are to judge of the moral intent of an accused person, and hold him guiltless, whatever his act, unless they find him to have acted with a criminal intent; that is, with a design to do what he knew to be criminal.

This principle is clear, because the question for a jury to determine is, whether the accused be *guilty*, or *not guilty*. *Guilt* is a personal quality of the actor, — not *necessarily* involved in the act, but depending also upon the intent or motive with which the act was done. Consequently, the jury must find that he acted from a criminal motive, before they can declare him *guilty*.

There is no moral justice in, nor any political necessity for, punishing a man for any act whatever that he may have committed, if he have done it without any criminal intent. There can be no *moral justice* in punishing for such an act, because, there having been no *criminal motive*, there can have been no other motive which justice can take cognizance of, as demanding or justifying punishment. There can be no *political necessity* for punishing, to warn against similar acts in future, because, if one man have injured another, however unintentionally, he is liable, and justly liable, to a *civil* suit for damages; and in this suit he will be compelled to make compensation for the injury, notwithstanding his innocence of any intention to injure. He must bear the consequences of his own act, instead of throwing them upon another, however innocent he may have been of any intention to do wrong. And the damages he will have to pay will be a sufficient warning to him not to do the like act again.

If it be alleged that there are crimes against the public, (as treason, for example, or any other resistance to government,) for which private persons can recover no damages, and that there is a political necessity for punishing for such offences, even though the party acted conscientiously, the answer is, — the government must bear with all resistance that is not so clearly wrong as to give evidence of criminal intent. In other words, the government, in all its acts, must keep itself so *clearly* within the limits of justice, as that twelve men, taken at random, will all agree that it is in the right, or it must incur the risk of resistance, without any power to punish it. This is the mode in which the trial by jury operates to prevent the government from falling into the hands of a party, or a faction, and to keep it within such limits as *all*, or substantially *all*, the people are agreed that it may occupy.

This necessity for a criminal intent, to justify conviction, is proved by the issue which the jury are to try, and the verdict they are to pronounce. The "issue" they are to try is, "*guilty*," or "*not guilty*." And those are the terms they are required to use in rendering their verdicts. But it is a plain falsehood to say that a man is "*guilty*," unless he have done an act which he knew to be criminal.

This necessity for a criminal intent — in other words, for *guilt* — as a preliminary to conviction, makes it impossible that a man can be rightfully convicted for an act that is intrinsically innocent, though forbidden by the government; because guilt is an intrinsic quality of actions and motives, and not one that can be imparted to them by arbitrary legislation. All the efforts of the government, therefore, to "*make offences by statute*," out of acts that are not criminal by nature, must necessarily be ineffectual, unless a jury will declare a man "*guilty*" for an act that is really innocent.

The corruption of judges, in their attempts to uphold the arbitrary authority of the government, by procuring the conviction of individuals for acts innocent in themselves, and forbidden only by some tyrannical statute, and the commission of which therefore indicates no criminal intent, is very apparent.

To accomplish this object, they have in modern times held it to be unnecessary that indictments should charge, as by the common law they were required to do, that an act was done "*wickedly*," "*feloniously*," "*with malice aforethought*," or in any other manner that implied a criminal intent, without which there can be no criminality; but that it is sufficient to charge simply that it was done "*contrary to the form of the statute in such case made and provided.*" This form of indictment proceeds plainly upon the assumption that the government is absolute, and that it has authority to prohibit any act it pleases, however innocent in its nature the act may be. Judges have been driven to the alternative of either sanctioning this new form of indictment, (which they never had any constitutional right to sanction,) or of seeing the authority of many of the statutes of the government fall to the ground; because the acts forbidden by the statutes were so plainly innocent in their nature, that even the government itself had not the face to allege that the commission of them implied or indicated any criminal intent.

To get rid of the necessity of showing a criminal intent, and thereby further to enslave the people, by reducing them to the necessity of a blind, unreasoning submission to the arbitrary will of the government, and of a surrender of all right, on their own part, to judge what are their constitutional and natural rights and liberties, courts have invented another idea, which they have incorporated among the pretended *maxims*, upon which they act in criminal trials, viz., that "*ignorance of the law excuses no one.*" As if it were in the nature of things possible that there could be an excuse more absolute and complete. What else than ignorance of the law is it that excuses persons under the years of discretion, and men of imbecile minds? What else than ignorance of the law is it that excuses judges themselves for all their erroneous decisions? Nothing. They are every day committing errors, which would be crimes, but for their ignorance of the law. And yet these same judges, who claim to be *learned* in the law, and who yet could not hold their offices for a day, but for the allowance which the law makes for their ignorance, are continually asserting it to be a "maxim" that "ignorance of the law excuses no one;" (by which, of course, they really mean that it excuses no one but themselves; and especially that it excuses no *unlearned* man, who comes before them charged with crime.)

This preposterous doctrine, that "ignorance of the law excuses no one," is asserted by courts because it is an indispensable one to the maintenance of absolute power in the government. It is indispensable for this purpose, because, if it be once admitted that the people *have* any rights and liberties which the government cannot lawfully take from them, then the question arises in regard to every statute of the government, whether it be law, or not; that is, whether it infringe, or not, the rights and liberties of the people. Of this question every man must of course judge according to the light in his own mind. And no man can be convicted unless the jury find, not only that the statute is *law*, — that it does *not* infringe the rights and liberties of the people, — but also that it was so clearly law, so clearly consistent with the rights and liberties of the people, as that the individual himself, who transgressed it, *knew it to be so*, and therefore had no moral excuse. for transgressing it. Governments see that if ignorance of the law were allowed to excuse a man for any act whatever, it must excuse him for transgressing all statutes whatsoever, which he himself thinks inconsistent with his rights and liberties. But such a doctrine would of course be inconsistent with the maintenance of arbitrary power by the government; and hence governments will not allow the plea, although they will not confess their true reasons for disallowing it.

The only reasons, (if they deserve the name of reasons), that I ever knew given for the doctrine that ignorance of the law excuses no one, are these:

1. "The reason for the maxim is that of necessity. It prevails, 'not that all men know the law, but because it is an excuse which every man will make, and no man can tell how to confute him.' — *Selden*, (as quoted in the 2d edition of *Starkie on Slander*, Prelim. Disc., p. 140, note.)" — *Law Magazine*, (*London*,) vol. 27, p. 97.

This reason impliedly admits that ignorance of the law is, *intrinsically*, an ample and sufficient excuse for a crime; and that the excuse ought to be allowed, if the fact of ignorance could but be ascertained. But it asserts that this fact is incapable of being ascertained, and that therefore there is a necessity for punishing the ignorant and the knowing — that is, the innocent and the guilty — without discrimination.

This reason is worthy of the doctrine it is used to uphold; as if a plea of ignorance, any more than any other plea, must necessarily be believed simply because it is urged; and as if it were not a common and every-day practice of courts and juries, in both civil and criminal cases, to determine the mental capacity of individuals; as, for example, to determine whether they are of sufficient mental capacity to make reasonable contracts; whether they are lunatic; whether they are *compotes mentis*, "of sound mind and memory," &c. &c. And there is obviously no more difficulty in a jury's determining whether an accused person knew the law in a criminal case, than there is in determining any of these other questions that are continually determined in regard to a man's mental capacity. For the question to be settled by the jury is not whether the accused person knew the particular *penalty* attached to his act, (for at common law no one knew what penalty a *jury* would attach to an offence,) but whether he knew that his act was *intrinsically criminal.* If it were *intrinsically criminal*, it was criminal at common law. If it was not intrinsically criminal, it was not criminal at common law. (At least, such was the general principle of the common law. There may have been exceptions in practice, owing to the fact that the opinions of men, as to what was intrinsically criminal, may not have been in all cases correct.)

A jury, then, in judging whether an accused person knew his act to be illegal, were bound first to use their own judgments, as to whether the act were *intrinsically* criminal. If their own judgments told them the act was *intrinsically* and *clearly* criminal, they would naturally and reasonably infer that the accused also understood that it was intrinsically criminal, (and consequently illegal,) unless it should appear that he was either below themselves in the scale of intellect, or had

had less opportunities of knowing what acts were criminal. In short, they would judge, from any and every means they might have of judging; and if they had any reasonable doubt that he knew his act to be criminal in itself, they would be bound to acquit him.

The second reason that has been offered for the doctrine that ignorance of the law excuses no one, is this:

"Ignorance of the municipal law of the kingdom, or of the penalty thereby inflicted on offenders, doth not excuse any that is of the age of discretion and compos mentis, from the penalty of the breach of it; because every person, of the age of discretion and compos mentis, *is bound to know the law*, and presumed to do so. *Ignorantia eorum, quæ quis scire tenetur non excusat.*" (Ignorance of those things which every one is bound to know, does not excuse.) — 1 *Hale's Pleas of the Crown*, 42. *Doctor and Student, Dialog.* 2, ch. 46. *Law Magazine*, (*London*,) vol. 27, p. 97.

The sum of this reason is, that ignorance of the law excuses no one, (who is of the age of discretion and is compos mentis,) because every such person "*is bound to know the law.*" But this is giving no reason at all for the doctrine, since saying that a man "is bound to know the law," is only saying, *in another form*, that "ignorance of the law does not excuse him." There is no difference at all in the two ideas. To say, therefore, that "ignorance of the law excuses no one, *because* every one is bound to know the law," is only equivalent to saying that "ignorance of the law excuses no one, *because* ignorance of the law excuses no one." It is merely reasserting the doctrine, without giving any reason at all.

And yet these reasons, which are really no reasons at all, are the only ones, so far as I know, that have ever been offered for this absurd and brutal doctrine.

The idea suggested, that "the age of discretion" determines the guilt of a person, — that there is a particular age, prior to which *all* persons alike should be held incapable of knowing *any* crime, and subsequent to which *all* persons alike should be held capable of knowing *all* crimes, — is another of this most ridiculous nest of ideas. All mankind acquire their knowledge of crimes, as they do of other things, *gradually*. Some they learn at an early age; others not till a later one. One individual acquires a knowledge of crimes, as he does of arithmetic, at an earlier age than others do. And to apply the same presumption to all, on the ground of age alone, is not only gross injustice, but gross folly. A universal presumption might, with nearly or quite as much reason, be founded upon weight, or height, as upon age.*

This doctrine, that "ignorance of the law excuses no one," is constantly repeated in the form that "every one is bound to know the law." The doctrine is true in *civil* matters, especially in contracts, so far as this: that no man, who has the *ordinary* capacity to make reasonable contracts, can escape the consequences of his own agreement, on the ground that he did not know the law applicable to it. When a man makes a contract, he gives the other party rights; and he must of necessity judge for himself, and take his own risk, as to what those rights are, — otherwise the contract would not be binding, and men could not make contracts that would convey rights to each other. Besides, the capacity to make reasonable con-

---

* This presumption, founded upon age alone, is as absurd in civil matters as in criminal. What can be more entirely ludicrous than the idea that all men (not manifestly imbecile) become mentally competent to make all contracts whatsoever on the day they become twenty-one years of age ? — and that, previous to that day, no man becomes competent to make any contract whatever, except for the present supply of the most obvious wants of nature ? In reason, a man's *legal* competency to make *binding* contracts, in any and every case whatever, depends wholly upon his *mental* capacity to make *reasonable* contracts in each particular case. It of course requires more capacity to make a reasonable contract in some cases than in others. It requires, for example, more capacity to make a reasonable contract in the purchase of a large estate, than in the purchase of a pair of shoes. But the mental capacity to make a reasonable contract, in any particular case, is, in reason, the only legal criterion of the legal competency to make a binding contract in that case. The age, whether more or less than twenty-one years, is of no legal consequence whatever, except that it is entitled to some consideration *as evidence of capacity.*

It may be mentioned, in this connection, that the rules that prevail, that every man is entitled to freedom from parental authority at twenty-one years of age, and no one before that age, are of the same class of absurdities with those that have been mentioned. The only ground on which a parent is ever entitled to exercise authority over his child, is that the child is incapable of taking reasonable care of himself. The child would be entitled to his freedom from his birth, if he were at that time capable of taking reasonable care of himself. Some become capable of taking care of themselves at an earlier age than others. And whenever any one becomes capable of taking reasonable care of himself, and not until then, he is entitled to his freedom, be his age more or less.

These principles would prevail under the true trial by jury, the jury being the judges of the capacity of every individual whose capacity should be called in question.

tracts, *implies and includes* a capacity to form a reasonable judgment as to the law applicable to them. But in *criminal* matters, where the question is one of punishment, or not; where no second party has acquired any right to have the crime punished, unless it were committed with criminal intent, (but only to have it compensated for by damages in a civil suit;) and when the criminal intent is the only moral justification for the punishment, the principle does not apply, and a man is bound to know the law *only as well as he reasonably may.* The criminal law requires neither impossibilities nor extraordinaries of any one. It requires only thoughtfulness and a good conscience. It requires only that a man fairly and properly use the judgment he possesses, and the means he has of learning his duty. It requires of him only the same care to know his duty in regard to the law, that he is morally bound to use in other matters of equal importance. *And this care it does require of him.* Any ignorance of the law, therefore, that is unnecessary, or that arises from indifference or disregard of one's duty, is no excuse. An accused person, therefore, may be rightfully held responsible for such a knowledge of the law as is common to men in general, having no greater natural capacities than himself, and no greater opportunities for learning the law. And he can rightfully be held to no greater knowledge of the law than this. To hold him responsible for a greater knowledge of the law than is common to mankind, when other things are equal, would be gross injustice and cruelty. The mass of mankind can give but little of their attention to acquiring a knowledge of the law. Their other duties in life forbid it. Of course, they cannot investigate abstruse or difficult questions. All that can rightfully be required of each of them, then, is that he exercise such a candid and conscientious judgment as it is common for mankind generally to exercise in such matters. If he have done this, it would be monstrous to punish him criminally for his errors; errors not of conscience, but only of judgment. It would also be contrary to the first principles of a free government (that is, a government formed by voluntary association) to punish men in such cases, because it would be absurd to suppose that any man would voluntarily assist to establish or support a govern-

ment that would punish himself for acts which he himself did
not know to be crimes. But a man may reasonably unite
with his fellow-men to maintain a government to punish those
acts which he himself considers criminal, and may reasonably
acquiesce in his own liability to be punished for such acts. As
those are the only grounds on which any one can be supposed
to render any voluntary support to a government, it follows
that a government formed by voluntary association, and of
course having no powers except such as *all* the associates have
consented that it may have, can have no power to punish a
man for acts which he did not himself know to be criminal.

The safety of society, which is the only object of the criminal law, requires only that those acts *which are understood by
mankind at large to be intrinsically criminal*, should be punished as crimes. The remaining few (if there are any) may
safely be left to go unpunished. Nor does the safety of society
require that any individuals, other than those who have sufficient mental capacity to understand that their acts are criminal, should be criminally punished. All others may safely be
left to their liability, under the *civil* law, to compensate for
their unintentional wrongs.

The only real object of this absurd and atrocious doctrine,
that "ignorance of the law (that is, of crime) excuses no one,"
and that "every one is bound to know the *criminal* law," (that
is, bound to know what is a crime,) is to maintain an entirely
arbitrary authority on the part of the government, and to deny
to the people all right to judge for themselves what their own
rights and liberties are. In other words, the whole object of
the doctrine is to deny to the people themselves all right to
judge what statutes and other acts of the government are consistent or inconsistent with their own rights and liberties; and
thus to reduce the people to the condition of mere slaves to a
despotic power, such as the people themselves would never
have voluntarily established, and the justice of whose laws the
people themselves cannot understand.

Under the true trial by jury all tyranny of this kind would
be abolished. A jury would not only judge what acts were
really criminal, but they would judge of the mental capacity
of an accused person, and of his opportunities for understand-

ing the true character of his conduct. In short, they would judge of his moral intent from all the circumstances of the case, and acquit him, if they had any reasonable doubt that he knew that he was committing a crime.*

---

* In contrast to the doctrines of the text, it may be proper to present more distinctly the doctrines that are maintained by judges, and that prevail in courts of justice.

Of course, no judge, either of the present day, or perhaps within the last five hundred years, has admitted the right of a jury to judge of the *justice* of a law, or to hold any law invalid for its injustice. Every judge asserts the power of the government to punish for acts that are intrinsically innocent, and which therefore involve or evince no criminal intent. To accommodate the administration of law to this principle, all judges, so far as I am aware, hold it to be unnecessary that an indictment should charge, or that a jury should find, that an act was done with a criminal intent, except in those cases where the act is *malum in se*, — criminal in itself. In all other cases, so far as I am aware, they hold it sufficient that the indictment charge, and consequently that the jury find, simply that the act was done " contrary to the form of the statute in such case made and provided ;" in other words, contrary to the orders of the government.

All these doctrines prevail universally among judges, and are, I think, uniformly practised upon in courts of justice ; and they plainly involve the most absolute despotism on the part of the government.

But there is still another doctrine that extensively, and perhaps most generally, prevails in practice, although judges are not agreed in regard to its soundness. It is this : that it is not even necessary that the jury should see or know, *for themselves*, what the law *is* that is charged to have been violated; nor to see or know, *for themselves*, that the act charged was in violation of any law whatever;— but that it is sufficient that they be simply *told by the judge* that any act whatever, charged in an indictment, is in violation of law, and that they are then bound blindly to receive the declaration as true, and convict a man accordingly, if they find that he has done the act charged.

This doctrine is adopted by many among the most eminent judges, and the reasons for it are thus given by Lord Mansfield :

" They (the jury) do not know, and are not presumed to know, the law. They are not sworn to decide the law;* they are not required to do it. . . The jury ought not to assume the jurisdiction of law. They do not know, and are not presumed to know, anything of the matter. They do not understand the language in which it is conceived, or the meaning of the terms. They have no rule to go by but their passions and wishes." — 3 *Term Rep.*, 428, note.

What is this but saying that the people, who are supposed to be represented in juries, and who institute and support the government, (of course for the protection of their own rights and liberties, *as they understand them*, for plainly no other motive can be attributed to them,) are really the slaves of a despotic power, whose arbitrary commands even they are not supposed competent to understand, but for the transgression of which they are nevertheless to be punished as criminals ?

This is plainly the sum of the doctrine, because the jury are the peers (equals) of the accused, and are therefore supposed to know the law as well as he does, and as well as it is known by the people at large. If *they* (the jury) are not presumed to know the

---

* This declaration of Mansfield, that juries in England " are not sworn to decide the law " in criminal cases, is a plain falsehood. They are sworn to try the whole case at issue between the king and the prisoner, and that includes the law as well as the fact. See *juror's oath*, page 86.

law, neither the accused nor the people at large can be presumed to know it. Hence, it follows that one principle of the *true* trial by jury is, that no accused person shall be held responsible for any other or greater knowledge of the law than is common to his political equals, who will generally be men of nearly similar condition in life. But the doctrine of Mansfield is, that the body of the people, from whom jurors are taken, are responsible to a law, *which it is agreed they cannot understand.* What is this but despotism ? — and not merely despotism, but insult and oppression of the intensest kind ?

This doctrine of Mansfield is the doctrine of all who deny the right of juries to judge of the law, although all may not choose to express it in so blunt and unambiguous terms. But the doctrine evidently admits of no other interpretation or defence.

CHAPTER X.

THE trial by jury must, if possible, be construed to be such that a man can rightfully sit in a jury, and unite with his fellows in giving judgment. But no man can rightfully do this, unless he hold in his own hand alone a veto upon any judgment or sentence whatever to be rendered by the jury against a defendant, which veto he must be permitted to use according to his own discretion and conscience, and not bound to use according to the dictation of either legislatures or judges.

The prevalent idea, that a juror may, at the mere dictation of a legislature or a judge, and without the concurrence of his own conscience or understanding, declare a man *"guilty,"* and thus in effect license the government to punish him ; and that the legislature or the judge, and not himself, has in that case all the moral responsibility for the correctness of the principles on which the judgment was rendered, is one of the many gross impostures by which it could hardly have been supposed that any sane man could ever have been deluded, but which governments have nevertheless succeeded in inducing the people at large to receive and act upon.

As a moral proposition, it is perfectly self-evident that, unless juries have all the legal rights that have been claimed for them in the preceding chapters, — that is, the rights of judging what the law is, whether the law be a just one, what evidence is admissible, what weight the evidence is entitled to, whether an act were done with a criminal intent, and the right also to *limit* the sentence, free of all dictation from any quarter, — they have no *moral* right to sit in the trial at all, and cannot do so without making themselves accomplices in any injustice that they may have reason to believe may result from their verdict. It is absurd to say that they have no moral responsibility for the use that may be made of their verdict by the government, when they have reason to suppose it will be used for purposes of injustice.

It is, for instance, manifestly absurd to say that jurors have no moral responsibility for the enforcement of an unjust law, when they consent to render a verdict of *guilty* for the transgression of it; which verdict they know, or have good reason to believe, will be used by the government as a justification for inflicting a penalty.

It is absurd, also, to say that jurors have no moral responsibility for a punishment inflicted upon a man *against law*, when, at the dictation of a judge as to what the law is, they have consented to render a verdict against their own opinions of the law.

It is absurd, too, to say that jurors have no moral responsibility for the conviction and punishment of an innocent man, when they consent to render a verdict against him on the strength of evidence, or laws of evidence, dictated to them by the court, if any evidence or laws of evidence have been excluded, which *they* (the jurors) think ought to have been admitted in his defence.

It is absurd to say that jurors have no moral responsibility for rendering a verdict of "*guilty*" against a man, for an act which he did not know to be a crime, and in the commission of which, therefore, he could have had no criminal intent, in obedience to the instructions of courts that "ignorance of the law (that is, of crime) excuses no one."

It is absurd, also, to say that jurors have no moral responsibility for any cruel or unreasonable *sentence* that may be inflicted even upon a *guilty* man, when they consent to render a verdict which they have reason to believe will be used by the government as a justification for the infliction of such sentence.

The consequence is, that jurors must have the whole case in their hands, and judge of law, evidence, and sentence, or they incur the moral responsibility of accomplices in any injustice which they have reason to believe will be done by the government on the authority of their verdict.

The same principles apply to civil cases as to criminal. If a jury consent, at the dictation of the court, as to either law or evidence, to render a verdict, on the strength of which they have reason to believe that a man's property will be taken from him and given to another, against their own notions of justice, they make themselves morally responsible for the wrong.

Every man, therefore, ought to refuse to sit in a jury, and to take the oath of a juror, unless the form of the oath be such as to allow him to use his own judgment, on every part of the case, free of all dictation whatsoever, and to hold in his own hand a veto upon any verdict that can be rendered against a defendant, and any sentence that can be inflicted upon him, even if he be guilty.

Of course, no man can rightfully take an oath as juror, to try a case "according to law," (if by law be meant anything other than his own ideas of justice,) nor "according to the law and the evidence, *as they shall be given him.*" Nor can he rightfully take an oath even to try a case "*according to the evidence,*" because in all cases he may have good reason to believe that a party has been unable to produce all the evidence legitimately entitled to be received. The only oath which it would seem that a man can rightfully take as juror, in either a civil or criminal case, is, that he "will try the case *according to his conscience.*" Of course, the form may admit of variation, but this should be the substance. Such, we have seen, were the ancient common law oaths.

CHAPTER XI.

PROBABLY no political compact between king and people was ever entered into in a manner to settle more authoritatively the fundamental law of a nation, than was Magna Carta. Probably no people were ever more united and resolute in demanding from their king a definite and unambiguous acknowledgment of their rights and liberties, than were the English at that time. Probably no king was ever more completely stripped of all power to maintain his throne, and at the same time resist the demands of his people, than was John on the 15th day of June, 1215. Probably no king every consented, more deliberately or explicitly, to hold his throne subject to specific and enumerated limitations upon his power, than did John when he put his seal to the Great Charter of the Liberties of England. And if any political compact between king and people was ever valid to settle the liberties of the people, or to limit the power of the crown, that compact is now to be found in Magna Carta. If, therefore, the constitutional authority of Magna Carta had rested solely upon the compact of John with his people, that authority would have been entitled to stand forever as the supreme law of the land, unless revoked by the will of the people themselves.

But the authority of Magna Carta does not rest alone upon the compact with *John*. When, in the next year, (1216,) his son, Henry III., came to the throne, the charter was ratified by him, and again in 1217, and again in 1225, in substantially the same form, and especially without allowing any new powers, legislative, judicial, or executive, to the king or his judges, and without detracting in the least from the powers of the jury. And from the latter date to this, the charter has remained unchanged.

In the course of two hundred years the charter was confirmed by Henry and his successors more than thirty times. And although they were guilty of numerous and almost continual breaches of it, and were constantly seeking to evade it, yet such were the spirit, vigilance and courage of the nation, that the kings held their thrones only on the condition of their renewed and solemn promises of observance. And it was not until 1429, (as will be more fully shown hereafter,) when a truce between themselves, and a formal combination against the mass of the people, had been enterèd into, by the king, the nobility, and the "*forty shilling freeholders*," (a class whom Mackintosh designates as "*a few freeholders then accounted wealthy,*"*) by the exclusion of all others than such freeholders from all voice in the election of knights to represent the counties in the House of Commons, that a repetition of these confirmations of Magna Carta ceased to be demanded and obtained.†

The terms and the formalities of some of these "confirmations" make them worthy of insertion at length.

Hume thus describes one which took place in the 38th year of Henry III. (1253):

"But as they (the barons) had experienced his (the king's) frequent breach of promise, they required that he should ratify the Great Charter in a manner still more authentic and solemn than any which he had hitherto employed. All the prelates and abbots were assembled. They held burning tapers in their hands. The Great Charter was read before them. They denounced the sentence of excommunication against every one who should thenceforth violate that fundamental law. They threw their tapers on the ground, and exclaimed, *May the soul of every one who incurs this sentence so stink and corrupt in hell!* The king bore a part in this ceremony, and subjoined, 'So help me God! I will keep all these articles inviolate, as I am a man, as I am a Christian, as I am a knight, and as I am a king crowned and anointed.' " —*Hume*, ch. 12. See also,

---

* *Mackintosh's Hist. of Eng.*, ch. 3.   45 *Lardner's Cab. Cyc.*, 354.

† " *Forty shilling freeholders* " were those " people dwelling and resident in the same counties, whereof every one of them shall have free land or tenement to the value of forty shillings by the year at the least above all charges." By statute 8 *Henry* 6, ch. 7, (1429,) these freeholders only were allowed to vote for members of Parliament from the *counties.*

Blackstone's Introd. to the Charters. Black. Law Tracts, Oxford ed., p. 332. *Mackintosh's Hist. of Eng.,* ch. 3. *Lardner's Cab. Cyc.,* vol. 45, p. 233–4.

The following is the form of "the sentence of excommunication" referred to by Hume :

"*The Sentence of Curse, Given by the Bishops, against the Breakers of the Charters.*

"The year of our Lord a thousand two hundred and fifty-three. the third day of May, in the great Hall of the King at Westminster, *in the presence, and by the assent, of the Lord Henry, by the Grace of God King of England,* and the Lords Richard, Earl of Cornwall, his brother, Roger (Bigot) Earl of Norfolk and Suffolk, marshal of England, Humphrey, Earl of Hereford, Henry, Earl of Oxford, John, Earl of Warwick, and other estates of the Realm of England : We, Boniface, by the mercy of God Archbishop of Canterbury, Primate of all England, F. of London, H. of Ely, S. of Worcester, E. of Lincoln, W. of Norwich, P. of Hereford, W. of Salisbury, W. of Durham, R. of Exeter, M. of Carlisle, W. of Bath, E. of Rochester, T. of Saint David's, Bishops, apparelled in Pontificals, with tapers burning, against the breakers of the Church's Liberties, and of the Liberties or free customs of the Realm of England, and especially of those which are contained in the Charter of the Common Liberties of the Realm, and the Charter of the Forest, have solemnly denounced the sentence of Excommunication in this form. By the authority of Almighty God, the Father, the Son, and the Holy Ghost, and of the glorious Mother of God, and perpetual Virgin Mary, of the blessed Apostles Peter and Paul, and of all apostles, of the blessed Thomas, Archbishop and Martyr, and of all martyrs, of blessed Edward of England, and of all Confessors and virgins, and of all the saints of heaven : We excommunicate, accurse, and from the thresholds (liminibus) of our Holy Mother the Church, We sequester, all those that hereafter willingly and maliciously deprive or spoil the Church of her right : And all those that by any craft or wiliness do violate, break, diminish, or change the Church's Liberties, or the ancient approved customs of the Realm, and especially the Liberties and free Customs contained in the Charters of the Common Liberties, and of the Forest, conceded by our Lord the King, to Archbishops, Bishops, and other Prelates of England ; and likewise to the Earls, Barons, Knights, and other Freeholders of the Realm : And all that secretly, or openly, by deed, word, or counsel, *do make statutes, or observe them being made,* and that bring in Customs, or keep them when they be brought in, against the said

ʿiberties, or any of them, the Writers and Counsellors of said
statutes, and the Executors of them, and all those that shall
presume to judge according to them. All and every which
persons before mentioned, that wittingly shall commit any-
hing of the premises, let them well know that they incur the
aforesaid sentence, *ipso facto*, (i. e., upon the deed being
done.) And those that ignorantly do so, and be admonished,
except they reform themselves within fifteen days after the
time of the admonition, and make full satisfaction for that
they have done, at the will of the ordinary, shall be from that
time forth included in the same sentence. And with the same
sentence we burden all those that presume to perturb the
peace of our sovereign Lord the King, and of the Realm. To
the perpetual memory of which thing, We, the aforesaid Prelates, have put our seals to these presents." — *Statutes of the
Realm*, vol. 1, p. 6. *Ruffhead's Statutes*, vol. 1, p. 20.

One of the Confirmations of the Charters, by Edward I.,
was by statute, in the 25th year of his reign, (1297,) in the
following terms. The statute is usually entitled " *Confirmatio
Cartarum*," (Confirmation of the Charters.)

Ch. 1. " Edward, by the Grace of God, King of England,
Lord of Ireland, and Duke of Guyan, To all those that these
presents shall hear or see, Greeting. Know ye, that We, to
the honor of God, and of Holy Church, and to the profit of
our Realm, have granted, for us and our heirs, that the Charter of Liberties, and the Charter of the Forest, which were
made by common assent of all the Realm, in the time of King
Henry our Father, shall be kept in every point without breach.
And we will that the same Charters shall be sent under our
seal, as well to our justices of the Forest, as to others, and to
all Sheriffs of shires, and to all our other officers, and to all our
cities throughout the Realm, together with our writs, in the
which it shall be contained, that they cause the aforesaid Charters to be published, and to declare to the people that We have
confirmed them at all points; and to our Justices, Sheriffs,
Mayors, and other ministers, which under us have the Laws
of our Land to guide, that they allow the same Charters, in
all their points, in pleas before them, and in judgment; that
is, to wit, the Great Charter as the Common Law, and the
Charter of the Forest for the wealth of our Realm.

Ch. 2. " And we will that if any judgment be given from
henceforth contrary to the points of the charters aforesaid by
the justices, or by any others our ministers that hold plea
before them, against the points of the Charters, it shall be
undone and holden for naught.

Ch. 3. "And we will, that the same Charters shall be sent, under our seal, to Cathedral Churches throughout our Realm, there to remain, and shall be read before the people two times in the year.

Ch. 4. "And that all Archbishops and Bishops shall pronounce the sentence of excommunication against all those that by word, deed, or counsel, do contrary to the foresaid charters, or that in any point break or undo them. And that the said Curses be twice a year denounced and published by the prelates aforesaid. And if the same prelates, or any of them, be remiss in the denunciation of the said sentences, the Archbishops of Canterbury and York, for the time being, shall compel and distrain them to make the denunciation in the form aforesaid." — *St.* 25 *Edward I.*, (1297.) *Statutes of the Realm*, vol. 1, p. 123.

It is unnecessary to repeat the terms of the various confirmations, most of which were less formal than those that have been given, though of course equally authoritative. Most of them are brief, and in the form of a simple statute, or promise, to the effect that "The Great Charter, and the Charter of the Forest, shall be firmly kept and maintained in all points." They are to be found printed with the other statutes of the realm. One of them, after having "again granted, renewed and confirmed" the charters, requires as follows:

"That the Charters be delivered to every sheriff of England under the king's seal, to be read four times in the year before the people in the full county," (that is, at the county court,) "that is, to wit, the next county (court) after the feast of Saint Michael, and the next county (court) after Christmas, and at the next county (court) after Easter, and at the next county (court) after the feast of Saint John." — 28 *Edward I.*, ch. 1, (1300.)

Lingard says, "The Charter was ratified four times by Henry III., twice by Edward I., fifteen times by Edward III., seven times by Richard II., six times by Henry IV., and once by Henry V.;" making thirty-five times in all. — 3 *Lingard*, 50, note, Philad. ed.

Coke says Magna Carta was confirmed thirty-two times. — *Preface to* 2 *Inst.*, p. 6.

Lingard calls these "thirty-five successive ratifications" of the charter, "a sufficient proof how much its provisions were

abhorred by the sovereign, and how highly they were prized
by the nation." — 3 *Lingard*, 50.

Mackintosh says, "For almost five centuries (that is, until
1688) it (Magna Carta) was appealed to as the decisive authority on behalf of the people, though commonly so far only
as the necessities of each case demanded." — *Mackintosh's
Hist. of Eng.* ch. 3.   45 *Lardner's Cab. Cyc.*, 221.

Coke, who has labored so hard to overthrow the most vital
principles of Magna Carta, and who, therefore, ought to be considered good authority when he speaks in its favor,* says :

"It is called Magna Carta, not that it is great in quantity,
for there be many voluminous charters commonly passed, specially in these later times, longer than this is; nor compara-
tively in respect that it is greater than *Charta de Foresta*, but
in respect of the great importance and weightiness of the matter, as hereafter shall appear; and likewise for the same cause
Charta de Foresta; and both of them are called *Magnæ Chartæ Libertatum Angliæ*, (The Great Charters of the Liberties
of England.) . .

"And it is also called *Charta Libertatum regni*, (Charter
of the Liberties of the kingdom;) and upon great reason it is
so called of the effect, *quia liberos facit*, (because it makes men
free.) Sometime for the same cause (it is called) *communis
libertas*, (common liberty,) and *le chartre des franchises*, (the
charter of franchises.) . .

"It was for the most part declaratory of the principal
grounds of the fundamental laws of England, and for the residue it is additional to supply some defects of the common
law. . .

"Also, by the said act of 25 Edward I., (called *Confirmatio
Chartarum*,) it is adjudged in parliament that the Great Charter and the Charter of the Forest shall be taken as the common
law. . .

"They (Magna Carta and Carta de Foresta) were, for the
most part, but declarations of the ancient common laws of
England, to the observation and keeping whereof, the king
was bound and sworn. . .

"After the making of Magna Charta, and Charta de Foresta, divers learned men in the laws, that I may use the words
of the record, kept schools of the law in the city of London,
and taught such as resorted to them the laws of the realm,

---

* He probably speaks in its favor only to blind the eyes of the people to the frauds
he has attempted upon its true meaning.

taking their foundation of Magna Charta and Charta de For
esta.

"And the said two charters have been confirmed, established, and commanded to be put in execution by thirty-two
several acts of parliament in all.

"This appeareth partly by that which hath been said, for
that it hath so often been confirmed by the wise providence of
so many acts of parliament.

"And albeit judgments in the king's courts are of high
regard in law, and *judicia* (judgments) are accounted as *juris-
dicta*, (the speech of the law itself,) yet it is provided by act
of parliament, that if any judgment be given contrary to any
of the points of the Great Charter and Charta de Foresta, by
the justices, or by any other of the king's ministers, &c., it
shall be undone, and holden for naught.

"And that both the said charters shall be sent under the
great seal to all cathedral churches throughout the realm, there
to remain, and shall be read to the people twice every year.

"The highest and most binding laws are the statutes which
are established by parliament; and by authority of that highest court it is enacted (only to show their tender care of Magna
Carta and Carta de Foresta) that if any statute be made contrary to the Great Charter, or the Charter of the Forest, that
shall be holden for none; by which words all former statutes
made against either of those charters are now repealed; and
the nobles and great officers were to be sworn to the observation of Magna Charta and Charta de Foresta.

"*Magna fuit quondam magnæ reverentia chartæ.*" (Great
was formerly the reverence for Magna Carta.) — *Coke's
Proem to 2 Inst.*, p. 1 to 7.

Coke also says, "All pretence of prerogative against Magna
Charta is taken away." — 2 *Inst.*, 36.

He also says, "That after this parliament (52 *Henry* III.,
in 1267) neither Magna Carta nor Carta de Foresta was ever
attempted to be impugned or questioned." — 2 *Inst.*, 102.*

---

* It will be noticed that Coke calls these confirmations of the charter " acts of parliament," instead of acts of the king alone. This needs explanation.

It was one of Coke's ridiculous pretences, that laws anciently enacted by the king, at
the *request*, or with the *consent*, or by the *advice*, of his parliament, was " an act of parliament," instead of the act of the king. And in the extracts cited, he carries this
idea so far as to pretend that the various confirmations of the Great Charter were
" acts of parliament," instead of the acts of the kings. He might as well have pretended that the original grant of the Charter was an " act of parliament ;" because it
was not only granted at the request, and with the consent, and by the advice, but on
the compulsion even, of those who commonly constituted his parliaments. Yet this did

To give all the evidence of the authority of Magna Carta, it would be necessary to give the constitutional history of England since the year 1215. This history would show that Magna Carta, although continually violated and evaded, was still acknowl-

---

not make the grant of the charter "an act of parliament." It was simply an act of the king.

The object of Coke, in this pretence, was to furnish some color for the palpable falsehood that the legislative authority, which parliament was trying to assume in his own day, and which it finally succeeded in obtaining, had a precedent in the ancient constitution of the kingdom.

There would be as much reason in saying that, because the ancient kings were in the habit of passing laws in special answer to the *petitions* of their subjects, therefore those *petitioners* were a part of the legislative power of the kingdom.

One great objection to this argument of Coke, for the legislative authority of the ancient parliaments, is that a very large — probably much the larger — number of legislative acts were done *without* the advice, consent, request, or even presence, of a parliament. Not only were many formal statutes passed without any mention of the consent or advice of parliament, but a simple order of the king in council, or a simple proclamation, writ, or letter under seal, issued by his command, had the same force as what Coke calls "an act of parliament." And this practice continued, to a considerable extent at least, down to Coke's own time.

The kings were always in the habit of consulting their parliaments, more or less, in regard to matters of legislation, — not because their consent was constitutionally necessary, but in order to make influence in favor of their laws, and thus induce the people to observe them, and the juries to enforce them.

The general duties of the ancient parliaments were not legislative, but judicial, as will be shown more fully hereafter. The *people* were not represented in the parliaments at the time of Magna Carta, but only the archbishops, bishops, earls, barons, and knights; so that little or nothing would have been gained for liberty by Coke's idea that parliament had a legislative power. He would only have substituted an aristocracy for a king. Even after the Commons were represented in parliament, they for some centuries appeared only as *petitioners*, except in the matter of taxation, when their *consent* was asked. And almost the only source of their influence on legislation was this : that they would sometimes refuse their consent to the taxation, unless the king would pass such laws as they petitioned for; or, as would seem to have been much more frequently the case, unless he would abolish such laws and practices as they remonstrated against.

The *influence* or power of parliament, and especially of the Commons, in the *general* legislation of the country, was a thing of slow growth, having its origin in a device of the king to get money contrary to law, (as will be seen in the next volume,) and not at all a part of the constitution of the kingdom, nor having its foundation in the consent of the people. The power, *as at present exercised*, was not fully established until 1688, (near five hundred years after Magna Carta,) when the House of Commons (falsely so called) had acquired such influence as the representative, *not of the people, but of the wealth,* of the nation, that they compelled the king to discard the oath fixed by the constitution of the kingdom; (which oath has been already given in a former chapter,[*] and was, in substance, to preserve and execute the Common Law, the Law of the Land,

edged as law by the government, and was held up by the people as the great standard and proof of their rights and liber-

---

— or, in the words of the oath, "*the just laws and customs which the common people had chosen;*") and to swear that he would " govern the people of this kingdom of England, and the dominions thereto belonging, *according to the statutes in parliament agreed on,* and the laws and customs of the same." *

The passage and enforcement of this statute, and the assumption of this oath by the king, were plain violations of the English constitution, inasmuch as they abolished, so far as such an oath could abolish, the legislative power of the king, and also "those just laws and customs which the common people (through their juries) had chosen," and substituted the will of parliament in their stead.

Coke was a great advocate for the legislative power of parliament, as a means of restraining the power of the king. As he denied all power to *juries* to decide upon the obligation of laws, and as he held that the legislative power was " *so transcendent and absolute as (that) it cannot be confined, either for causes or persons, within any bounds,*" † he was perhaps honest in holding that it was safer to trust this terrific power in the hands of parliament, than in the hands of the king. His error consisted in holding that either the king or parliament had any such power, or that they had any power at all to pass laws that should be binding upon a jury.

These declarations of Coke, that the charter was confirmed by thirty-two " acts of parliament," have a mischievous bearing in another respect. They tend to weaken the authority of the charter, by conveying the impression that the charter itself might be *abolished* by " act of parliament." Coke himself admits that it could not be revoked or rescinded by the *king;* for he says, " All pretence of prerogative against Magna Carta is taken away." (2 *Inst.,* 36.)

He knew perfectly well, and the whole English nation knew, that the *king* could not lawfully infringe Magna Carta. Magna Carta, therefore, made it impossible that absolute power could ever be practically established in England, *in the hands of the king.* Hence, as Coke was an advocate for absolute power, — that is, for a legislative power " so transcendent and absolute as (that) it cannot be confined, either for causes or persons, within any bounds," — there was no alternative for him but to vest this absolute power in parliament. Had he not vested it in parliament, he would have been obliged to abjure it altogether, and to confess that the people, *through their juries,* had the right to judge of the obligation of all legislation whatsoever; in other words, that they had the right to confine the government within the limits of "those just laws and customs which the common people (acting as jurors) had chosen." True to his instincts, as a judge, and as a tyrant, he *assumed* that this absolute power was vested in the hands of parliament.

But the truth was that, as by the English constitution parliament had no authority at all for *general* legislation, it could no more confirm, than it could abolish, Magna Carta.

These thirty-two confirmations of Magna Carta, which Coke speaks of as " acts of parliament," were merely acts of the king. The parliaments, indeed, by refusing to grant him money, except on that condition, and otherwise, had contributed to oblige him to make the confirmations; just as they had helped to oblige him by arms to grant the charter in the first place. But the confirmations themselves were nevertheless constitutionally, as well as formally, the acts of the king alone.

* St. 1 *William and Mary,* ch. 6, (1688.)   † 4 *Inst.,* 36.

ties. It would show also that the judicial tribunals, *whenever it suited their purposes to do so*, were in the habit of referring to Magna Carta as authority, in the same manner, and with the same real or pretended veneration, with which American courts now refer to the constitution of the United States, or the constitutions of the states. And, what is equally to the point, it would show that these same tribunals, the mere tools of kings and parliaments, would resort to the same artifices of assumption, *precedent*, construction, and false interpretation, to evade the requirements of Magna Carta, and to emasculate it of all its power for the preservation of liberty, that are resorted to by American courts to accomplish the same work on our American constitutions.

I take it for granted, therefore, that if the authority of Magna Carta had rested simply upon its character as a *compact* between the king and the people, it would have been forever binding upon the king, (that is, upon the government, for the king was the government,) in his legislative, judicial, and executive character; and that there was no *constitutional* possibility of his escaping from its restraints, unless the people themselves should freely discharge him from them.

But the authority of Magna Carta does not rest, either wholly or mainly, upon its character as a compact. For centuries before the charter was granted, its main principles constituted "the Law of the Land," — the fundamental and constitutional law of the realm, which the kings were sworn to maintain. And the principal benefit of the charter was, that it contained a *written* description and acknowledgment, by the king himself, of what the constitutional law of the kingdom was, which his coronation oath bound him to observe. Previous to Magna Carta, this constitutional law rested mainly in precedents, customs, and the memories of the people. And if the king could but make one innovation upon this law, without arousing resistance, and being compelled to retreat from his usurpation, he would cite that innovation as a precedent for another act of the same kind; next, assert a custom; and, finally, raise a controversy as to what the Law of the Land really was. The great object of the barons and people, in demanding from the king a written description and acknowledgment of the Law of the Land, was to put an end to all disputes of this kind, and to put it out of the power of the king to plead any misunderstanding of the constitutional law of the kingdom. And the charter, no doubt, accomplished very much in this way. After Magna Carta, it required much more audacity, cunning, or strength, on the part of the king, than it had before, to invade the people's liberties with impunity. Still, Magna Carta, like all other written constitutions, proved inadequate to the full accomplishment of its purpose; for when did a parchment ever have power adequately to restrain a government, that had either cunning to evade its requirements, or strength to overcome those who attempted its defence? The work of usurpation, therefore, though seriously checked, still went on, to a great extent, after Magna Carta. Innovations upon the Law of the Land are still made by the government. One innovation was cited as a precedent; precedents made customs; and customs became laws, so far as practice was concerned; until the government, composed of the king, the high functionaries of the church, the nobility, a House of Commons representing the "forty shilling freeholders," and a dependent and servile judiciary, all acting in conspiracy against the mass of the people, became practically absolute, as it is at this day.

As proof that Magna Carta embraced little else than what was previously recognized as the common law, or Law of the Land, I repeat some authorities that have been already cited.

Crabbe says, " It is admitted on all hands that it (Magna Carta) contains nothing but what was confirmatory of the common law and the ancient usages of the realm; and is, properly speaking, only an enlargement of the charter of Henry I. and his successors." — *Crabbe's Hist. of the Eng. Law,* p. 127.

Blackstone says, " It is agreed by all our historians that the Great Charter of King John was, for the most part, compiled from the ancient customs of the realm, or the laws of Edward the Confessor; by which they mean the old common law which was established under our Saxon princes." — *Blackstone's Introd. to the Charters.* See *Blackstone's Law Tracts,* Oxford ed., p. 289.

Coke says, " The common law is the most general and ancient law of the realm. . . The common law appeareth in the statute of *Magna Carta*, and other ancient statutes, (which for the most part are affirmations of the common law,) in the original writs, in judicial records, and in our books of terms and years." — 1 *Inst.*, 115 b.

Coke also says, "It (Magna Carta) was for the most part declaratory of the principal grounds of the fundamental laws of England, and for the residue it was additional to supply some defects of the common law. . . They (Magna Carta and Carta de Foresta) were, for the most part, but declarations of the ancient common laws of England, *to the observation and keeping whereof the king was bound and sworn.*" — *Preface to* 2 *Inst.*, p. 3 and 5.

Hume says, "We may now, from the tenor of this charter, (Magna Carta,) conjecture what those laws were of King Edward, (the Confessor,) which the English nation during so many generations still desired, with such an obstinate perseverance, to have recalled and established. They were chiefly these latter articles of Magna Carta; and the barons who, at the beginning of these commotions, demanded the revival of the Saxon laws, undoubtedly thought that they had sufficiently satisfied the people, by procuring them this concession, which comprehended the principal objects to which they had so long aspired." — *Hume*, ch. 11.

Edward the First confessed that the Great Charter was substantially identical with the common law, as far as it went, when he commanded his justices to allow "the Great Charter as the Common Law," "in pleas before them, and in judgment," as has been already cited in this chapter. — 25 *Edward* I., ch. 1, (1297.)

In conclusion of this chapter, it may be safely asserted that the veneration, attachment, and pride, which the English nation, for more than six centuries, have felt towards Magna Carta, are in their nature among the most irrefragable of all proofs that it was the fundamental law of the land, and constitutionally binding upon the government; for, otherwise, it would have been, in their eyes, an unimportant and worthless thing. What those sentiments were I will use the words of others to describe, — the words, too, of men, who, like all modern authors who have written on the same topic, had utterly inadequate ideas of the true character of the instrument on which they lavished their eulogiums.

Hume, speaking of the Great Charter and the Charter of the Forest, as they were confirmed by Henry III., in 1217, says:

"Thus these famous charters were brought nearly to the shape in which they have ever since stood; and they were, during many generations, the peculiar favorites of the English nation, and esteemed the most sacred rampart to national liberty and independence. As they secured the rights of all orders of men, they were anxiously defended by all, and became the basis, in a manner, of the English monarchy, and a kind of original contract, which both limited the authority of the king and ensured the conditional allegiance of his subjects. Though often violated, they were still claimed by the nobility and people; and, as no precedents were supposed valid that infringed them, they rather acquired than lost authority, from the frequent attempts made against them in several ages, by regal and arbitrary power." — *Hume*, ch. 12.

Mackintosh says, "It was understood by the simplest of the unlettered age for whom it was intended. It was remembered by them. . . For almost five centuries it was appealed to as the decisive authority on behalf of the people. . . To have produced it, to have preserved it, to have matured it, constitute the immortal claim of England on the esteem of mankind. Her Bacons and Shakspeares, her Miltons and Newtons, with all the truth which they have revealed, and all the generous virtues which they have inspired, are of inferior value when compared with the subjection of men and their rulers to the principles of justice; if, indeed, it be not more true that these mighty spirits could not have been formed except under equal laws, nor roused to full activity without the influence of that spirit which the Great Charter breathed over their forefathers." — *Mackintosh's Hist. of Eng.*, ch. 3.*

Of the Great Charter, the trial by jury is the vital part, and the only part that places the liberties of the people in their own keeping. Of this Blackstone says:

"The trial by jury, or the country, *per patriam*, is also that trial by the peers of every Englishman, which, as the grand bulwark of his liberties, is secured to him by the Great Charter; *nullus liber homo capiatur, vel imprisonetur, aut exuletur, aut aliquo modo destruatur, nisi per legale judicium parium suorum, vel per legem terrae.* . .

The liberties of England cannot but subsist so long as this palladium remains sacred and inviolate, not only from all

---

* Under the head of "*John.*"

open attacks, which none will be so hardy as to make, but also from all secret machinations which may sap and undermine it." *

"The trial by jury ever has been, and I trust ever will be, looked upon as the glory of the English law. . . It is the most transcendent privilege which any subject can enjoy or wish for, that he cannot be affected in his property, his liberty, or his person, but by the unanimous consent of twelve of his neighbors and equals." †

Hume calls the trial by jury "An institution admirable in itself, and the best calculated for the preservation of liberty and the administration of justice, that ever was devised by the wit of man." ‡

An old book, called " English Liberties," says:

" English Parliaments have all along been most zealous for preserving this great Jewel of Liberty, trials by juries having no less than fifty-eight several times, since the Norman Conquest, been established and confirmed by the legislative power, no one privilege besides having been ever so often remembered in parliament." §

---

* 4 *Blackstone,* 349–50. † 3 *Blackstone,* 379. ‡ *Hume,* ch. 2.
§ Page 203, 5th edition, 1721.

CHAPTER XII.

LIMITATIONS IMPOSED UPON THE MAJORITY BY THE TRIAL BY JURY.

THE principal objection, that will be made to the doctrine of this essay, is, that under it, a jury would paralyze the power of the majority, and veto all legislation that was not in accordance with the will of the whole, or nearly the whole, people.

The answer to this objection is, that the limitation, which would be thus imposed upon the legislative power, (whether that power be vested in the majority, or minority, of the people,) is the crowning merit of the trial by jury. It has other merits; but, though important in themselves, they are utterly insignificant and worthless in comparison with this.

It is this power of vetoing all partial and oppressive legislation, and of restricting the government to the maintenance of such laws as the *whole*, or substantially the whole, people *are agreed in*, that makes the trial by jury " the palladium of liberty." Without this power it would never have deserved that name.

The will, or the pretended will, of the majority, is the last lurking place of tyranny at the present day. The dogma, that certain individuals and families have a divine appointment to govern the rest of mankind, is fast giving place to the one that the larger number have a right to govern the smaller; a dogma, which may, or may not, be less oppressive in its practical operation, but which certainly is no less false or tyrannical in principle, than the one it is so rapidly supplanting. Obviously there is nothing in the nature of majorities, that insures justice at their hands. They have the same passions as minorities, and they have no qualities whatever that should be expected to prevent them from practising the same tyranny

as minorities, if they think it will be for their interest to
do so.

There is no particle of truth in the notion that the majority
have a *right* to rule, or to exercise arbitrary power over, the
minority, simply because the former are more numerous than
the latter. Two men have no more natural right to rule one,
than one has to rule two. Any single man, or any body of
men, many or few, have a natural right to maintain justice
for themselves, and for any others who may need their assistance, against the injustice of any and all other men, without
regard to their numbers; and majorities have no right to do
any more than this. The relative numbers of the opposing
parties have nothing to do with the question of right. And
no more tyrannical principle was ever avowed, than that the
will of the majority ought to have the force of law, without
regard to its justice; or, what is the same thing, that the will
of the majority ought always to be presumed to be in accordance with justice. Such a doctrine is only another form of
the doctrine that might makes right.

When *two* men meet *one* upon the highway, or in the wilderness, have they a right to dispose of his life, liberty, or
property at their pleasure, simply because they are the more
numerous party? Or is he bound to submit to lose his life,
liberty, or property, if they demand it, merely because he is
the less numerous party? Or, because they are more numerous than he, is he bound to presume that they are governed
only by superior wisdom, and the principles of justice, and by
no selfish passion that can lead them to do him a wrong?
Yet this is the principle, which it is claimed should govern
men in all their civil relations to each other. Mankind fall in
company with each other on the highway or in the wilderness
of life, and it is claimed that the more numerous party, simply
by virtue of their superior numbers, have the right arbitrarily
to dispose of the life, liberty, and property of the minority; and
that the minority are bound, by reason of their inferior numbers, to practise abject submission, and consent to hold their
natural rights,— any, all, or none, as the case may be,— at
the mere will and pleasure of the majority; as if all a man's
natural rights expired, or were suspended by the operation of

a paramount law, the moment he came into the presence of superior numbers.

If such be the true nature of the relations men hold to each other in this world, it puts an end to all such things as crimes, unless they be perpetrated upon those who are equal or superior, in number, to the actors. All acts committed against persons *inferior* in number to the aggressors, become but the exercise of rightful authority. And consistency with their own principles requires that all governments, founded on the will of the majority, should recognize this plea as a sufficient justification for all crimes whatsoever.

If it be said that the majority should be allowed to rule, not because they are stronger than the minority, but because their superior numbers furnish a *probability* that they are in the right; one answer is, that the lives, liberties, and properties of men are too valuable to them, and the natural presumptions are too strong in their favor, to justify the destruction of them by their fellow-men on a mere balancing of probabilities, *or on any ground whatever short of certainty beyond a reasonable doubt.* This last is the moral rule universally recognized to be binding upon single individuals. And in the forum of conscience the same rule is equally binding upon governments, for governments are mere associations of individuals. This *is* the rule on which the trial by jury is based. And it is plainly the only rule that ought to induce a man to submit his rights to the adjudication of his fellow-men, or dissuade him from a forcible defence of them.

Another answer is, that if two opposing parties could be supposed to have no personal interests or passions involved, to warp their judgments, or corrupt their motives, the fact that one of the parties was more numerous than the other, (a fact that leaves the comparative intellectual competency of the two parties entirely out of consideration,) might, perhaps, furnish a slight, but at best only a very slight, probability that such party was on the side of justice. But when it is considered that the parties are liable to differ in their intellectual capacities, and that one, or the other, or both, are undoubtedly under the influence of such passions as rivalry, hatred, avarice, and ambition,— passions that are nearly certain to pervert their judgments, and very likely to corrupt their motives,— all probabilities founded upon a mere numerical majority, in one party, or the other, vanish at once; and the decision of the majority becomes, to all practical purposes, a mere decision of chance. And to dispose of men's properties, liberties, and lives, by the mere process of enumerating such parties, is not only as palpable gambling as was ever practised, but it is also the most atrocious that was ever practised, except in matters of government. And where government is instituted on this principle, (as in the United States, for example,) the nation is at once converted into one great gambling establishment; where all the rights of men are the stakes; a few bold bad men throw the dice—(dice loaded with all the hopes, fears, interests, and passions which rage in the breasts of ambitious and desperate men,) —and all the people, from the interests they have depending, become enlisted, excited, agitated, and generally corrupted, by the hazards of the game.

The trial by jury disavows the majority principle altogether; and proceeds upon the ground that every man should be presumed to be entitled to life, liberty, and such property as he has in his possession; and that the government should lay its hand upon none of them, (except for the purpose of bringing them before a tribunal for adjudication,) unless it be first ascertained, *beyond a reasonable doubt*, in every individual case, that justice requires it.

To ascertain whether there be such reasonable doubt, it takes twelve men *by lot* from the whole body of mature men. If any of these twelve are proved to be under the influence of any *special* interest or passion, that may either pervert their judgments, or corrupt their motives, they are set aside as unsuitable for the performance of a duty requiring such absolute impartiality and integrity; and others substituted in their stead. When the utmost practicable impartiality is attained on the part of the whole twelve, they are sworn to the observance of justice; and their unanimous concurrence is then held to be necessary to remove that reasonable doubt, which, unremoved, would forbid the government to lay its hand on its victim.

Such is the caution which the trial by jury both practises

and inculcates, against the violation of justice, on the part of the government, towards the humblest individual, in the smallest matter affecting his civil rights, his property, liberty, or life.   And such is the contrast, which the trial by jury presents, to that gambler's and robber's rule, that the majority have a right, by virtue of their superior numbers, and without regard to justice, to dispose at pleasure of the property and persons of all bodies of men less numerous than themselves.

The difference, in short, between the two systems, is this. The trial by jury protects person and property, inviolate to their possessors, from the hand of the law, unless *justice, beyond a reasonable doubt,* require them to be taken.   The majority principle takes person and property from their possessors, at the mere arbitrary will of a majority, who are liable and likely to be influenced, in taking them, by motives of oppression, avarice, and ambition.

If the relative numbers of opposing parties afforded sufficient evidence of the comparative justice of their claims, the government should carry the principle into its courts of justice; and instead of referring controversies to impartial and disinterested men,— to judges and jurors, sworn to do justice, and bound patiently to hear and weigh all the evidence and arguments that can be offered on either side,— it should simply *count* the plaintiffs and defendants in each case, (where there were more than one of either,) and then give the case to the majority; after ample opportunity had been given to the plaintiffs and defendants to reason with, flatter, cheat, threaten, and bribe each other, by way of inducing them to change sides. Such a process would be just as rational in courts of justice, as in halls of legislation; for it is of no importance to a man, who has his rights taken from him, whether it be done by a legislative enactment, or a judicial decision.

In legislation, the people are all arranged as plaintiffs and defendants in their own causes; (those who are in favor of a particular law, standing as plaintiffs, and those who are opposed to the same law, standing as defendants); and to allow these causes to be decided by majorities, is plainly as absurd as it would be to allow judicial decisions to be determined by the relative number of plaintiffs and defendants.

If this mode of decision were introduced into courts of justice, we should see a parallel, and only a parallel, to that system of legislation which we witness daily. We should see large bodies of men conspiring to bring perfectly groundless suits, against other bodies of men, for large sums of money, and to carry them by sheer force of numbers; just as we now continually see large bodies of men conspiring to carry, by mere force of numbers, some scheme of legislation that will, directly or indirectly, take money out of other men's pockets, and put it into their own. And we should also see distinct bodies of men, parties in separate suits, combining and agreeing all to appear and be counted as plaintiffs or defendants in each other's suits, for the purpose of ekeing out the necessary majority; just as we now see distinct bodies of men, interested in separate schemes of ambition or plunder, conspiring to carry through a batch of legislative enactments, that shall accomplish their several purposes.

This system of combination and conspiracy would go on, until at length whole states and a whole nation would become divided into two great litigating parties, each party composed of several smaller bodies, having their separate suits, but all confederating for the purpose of making up the necessary majority in each case. The individuals composing each of these two great parties, would at length become so accustomed to acting together, and so well acquainted with each others' schemes, and so mutually dependent upon each others' fidelity for success, that they would become organized as permanent asso<iations; bound together by that kind of honor that prevails among thieves; and pledged by all their interests, sympathies, and animosities, to mutual fidelity, and to unceasing hostility to their opponents; and exerting all their arts and all their resources of threats, injuries, promises, and bribes, to drive or seduce from the other party enough to enable their own to retain or acquire such a majority as would be necessary to gain their own suits, and defeat the suits of their opponents. All the wealth and talent of the country would become enlisted in the service of these rival associations; and both would at length become so compact, so well organized, so powerful, and yet always so much in need of recruits,

that a private person would be nearly or quite unable to obtain justice in the most paltry suit with his neighbor, except on the condition of joining one of these great litigating associations, who would agree to carry through his cause, on condition of his assisting them to carry through all the others, good and bad, which they had already undertaken. If he refused this, they would threaten to make a similar offer to his antagonist, and suffer their whole numbers to be counted against him.

Now this picture is no caricature, but a true and honest likeness. And such a system of administering justice, would be no more false, absurd, or atrocious, than that system of working by majorities, which seeks to accomplish, by legislation, the same ends which, in the case supposed, would be accomplished by judicial decisions.

Again, the doctrine that the minority ought to submit to the will of the majority, proceeds, not upon the principle that government is formed by voluntary association, and for an *agreed purpose*, on the part of all who contribute to its support, but upon the presumption that all government must be practically a state of war and plunder between opposing parties; and that, in order to save blood, and prevent mutual extermination, the parties come to an agreement that they will count their respective numbers periodically, and the one party shall then be permitted quietly to rule and plunder, (restrained only by their own discretion,) and the other submit quietly to be ruled and plundered, until the time of the next enumeration.

Such an agreement may possibly be wiser than unceasing and deadly conflict; it nevertheless partakes too much of the ludicrous to deserve to be seriously considered as an expedient for the maintenance of civil society. It would certainly seem that mankind might agree upon a cessation of hostilities, upon more rational and equitable terms than that of unconditional submission on the part of the less numerous body. Unconditional submission is usually the last act of one who confesses himself subdued and enslaved. How any one ever came to imagine that condition to be one of freedom, has never been explained. And as for the system being adapted to the maintenance of justice among men, it is a mystery that any human mind could ever have been visited with an insanity wild enough to originate the idea.

If it be said that other corporations, than governments, surrender their affairs into the hands of the majority, the answer is, that they allow majorities to determine only trifling matters, that are in their nature mere questions of discretion, and where there is no natural presumption of justice or right on one side rather than the other. They *never* surrender to the majority the power to dispose of, or, what is practically the same thing, to *determine*, the *rights* of any individual member. The *rights* of every member are determined by the written compact, to which all the members have voluntarily agreed.

For example. A banking corporation allows a majority to determine such questions of discretion as whether the note of A or of B shall be discounted; whether notes shall be discounted on one, two, or six days in the week; how many hours in a day their banking-house shall be kept open; how many clerks shall be employed; what salaries they shall receive, and such like matters, which are in their nature mere subjects of discretion, and where there are no natural presumptions of justice or right in favor of one course over the other. But no banking corporation allows a majority, or any other number of its members less than the whole, to divert the funds of the corporation to any other purpose than the one to which *every member* of the corporation has legally agreed that they may be devoted; nor to take the stock of one member and give it to another; nor to distribute the dividends among the stockholders otherwise than to each one the proportion which he has agreed to accept, and all the others have agreed that he shall receive. Nor does any banking corporation allow a majority to impose taxes upon the members for the payment of the corporate expenses, except in such proportions as *every member* has consented that they may be imposed. All these questions, involving the *rights* of the members as against each other, are fixed by the articles of the association, — that is, by the agreement to which *every member* has personally assented.

What is also specially to be noticed, and what constitutes a

vital difference between the banking corporation and the political corporation, or government, is, that in case of controversy
among the members of the banking corporation, as to the
rights of any member, the question is determined, not by any
number, either majority, or minority, of the corporation itself,
but by persons out of the corporation; by twelve men acting as
jurors, or by other tribunals of justice, of which no member
of the corporation is allowed to be a part. But in the case of
the political corporation, controversies among the parties to it,
as to the rights of individual members, must of necessity be
settled by members of the corporation itself, because there are
no persons out of the corporation to whom the question can be
referred.

Since, then, all questions as to the *rights* of the members of
the political corporation, must be determined by members of
the corporation itself, the trial by jury says that no man's
rights,— neither his right to his life, his liberty, nor his property,— shall be determined by any such standard as the mere
will and pleasure of majorities; but only by the unanimous
verdict of a tribunal fairly representing the whole people,—
that is, a tribunal of twelve men, taken at random from the
whole body, and ascertained to be as impartial as the nature
of the case will admit, *and sworn to the observance of justice.*
Such is the difference in the two kinds of corporations; and
the custom of managing by majorities the mere discretionary
matters of business corporations, (the majority having no power
to determine the *rights* of any member,) furnishes no analogy
to the practice, adopted by political corporations, of disposing
of all the *rights* of their members by the arbitrary will of
majorities.

But further. The doctrine that the majority have a *right*
to rule, proceeds upon the principle that minorities have no
rights in the government; for certainly the minority cannot
be said to have any *rights* in a government, so long as the
majority alone determine what their rights shall be. They
hold everything, or nothing, as the case may be, at the mere
will of the majority.

It is indispensable to a *"free government,"* (in the political
sense of that term,) that the minority, the weaker party, have

a veto upon the acts of the majority. Political liberty is liberty for the *weaker party* in a nation. It is only the weaker party that lose their liberties, when a government becomes oppressive. The stronger party, in all governments, are free by virtue of their superior strength. They never oppress themselves.

Legislation is the work of this stronger party; and if, in addition to the sole power of legislating, they have the sole power of determining what legislation shall be enforced, they have all power in their hands, and the weaker party are the subjects of an absolute government.

Unless the weaker party have a veto, either upon the making, or the enforcement of laws, they have no power whatever in the government, and can of course have no liberties except such as the stronger party, in their arbitrary discretion, see fit to permit them to enjoy.

In England and the United States, the trial by jury is the only institution that gives the weaker party any veto upon the power of the stronger. Consequently it is the only institution, that gives them any effective voice in the government, or any guaranty against oppression.

Suffrage, however free, is of no avail for this purpose; because the suffrage of the minority is overborne by the suffrage of the majority, and is thus rendered powerless for purposes of legislation. The responsibility of officers can be made of no avail, because they are responsible only to the majority. The minority, therefore, are wholly without rights in the government, wholly at the mercy of the majority, unless, through the trial by jury, they have a veto upon such legislation as they think unjust.

Government is established for the protection of the weak against the strong. This is the principal, if not the sole, motive for the establishment of all legitimate government. Laws, that are sufficient for the protection of the weaker party, are of course sufficient for the protection of the stronger party; because the strong can certainly need no more protection than the weak. It is, therefore, right that the weaker party should be represented in the tribunal which is finally to determine what legislation may be enforced; and that no legislation shall be enforced against their consent. They being presumed to be competent judges of what kind of legislation makes for their safety, and what for their injury, it must be presumed that any legislation, which *they* object to enforcing, tends to their oppression, and not to their security.

There is still another reason why the weaker party, or the minority, should have a veto upon all legislation which they disapprove. *That reason is, that that is the only means by which the government can be kept within the limits of the contract, compact, or constitution, by which the whole people agree to establish government.* If the majority were allowed to interpret the compact for themselves, and enforce it according to their own interpretation, they would, of course, make it authorize them to do whatever they wish to do.

The theory of free government is that it is formed by the voluntary contract of the people individually with each other. This is the theory, (although it is not, as it ought to be, the fact,) in all the governments in the United States, as also in the government of England. The theory assumes that each man, who is a party to the government, and contributes to its support, has individually and freely consented to it. Otherwise the government would have no right to tax him for its support,— for taxation without consent is robbery. This theory, then, necessarily supposes that this government, which is formed by the free consent of all, has no powers except such as *all* the parties to it have individually agreed that it shall have; and especially that it has no power to pass any *laws*, except such as *all* the parties have agreed that it may pass.

This theory supposes that there may be certain laws that will be beneficial to *all*,— so beneficial that *all* consent to be taxed for their maintenance. For the maintenance of these specific laws, in which all are interested, all associate. And they associate for the maintenance of those laws *only*, in which *all* are interested. It would be absurd to suppose that all would associate, and consent to be taxed, for purposes which were beneficial only to a part; and especially for purposes that were injurious to any. A government of the whole, therefore, can have no powers except such as *all* the parties consent that it may have. It can do nothing except what *all* have consented that it may do. And if any portion of the people,— no matter how large their number, if it be less than the whole,— desire a government for any purposes other than those that are common to all, and desired by all, they must form a separate association for those purposes. They have no right,— by perverting this government of the whole, to the accomplishment of purposes desired only by a part,— to compel any one to contribute to purposes that are either useless or injurious to himself.

Such being the principles on which the government is formed, the question arises, how shall this government, when formed, be kept within the limits of the contract by which it was established? How shall this government, instituted by the whole people, agreed to by the whole people, supported by the contributions of the whole people, be confined to the accomplishment of those purposes alone, which the whole people desire? How shall it be preserved from degenerating into a mere government for the benefit of a part only of those who established, and who support it? How shall it be prevented from even injuring a part of its own members, for the aggrandizement of the rest? Its laws must be, (or at least now are,) passed, and most of its other acts performed, by mere agents,— agents chosen by a part of the people, and not by the whole. How can these agents be restrained from seeking their own interests, and the interests of those who elected them, at the expense of the rights of the remainder of the people, by the passage and enforcement of laws that shall be partial, unequal, and unjust in their operation? That is the great question. And the trial by jury answers it. And how does the trial by jury answer it? It answers it, as has already been shown throughout this volume, by saying that these mere agents and attorneys, who are chosen by a part only of the people, and are liable to be influenced by partial and unequal purposes, shall not have unlimited authority in the enactment and enforcement of laws; that they shall not exercise *all* the functions of government. It says that they shall never exercise that ultimate power of compelling obedience to the laws by punishing for disobedience, or of executing the laws against the person or property of any man, without first

getting the consent of the people, through a tribunal that may
fairly be presumed to represent the whole, or substantially
the whole, people. It says that if the power to make laws,
and the power also to enforce them, were committed to these
agents, they would have all power,— would be absolute
masters of the people, and could deprive them of their rights
at pleasure. It says, therefore, that the people themselves
will hold a veto upon the enforcement of any and every law,
which these agents may enact, and that whenever the occasion arises for them to give or withhold their consent,— inasmuch as the whole people cannot assemble, or devote the time
and attention necessary to the investigation of each case,—
twelve of their number shall be taken by lot, or otherwise at
random, from the whole body; that they shall not be chosen
by majorities, (the same majorities that elected the agents who
enacted the laws to be put in issue,) nor by any interested or
suspected party; that they shall not be appointed by, or be in
any way dependent upon, those who enacted the law; that
their opinions, whether for or against the law that is in issue,
shall not be inquired of beforehand; and that if these twelve
men give their consent to the enforcement of the law, their
consent shall stand for the consent of the whole.

This is the mode, which the trial by jury provides, for keeping the government within the limits designed by the whole
people, who have associated for its establishment. And it is
the only mode, provided either by the English or American
constitutions, for the accomplishment of that object.

But it will, perhaps, be said that if the minority can defeat
the will of the majority, then the minority *rule* the majority.
But this is not true in any unjust sense. The minority enact
no laws of their own. They simply refuse their assent to such
laws of the majority as they do not approve. The minority
assume no authority over the majority; they simply defend
themselves. They do not interfere with the right of the
majority to seek their own happiness in their own way, so
long as they (the majority) do not interfere with the minority.
They claim simply not to be oppressed, and not to be compelled to assist in doing anything which they do not approve.
They say to the majority, " We will unite with you, if you

desire it, for the accomplishment of all those purposes, in which we have a common interest with you. You can certainly expect us to do nothing more. If you do not choose to associate with us on those terms, there must be two separate associations. You must associate for the accomplishment of your purposes; we for the accomplishment of ours."

In this case, the minority assume no authority over the majority; they simply refuse to surrender their own liberties into the hands of the majority. They propose a union; but decline submission. The majority are still at liberty to refuse the connection, and to seek their own happiness in their own way, except that they cannot be gratified in their desire to become absolute masters of the minority.

But, it may be asked, how can the minority be trusted to enforce even such legislation as is equal and just? The answer is, that they are as reliable for that purpose as are the majority; they are as much presumed to have associated, and are as likely to have associated, for that object, as are the majority; and they have as much interest in such legislation as have the majority. They have even more interest in it; for, being the weaker party, they must rely on it for their security, — having no other security on which they can rely. Hence their consent to the establishment of government, and to the *taxation* required for its support, is *presumed*, (although it ought not to be presumed,) without any express consent being given. This presumption of their consent to be taxed for the maintenance of laws, would be absurd, if they could not themselves be trusted to act in good faith in enforcing those laws. And hence they cannot be presumed to have consented to be taxed for the maintenance of any laws, except such as they are themselves ready to aid in enforcing. It is therefore unjust to tax them, unless they are eligible to seats in a jury, with power to judge of the justice of the laws. Taxing them for the support of the laws, on the assumption that they are in favor of the laws, and at the same time refusing them the right, as jurors, to judge of the justice of the laws, on the assumption that they are opposed to the laws, are flat contradictions.

But, it will be asked, what motive have the majority, when

they have all power in their own hands, to submit their will
to the veto of the minority?

One answer is, that they have the motive of justice. It
would be *unjust* to compel the minority to contribute, by taxation, to the support of any laws which they did not approve.

Another answer is, that if the stronger party wish to use
their power only for purposes of justice, they have no occasion
to fear the veto of the weaker party; for the latter have as
strong motives for the maintenance of *just* government, as
have the former.

Another answer is, that if the stronger party use their power
unjustly, they will hold it by an uncertain tenure, especially
in a community where knowledge is diffused; for knowledge
will enable the weaker party to make itself in time the
stronger party. It also enables the weaker party, even while
it remains the weaker party, perpetually to annoy, alarm, and
injure their oppressors. Unjust power,— or rather power that
is *grossly* unjust, and that is known to be so by the minority,
— can be sustained only at the expense of standing armies,
and all the other machinery of force; for the oppressed party
are always ready to risk their lives for purposes of vengeance,
and the acquisition of their rights, whenever there is any tol-
erable chance of success. Peace, safety, and quiet for all, can
be enjoyed only under laws that obtain the consent of all.
Hence tyrants frequently yield to the demands of justice from
those weaker than themselves, as a means of buying peace
and safety.

Still another answer is, that those who are in the majority
on one law, will be in the minority on another. All, therefore, need the benefit of the veto, at some time or other, to
protect themselves from injustice.

That the limits, within which legislation would, by this
process, be confined, would be exceedingly narrow, in comparison with those it at present occupies, there can be no
doubt. All monopolies, all special privileges, all sumptuary
laws, all restraints upon any traffic, bargain, or contract, that
was naturally lawful,* all restraints upon men's natural

---

* Such as restraints upon banking, upon the rates of interest, upon traffic with for-
eigners, &c., &c.

rights, the whole catalogue of *mala prohibita*, and all taxation to which the taxed parties had not individually, severally, and freely consented, would be at an end; because all such legislation implies a violation of the rights of a greater or less minority. This minority would disregard, trample upon, or resist, the execution of such legislation, and then throw themselves upon a jury of the whole people for justification and protection. In this way all legislation would be nullified, except the legislation of that general nature which impartially protected the rights, and subserved the interests, of all. The only legislation that could be sustained, would probably be such as tended directly to the maintenance of justice and liberty; such, for example, as should contribute to the enforcement of contracts, the protection of property, and the prevention and punishment of acts intrinsically criminal. In short, government in practice would be brought to the necessity of a strict adherence to natural law, and natural justice, instead of being, as it now is, a great battle, in which avarice and ambition are constantly fighting for and obtaining advantages over the natural rights of mankind.

APPENDIX.

TAXATION.

It was a principle of the Common Law, as it is of the law of nature, and of common sense, that no man can be taxed without his personal consent. The Common Law knew nothing of that system, which now prevails in England, of *assuming* a man's own consent to be taxed, because some pretended representative, whom he never authorized to act for him, has taken it upon himself to consent that he may be taxed. That is one of the many frauds on the Common Law, and the English constitution, which have been introduced since Magna Carta. Having finally established itself in England, it has been stupidly and servilely copied and submitted to in the United States.

If the trial by jury were reëstablished, the Common Law principle of taxation would be reëstablished with it ; for it is not to be supposed that juries would enforce a tax upon an individual which he had never agreed to pay. Taxation without consent is as plainly robbery, when enforced against one man, as when enforced against millions ; and it is not to be imagined that juries could be blind to so self-evident a principle. Taking a man's money without his consent, is also as much robbery, when it is done by millions of men, acting in concert, and calling themselves a government, as when it is done by a single individual, acting on his own responsibility, and calling himself a highwayman. Neither the numbers engaged in the act, nor the different characters they assume as a cover for the act, alter the nature of the act itself.

If the government can take a man's money without his consent, there is no limit to the additional tyranny it may practise upon him ; for, with his money, it can hire soldiers to stand over him, keep him in subjection, plunder him at discretion, and kill him if he resists. And governments always will do this, as they everywhere and always have done it, except where the Common Law principle has been established. It is therefore a first principle, a very *sine qua non* of political freedom, that a man can be taxed only by his personal consent. And the establishment of this principle, *with trial by jury*, insures freedom of course ; because : 1. No man would pay his money unless he had first contracted for such a government as he was willing to support ; and, 2. Unless the government then kept itself within the terms of its contract, juries would not enforce the payment of the tax. Besides, the agreement to be taxed would probably be entered into but for a year at a time. If, in that year, the government proved itself either inefficient or tyrannical, to any serious degree, the contract would not be renewed.

The dissatisfied parties, if sufficiently numerous for a new organization, would form themselves into a separate association for mutual protection. If not sufficiently numerous for that purpose, those who were conscientious would forego all governmental protection, rather than contribute to the support of a government which they deemed unjust.

All legitimate government is a mutual insurance company, voluntarily agreed upon by the parties to it, for the protection of their rights against wrong-doers. In its voluntary character it is precisely similar to an association for mutual protection against fire or shipwreck. Before a man will join an association for these latter purposes, and pay the premium for being insured, he will, if he be a man of sense, look at the articles of the association ; see what the company promises to do ; what it is likely to do ; and what are the rates of insurance. If he be satisfied on all these points, he will become a member, pay his premium for a year, and then hold the company to its contract. If the conduct of the company prove unsatisfactory, he will let his policy expire at the end of the year for which he has paid ; will decline to pay any further premiums, and either seek insurance elsewhere, or take his own risk without any insurance. And as men act in the insurance of their ships and dwellings, they would act in the insurance of their properties, liberties and lives, in the political association, or government.

The political insurance company, or government, have no more right, in nature or reason, to *assume* a man's consent to be protected by them, and to be taxed for that protection, when he has given no actual consent, than a fire or marine insurance company have to assume a man's consent to be protected by them, and to pay the premium, when his actual consent has never been given. To take a man's property without his consent is robbery ; and to assume his consent, where no actual consent is given, makes the taking none the less robbery. If it did, the highwayman has the same right to assume a man's consent to part with his purse, that any other man, or body of men, can have. And his assumption would afford as much moral justification for his robbery as does a like assumption, on the part of the government, for taking a man's property without his consent. The government's pretence of protecting him, as an equivalent for the taxation, affords no justification. It is for himself to decide whether he desires such protection as the government offers him. If he do not desire it, or do not bargain for it, the government has no more right than any other insurance company to impose it upon him, or make him pay for it.

Trial by the country, and no taxation without consent, were the two pillars of English liberty, (when England had any liberty,) and the first principles of the Common Law. They mutually sustain each other ; and neither can stand without the other. Without both, no people have any guaranty for their freedom ; with both, no people can be otherwise than free.*

---

* Trial by the country, and no taxation without consent, mutually sustain each other, and can be sustained only by each other, for these reasons : 1. Juries would refuse to enforce a tax against a man who had never agreed to pay it. They would also protect men in forcibly resisting the collection of taxes to which they had never consented. Otherwise the jurors would authorize the government to tax themselves without their consent, — a thing which no jury would be likely to do. In these two ways, then, trial by the country would sustain the principle of no taxation without consent. 2. On the other hand, the principle of no taxation without consent would sustain the trial by the country, because men in general would not consent to be taxed for the support of a

By what force, fraud, and conspiracy, on the part of kings, nobles, and "a few wealthy freeholders," these pillars have been prostrated in England, it is designed to show more fully in the next volume, if it should be necessary.

---

government under which trial by the country was not secured. Thus these two principles mutually sustain each other.

But, if either of these principles were broken down, the other would fall with it, and for these reasons: 1. If trial by the country were broken down, the principle of no taxation without consent would fall with it, because the government would then be *able* to tax the people without their consent, inasmuch as the legal tribunals would be mere tools of the government, and would enforce such taxation, and punish men for resisting such taxation, as the government ordered. 2. On the other hand, if the principle of no taxation without consent were broken down, trial by the country would fall with it, because the government, if it could tax people without their consent, would, of course, take enough of their money to enable it to employ all the force necessary for sustaining its own tribunals, (in the place of juries,) and carrying their decrees into execution.